DEDICATION

The Holy Spirit,
who makes "...my tongue as the pen of a ready writer."
(Psalm 45:1 NAS)

&

My wife,
Linda,
who kept hope alive with her support and prayers.

A MEETING IN THE AIR

BY
DENNIS A. BEAUDRY

PublishAmerica
Baltimore

ISBN: 1-59286-998-X
PUBLISHED BY PUBLISHAMERICA, LLLP
www.publishamerica.com
Baltimore

Printed in the United States of America

INTRODUCTION

"Dear heavenly Father," my midnight prayer started as I stood gazing out through the large living room picture window. It was mid November, and the heavy, wet snow kept falling, piling higher and higher with each moment that passed. "There's no retreat or status quo left in me, thanks to You. Forward movement in Your kingdom is all I want. Unlike Lot's wife, I don't even want to look back. You know that; after all, who could possibly know me better than You? I search the inner depths of me, finding You and the evidence of Your presence everywhere I look – Your Spirit, Your truth, Your peace and Your revelation. I see things so differently now, and I'm thankful for it. These words: spirit, truth, peace, revelation, were only words with dictionary meanings to me before encountering Your Holy Spirit. They were just words in the Bible, the ultimate book of truth – yet so unyielding to my casual reading.

"How have these recent changes in my life taken place? How is it that where there once was spiritual mediocrity, there now is desire for excellence? How is it, Lord God, that where there once was loneliness, there now is fulfillment? Father, You know these questions have already been answered. You answered them all and Your Spirit confirms that to me. You answered most of them through the life of the one You placed in my pathway, who sleeps upstairs even now as I pray.

"I'm thankful to You, God, for her entry into my life. Without her, I would still be struggling with my relationship to You, if indeed even trying to struggle at all. I would be living a powerless life, and worse yet, I would be walking through this earthly life ignorant of the challenges to my soul. Father, bless her, and enable me to be that blessing. Deepen our affections for each other and cause our life together to be pleasing unto You. In Jesus' name I pray. Amen and Amen."

The Bible says "...And the Lord God said, It is not good that the man should be alone; I will make him a help meet for him.... And the Lord God caused a deep sleep to fall upon Adam, and he slept: and He took one of his ribs, and closed up the flesh instead thereof; And the rib, which the Lord God had taken from man, made he a woman, and brought her unto the man. And Adam said, This is now bone of my bones, and flesh of my flesh: she shall be called Woman, because she was taken out of Man. Therefore shall a man leave his father and his mother, and shall cleave unto his wife: and they shall be one flesh. And they were both naked, the man and his wife, and were not ashamed."

My name is David Post, and I knew there had to be someone out there for me somewhere. That's what I'd heard so many times from so many family members, friends and associates. Maybe there was a time when I believed it; I don't really know. What I did know was that I had stopped actively seeking a wife long ago. My life had rambled through as much of that seeking, dating, relating and compromising as I could stand.

After becoming a born-again believer in Jesus Christ I was nothing more than a spiritual baby. I lived a day-to-day existence; powerless to do much more than attend services, pray halfheartedly, and meander fruitlessly through the Bible. That is, until a lunch-time encounter with a previously nondescript acquaintance from my past.

The turn of events that followed, coming in rapid-fire succession, can only be described as God's intervention. What wonderful thoughts, dreams and hopes escape the carnal existence of man when the spiritual life is neglected. The mighty plans of God Himself await their implementation, predicated by an awakened spirit, a diligent search, a responsive heart, and a submissive will. While prayer is one of the keys to attaining this state; the baptism of the Holy Ghost is the master key. It unlocks a spiritual awareness conducive to attaining God's best, which is really all He wants to give us.

But now, here are the events of this story.

CHAPTER ONE

The first frost came like clockwork. Labor Day was over and with it went summer, and the nearly perfect weather of the past four months. But unlike other places where I had lived, Michigan's Upper Peninsula was predictable in only one way each day brought us closer to a certain and long lived winter.

Today was Wednesday, and my first step outside the house coldly alerted me that for at least this day autumn had been skipped, and winter was taking control. After starting my car's engine, I stepped back out into the brisk, unlit, morning air to scrape nature's icy residue from the windshield and side glass. Yes, there was a substantial touch of frost but eventually that would mean something beautiful. The annual spectacular color-rama of the northern Michigan trees would soon be taking my breath away. In fact some of the maples and birches had already displayed a touch of that thrilling color. Though nearly two full weeks from peak color, today would still be a great day for walking through the woods in back of my house. While there I could survey, up close, the beginning of the fall extravaganza. As much as I would like to take that walk in the morning's first light, I knew it would have to await completion of the demands of my job.

Although I am a freelance photographer, able in most cases to set my own agenda, regrettably the office work has to be done too. Today was to be an office day and upon entering my studio I paused to glance at the calendar on my desk. It verified what I already knew. I had no appointments, but highlighted in red was "Do Billing." The written comment triggered a grimace that I'm certain reflected my disdain for that chore. But alas, I had put it off for several days, and now realized that if the bills didn't go out, the pay wouldn't come in.

After filling my cup with coffee, I started the routines on the computer, doing so with the same groggy-eyed, half-asleep, trance-like enthusiasm of a night watchman after his first graveyard shift. In the background, one of my favorite contemporary Christian songs played on the radio, which soothed me and brought thoughts of God to mind. I had started my day with Him, praying as I inched my way out of bed, and methodically dedicating the day back to Him. It was morning meditation as usual and best described as on the fly. More often than I cared to admit the workday seldom relinquished time for contemplating the wonders or nearness of God. This morning, though, while my fingers independently worked the computer keyboard, my mind lingered on thoughts of my Heavenly Father.

His power and greatness were the first things I locked in on. The scenic beauty of this Earth has always been important to me. His great handiwork is vividly displayed in all He has created. That was why taking pictures of God's creation was such a pleasure to me. The wondrous old hymn "How Great Thou Art," states it well but I had found a way to do it one better. I had unintentionally started softly singing those famous words, meditating on them, while walking through God's masterpiece one day. There in the solitude of the wooded trail, while observing the complexity and grandeur of the world in which we live, I came to a significantly deeper appreciation of the praise we give unto Him by acknowledging "...how great Thou art!"

Recovering from the distraction of several phone calls, I started reflecting on life's events that had led me to where I was now. I pondered how I had achieved so much. Why had I been so richly blessed? How was it that my life had provided so many of the things I desired? The verse of David's Psalm resounded in my mind, "Who is man that Thou art mindful of him?" I paraphrased it to ask, who am I that You are mindful of me?

My thoughts carried me back in time. I was the second in a family of four children. The only one who claimed Christ as Savior. Life had led us all in different directions – One now living in Maine; one in Illinois; the youngest in Pennsylvania; and I in Michigan. Three married while I remained single. Two had children. One on the road of alcoholism; one excelling in the area of career growth; one into materialism; and then me; for some unknown reason, the black sheep of the family.

I wasn't anyone special as I grew up, and adult life had led me into military service, which in turn, had steered me down paths I would rather not admit to now. My parent's teaching and church attendance during my younger years had proven useless, amounting to nothing more than a tradition and memory that annoyingly hung around when I'd just as soon it left.

Yet from a meaningless existence, stagnating in mediocrity, I was aimless in my goals and drifting recklessly with the tide of sinful influence, when God saved me. Though able to point out a clearly identifiable encounter with God in my past, I lacked the spiritual awareness to question "Why me?"– let alone, find the answer.

The front door of my studio opened abruptly, and just as abruptly jerked me back to reality. How much time, I wondered, had elapsed during this reminiscing. The inquisitive customer had finally settled down to reviewing my service and price listing, allowing me to return to the computer momentarily.

After I exchanged my business card for the price list, the customer left. Now nearly lunchtime, my stomach insisted the meat loaf platter at the Downtowner Café would be the only payment it would accept for a morning of office work. I acquiesced.

Wrapping myself in my coat, I left the studio. The early morning weather report had predicted temperatures would drop throughout the day with a chance of rain late in the afternoon. Checking the sky as I walked, the clouds seemed out of place. They bore a resemblance more to November snow clouds than September rain. But my exposed face and hands determined the temperatures, though chilly, were not cold enough for snow.

I turned up Washington Street, bracing myself for the wind normally associated with a trek up that street. The wind was there as expected, and with it wafted the familiar aroma of the Downtowner Cafe's meat loaf special. Nowhere in my travels was there meat loaf as delicious as the Downtowner's.

Stepping inside to a bustling, noisy café, I located an empty booth at the far end of the room. I slid in, loosened my coat, and placed my order with Julie, the frazzled but courteous waitress. The din of the busy café was blocked out by my mental drifting until I suddenly detected someone had sat down in the booth with me. I looked across the table spying the face of a former associate from my Air Force days. It had been more years than I cared to guess since we last met, although there was no proof of that on his still youthful face. Starting the one-sided conversation before I could recall his name, his small talk centered on his life since military discharge. He then asked for an update from me. Jerry, that's it, Jerry McFarland was his name, I eventually remembered.

Jerry couldn't stay for lunch, but related he had seen me from across the street and wanted to say a quick hello. He also hoped for a get-together later to talk about something more specific. He seemed happy, but more. Actually, I thought, he appeared to be overly enthusiastic about this coincidental meeting but I couldn't tell why; after all, it had been well over two years since our last brief encounter, and we hadn't really been all that close back in the Air Force. Jerry left as quickly as he had arrived but not without sliding one of his business cards across the table to me with instructions to call him as soon as I could.

I started devouring my lunch with little more thought about the chance encounter until the waitress brought my bill. She placed it on the table on top of Jerry's upside-down business card. While picking up the lunch bill, I likewise retrieved the card. Flipping it over I read, "Jerry McFarland, President & General Manager, WPFH-AM". The very Christian radio station I normally listened to. Now the chance encounter had developed greater significance, but I was at a loss to know why.

I placed Jerry's card in my shirt pocket, paid my bill and headed back to the studio. As I walked my mind would not let go of the meeting, nor would Jerry's request for me to contact him. I knew he was a Christian. In fact, a long time ago, in his own awkward way he had witnessed to me before I became a believer. Maybe he had become bolder and just wanted to witness to me again. There was no way for him to know I was now a brother in the Lord.

The afternoon's work went smoothly. With all my office tasks completed, it was time to prepare the coffee maker for the next day and go home. On the way I stopped at the post office to place the bills in the afternoon's mail.

Whether I fit the description of what most people imagine a freelance photographer to be, I can't say. Contrary to my smiling face, triggered by the fact that I genuinely enjoy my work and life style, I'm not all that wealthy, at least not in the area of income. However taking pictures for a living is probably just as enjoyable to me as recreational fishing is to others. I drive a family car–a station wagon at that– which fits nicely into my photography business. My house is a more-than-adequate, redwood A-frame tucked away on the side of a wooded hill, and situated about a thousand feet back from the road. It is complete with frontal glass, spiral staircase to the loft, and a central fireplace. The winding gravel driveway was fashioned so that not one tree had to be removed. The placement of the house required only three large trees to be removed and several smaller trees transplanted. Construction crews exercised extreme care in hauling the building materials to the job site. It took just over a year from the date I purchased the land through completion of construction.

It was nearly dark as I arrived home. The rain had started as the weatherman had predicted, and the chilling damp breeze gnawed at my unprotected ears. The inclement weather and darkness canceled my plans for a walk in the woods. I comforted myself with the hope that tomorrow would provide an opportunity for that pleasure.

I started a fire in the fireplace to take the damp chill from the house. As was my habit, I turned the TV on to the 24-hour news service and started my supper. Not paying much attention to it as I went about my routines, a story was being reported about a radio station somewhere. Quickly my thoughts returned to Jerry, the luncheon encounter, and the business card still in my shirt pocket. I looked to see if it had his home phone number; it did. I dialed the number but Jerry wasn't home but his wife, Carol, was. She agreed to have him call me when he got in.

I had barely finished eating when the phone rang. It was Jerry. He asked to come over and I agreed, and gave him directions. There seemed to be sense of eagerness in both of us to rekindle the acquaintance, but I wondered why.

He arrived about forty minutes later, just as I finished the dishes, and we sat in the living room near the fireplace, savoring a hot cup of freshly brewed coffee. We related the significant events of the years that had elapsed. Jerry had finally graduated from Northern Michigan University in Marquette and had decided to stay in the Upper Peninsula rather than returning to his hometown in the Chicago suburbs. He and his wife were renting a house on the north end of town. He had risen to his present position as President of the radio station then called WCDP.

I sat attentively as Jerry related his start in radio; a start that, as he put it, was a struggle financially until finally obtaining full-time employment. The rest, he stated, was just normal advancement to general manager. Two months later the president of the station's charter company sold out to a Christian fellow who knew absolutely nothing about the broadcasting business.

Jerry continued, "He just asked me to fill in until he could hire someone to serve as president. I'm still filling in, but now it's permanent."

I told Jerry that I had expected him to start witnessing to me about Christ, and was somewhat surprised he hadn't. He said he had intended to and was glad I broached the subject. Of course I was likewise thrilled to tell him that he didn't need to, and we rejoiced in the common bond of brotherhood in Christ.

Then Jerry looked at me intently. His expression told me he was about to make a profound statement, but I was totally unprepared for what he asked. "How satisfied are you with your work in photography?" he inquired.

"Well, it's my second love," I replied. "Jesus being my first, of course."

"I would like you to consider coming to work for me at the station? We're soon to have an AM/FM combination and it's getting to be too much for me. The radio business is not what I went to college for. What knowledge I have I've gained by the seat of my pants, so to speak. I really need help, and I need it now. Together we could manage a lot easier than I can by myself."

I sat there studying his face yet saying nothing. After a pause for a sip of coffee, Jerry continued, "I know this has to hit you like a bolt out of the blue. I can't say why, other than by God's direction, our paths crossed again when they did. I believe both you and I have been especially prepared by God for this very endeavor."

I quickly asked, "How do you know that, Jerry?"

"Because I've placed the needs of the radio station before God in such a way the answer could only come from God. It's obvious to me that you have been prepared by the way your life has gone prior to our meeting. The last time we had a real opportunity to talk neither of us was where we are now. See what's transpired since then? Look at the managerial skills you've developed over all those years with the Air Force; well over twenty, right? Surely as a born-again believer, you know that God works in people's lives. You've probably learned by now that God has a plan for each of us. And to be perfectly honest with you, you hadn't even entered my mind until I saw you walk into the café. I recognized you on the spot. My spirit was quickened, and I asked God, 'Are you sure about Dave? I don't believe he's even a Christian.' and yet God gave me peace and said you were the one I was to ask.

"You see, Dave, we've both been prepared. I was placed in the station to get it running in a different direction. But God knew it would be too much for me so He prepared you by the working of the Holy Ghost, brought you to salvation and then had our paths cross one more time."

"But Jerry," I protested. "What if I'm happy where I am? After all, I'm finally doing what I've longed to do all my life, and doing quite well at that. Forgive me for asking, but why would God want me to leave what He's already given me, including my established business and clientele? What do I know about radio? By your own admission, you have some 'seat of the pants' training. I don't even have that. I haven't any background or education in those areas. What makes you so sure?"

Jerry's reply was not anything near what I wanted to hear. His assessment of my life could not have been any more truly described.

"Dave, you've been blessed. You know that, don't you?" He didn't wait for my reply. "You have a very comfortable life. You've succeeded in so many areas of life where most people only dream. Look at what you have. Has God asked for anything from you except your love? I'd venture He hasn't. But God hasn't given you all of this for selfish enjoyment. I know this is hard to imagine, but He's not asking you to leave it all behind. He's not asking for you to travel to a jungle. He's not even asking you to give up this beautiful house. He just wants you to help him spread the Gospel right here in Ridgemont. There will be nothing, I repeat, nothing you'll ever do in life more rewarding or lasting than making contributions to Heaven in the form of souls. Who knows what else He has planned for you if you will but follow Him. You can't out give Him and you can't plan a better life than He will provide if you but say yes to Him.

"I won't ask you for your answer right now. In fact, Dave, I'll give you a week, only because I am desperately in need of getting you in and helping. But I will share this with you. You will have an answer from God by Saturday, in a very real and dramatic way. And what's more, God will start dealing with you about this tonight."

"Well, let me ask you this, Jerry; what is it that you seem to think I can do for you at the station?"

"I could talk to you on that subject 'til next month but I won't. Suffice it to say that the AM side is operating adequately, but its aging electronic equipment and outdated technology are in desperate need of replacement. When we gradually replace the equipment, as we've already started doing, we call it – phasing. Most of the time it's done at night, when we're off the air. It's very tedious and time-consuming work, requiring many hours of overtime for the staff and myself. The FM side has been licensed but hasn't gone on the air yet. We have an FCC deadline that stipulates we get on the air or lose the license. In a nutshell, you would finish the set-up and run the FM side while I continue getting the AM side updated. After that...and these are long-range plans that I hope won't scare you off...we'll probably be involved in the initial stages of a Christian television station."

Immediately I became doubtful and defensive; certain he had the wrong man. "Photography is one thing, Jerry; television is quite another. They're both visual media forms, but the resemblance ends there. You've succeeded in totally overwhelming me. I can share your enthusiasm. I can even appreciate your dream, but whether I can share in the achievement of that dream is still a long way from being determined," I slowly responded. "But don't you dare leave me alone to this decision. I'll pray about this – believe me I'll pray – but you'd better pray too. I've been a Christian long enough to know God hears our prayers and answers, but His answer on this one better be an unmistakable one, and I mean REALLY unmistakable."

With that, Jerry looked at his watch and started for the door. We shook hands saying good night. As I sat in front of the dying fire, I was flooded with varied opinions. On the one hand, a good challenge never scared me off, but likewise, I've always been keenly aware of my abilities, never picking a fight I couldn't win. As my mind filled with questions, I said the first of many prayers that night.

"Lord, I don't know where to start praying, but I do know that if I ask, You will unclutter my mind. If I ask, You will place Your will in my spirit, and let me know the peace of Christ in this decision."

Sitting in the dark for what seemed like only a few minutes when in fact hours had passed, the events of the day went running, no, rambling through my mind. I say rambling because they all ran together with no apparent order or focus. Then a slight chill brought me to my senses. The fire had gone completely out and with the thermostat set at 50 degrees the house was now chilly. Checking my watch, I couldn't believe the time. Jerry had left just before ten, now it was 3:00 a.m. Where had I been? Had I dozed off? I didn't know, but I knew I wasn't any closer to a decision than when Jerry left. Confusion ruled in my mind. I could make only one decision tonight and that was to surrender to the call for rest. Closing my eyes, I breathed a short prayer, falling asleep before the "Amen" was heard in heaven.

The radio woke me up at 7 a.m. The soft music wanted to coax me back to slumber but the call of a new day was not to be denied. With more office work in the morning and a social engagement to shoot in the early evening, perhaps I could have that delayed afternoon walk in the woods, if the weather cooperated. A few moments later the weather forecast came on calling for partly cloudy skies with a high of 60 to 65 degrees. Those high temperatures would occur in the afternoon and would add to the pleasure of the woods and the solitude I enjoyed while there. Then came those letters as the radio announcer identified the station...W P F H.

I was starting to wonder why those call letters attracted me more than before. Was it because I knew who ran the station? Was it because of Jerry's offer? Or was there something else? My concern triggered a spontaneous prayer. "God, Jerry said I would have your answer by Saturday, yet right now I feel no closer. You know I love my job. Do you want me to give that up? Please let me know the answers to all my questions. This really has happened much too quickly and unexpectedly for me to make a rational decision by myself."

"What problems face humanity?"

I wondered where that question came from. What problems face humanity? Indeed, all kinds of problems face humanity, I answered internally. War, famine, pestilence, all the things God's word tells us about in Matthew 24:7 are problems that face humanity.

"Yes, but something else faces humanity."

The eminent return of Jesus Christ is a problem facing humanity—at least that portion of humanity that hasn't accepted Him as Savior. But there are evangelists, missionaries and preachers warning the people about that future event, I reasoned. How does that affect me? And how does that affect my current decision process? Then I realized – the question was composed of four words. What Problems Face Humanity? WPFH. "Oh God, surely that's just a coincidence. That isn't an unmistakable answer. God, you can surely do much better than that...you know, lightning or something."

"Answer the question!" came the command to my inner ears. Just as quickly came the answer so I spoke it out loud.

"Hearing the Gospel of Jesus Christ."

"How do they hear?" came another question.

"Lord, are you going to play twenty questions with me? Where is all this leading?" I asked aloud.

I dressed, gulped some orange juice, and listened momentarily to the silence of the house. Apparently God didn't care to continue with someone who was being argumentative, so He stopped. I took advantage of the silence, retreating to my car. Because I had dallied at the house for so long the sky was already brilliantly ablaze from the morning sun. There was a spattering of white fluffy clouds, the kind that made the blue of the sky appear deeper than usual. I projected my thoughts beyond the morning's work to the afternoon's walk in the woods. That's when I would be able to continue the conversation with God, I reasoned. That is of course, if He desired to do so with me.

The morning's work lasted into the early afternoon. Finally finished, I locked up the studio and headed for home, with one stop on the way at the discount store for film; just in case I encountered any critters or promising scenery. By the time I got home, ate a sandwich, loaded the camera and changed clothes, it was nearly two o'clock. The social event I was to shoot started at 5:30 and would run through nine. That left me better than an hour to walk. More than enough, I figured.

I had walked through the wooded section of my back yard so many times that an established trail now existed. It was filled with various photographic delights such as scrub oaks, white birch, poplars, fully grown maples and pine trees of varying shades, sizes and needle types. Often ground squirrels and other ground critters would scurry for safety as the sound of crunching leaves and twigs under my feet announced human trespass into their world. I had had many close-up encounters with deer, raccoons, and rabbits on my many jaunts along the nature trail. I hoped today's trek would be likewise rewarded. God had something else waiting for me.

Jerry's words came quickly to the forefront of my mind. Yes, God had been extremely good to me. Although I had never married, He found ways to keep me comforted and happy without a wife. In fact, the desire to be married had faded into my past long ago. It was almost funny how it had come to my mind while remembering both the decision that confronted me, and the words Jerry spoke the night before. No matter what decisions I made; no matter where life took me, my decisions would not have any effects on a wife, a family or a marriage. Fortunately in this case, those things weren't factors. I searched for things that were involved—there were really none, other than my photography business. Then my mind rapidly listed other things that weren't factors that required consideration. Money wasn't a problem so long as Jerry offered a reasonable salary. Moving wasn't a factor; the station was in the same community. Surprisingly even the work wasn't a factor; though I lacked experience, I felt confident enough in my abilities to adapt and learn. Then why wouldn't the answer come?

Quite accidentally I noticed an oddity at the side of the path that I hadn't noticed on any of my previous treks. I framed the scene in the viewfinder of the camera, firing off six or seven shots from various angles. The subject of the pictures was that of a one or two year old pine sapling growing up from the softened center of a rotten tree stump.

"Look at that," I thought out loud. "A new tree up from the stump of the old." How great was God's design to allow for that to happen. He did the same thing with me when He saved me. Then I realized the truth of the new birth. Everyone who has accepted Jesus as savior and made Him Lord of their life, experiences a rebirth, just like that new pine tree rising out of the ruins of the old decomposing one.

Was God just showing me something about my past in that old tree stump with the new tree growing out of it? Or was He showing me something about the future? Was the job offer from Jerry God's way of getting me to start a new life from my old? He had done that with me once, spiritually, with salvation. Now He might be doing that with my physical life.

"Where do people find Him?" God apparently started.

I had found Him during the final years of military service. As was my case, the usual common denominator seemed to be need. Most people, I suspect, find Jesus, and spiritual life, through a need, be it internal, external or both.

"Where do people find Him?"

At church, I suspect, Lord. And in the preached word, in the music... yes, in the music like I do.

"That's where people find Him. Where People Find Him!"

"Yes Lord, WHERE PEOPLE FIND HIM! W P F H!"

That was the second time that had happened. The second time those letters had been displayed to me in mind and spirit. It was time to determine if it was God's way of alerting me to His will. But just how would I do that? No, just how would He do that?

Before showering for my 5:30 booking, I left a message with the station receptionist. "Tell Jerry, David Post called. I'm not certain I have God's answer yet, but I know He's talking. If he can spend some time with me later tonight or tomorrow, have him call me back."

When I returned home about ten I went immediately to my answering machine. Jerry's message was the last one of three. He could meet with me for breakfast in the morning at the Downtowner at six. I got ready for bed.

CHAPTER TWO

I awoke only moments before the alarm went off. The furnace was running, certain evidence that temperatures had fallen through the night. I settled back into the warm sanctuary of the waterbed, pulling the quilt over my head and lie there waiting for the news and weather on the radio. Soon the newscaster announced a temperature of 28 degrees and an accumulation of one to two inches of snow. Certain he was playing a *War of the Worlds* joke on his audience, I hit the floor running, spying out through the frosted window. Sure enough, the scene was as perfect as a Christmas card; everything was blanketed with the season's first, fluffy flakes of snow. A black and white photographer's delight!

Remembering the breakfast appointment with Jerry, I quickly readied myself for the day and headed out into the white, winter wonderland. Cautiously I drove into town where the roads changed from slick and snow covered to just wet.

The sidewalks, however, left a lot to be desired. Whereas the city streets had been salted, at ten till six in the morning, the sidewalks had not. I tried desperately to remember and apply the proper procedures for safe walking under such wintry conditions. Regrettably though, I had chosen the wrong kind of shoes for the occasion and down I went.

"First casualty of the winter," someone behind me said. Then I spied the gloved hand of that someone offering to help me stand. It was Jerry. "I thought that was you, Dave," he said. "I did the same thing about a block back. By the time I got up, you were coming out of the parking garage. Are you okay?" My reply assured him that I was fine, but it had not assured me. My first step triggered pain in my right hip, which in turn caused a slight limp.

"Let me pray for that," Jerry said as he placed his hand on the side of my hip and spoke in a foreign language; or at least what I presumed in my ignorance to be a foreign language. Remarkably, as soon as he started praying, the pain in my hip subsided. Maybe subsided isn't the right word...the pain was gone, not just fading away, but gone!

"Say Jerry, that was quicker than an aspirin. How did you do that?" I asked.

Jerry started explaining the power of divine healing. As he did so, we continued the treacherous trek toward the Downtowner Café. Although the pain in my hip was gone, and my pride had been somewhat restored, I was still very hungry, both for food and for what Jerry was telling me. In my few short years as a Christian I had turned away from what I had heard termed as faith healings. But maybe, I thought, there was something more to this that my lack of Christian depth had caused me to reject.

Soon we were seated, awaiting our breakfast orders. Jerry hadn't stopped talking, and I hadn't stopped listening. When he finished explaining the healing power of Jesus and His being "...the same yesterday, today and forever...." I waited a few moments for all of what he said to settle into my mind and spirit. Then I asked, "But what was it you said as you placed your hand on the side of my hip?"

"I simply prayed in the Holy Ghost; tongues if you prefer. Haven't you ever done that?" Jerry's question sparked a whole new series of questions in my head. Yes, I had heard of that, but just as I had without investigation dismissed faith healing, I had likewise dismissed as fanaticism the practice of speaking in tongues.

"Dave? Oh Dave. Did you hear me?" Jerry prodded. "Hey guy, where you at?"

I quietly replied, "I was just considering all that you've said this morning. Certainly I've heard of speaking in tongues, but I've never done it. I'm not certain I would know how. You're the first person I've ever seen do it, right in front of me, not on T.V."

"Dave, a more pointed question would be, have you..." Jerry's next question was interrupted midstream by the waitress bringing our breakfasts. "...have you ever received the baptism of the Holy Ghost?" He didn't leave me time to answer as he continued, "I know you're a Christian, but what's happened beyond your new birth? Maybe we need to talk specifics. Could you start by sharing your testimony with me?"

That wasn't a problem; I had done that before at church. God's generous gift of salvation had finally found me on one of my many Air Force trips. This memorable one was to Mississippi. I would always include my Catholic background and its part in both hindering and aiding me to recognize my fallen and sinful state. (Hindered by not being taught the complete plan of salvation; aided by convincing me of my sinful nature.) It may have also been the source of a deep-rooted belief that there was a God somewhere to be reckoned with. Certainly I knew that death would someday find me. And just as certainly, there would be an inevitable accountability for what had been done in this life. All of that was part of me, tucked away very deep inside of me; yet more often than not, I pushed it aside, living the kind of life that I wanted to, not what I knew was right. But one day, while feeling desperate and alone, in the privacy of my dormitory room, without the help of a preacher, I confessed my sins and determined in my heart to turn to God. In retrospect, I know what happened. The Holy Ghost with His convicting power had performed a mighty work in my life, displaying the way of salvation through the cleansing blood of Christ. I accepted, not with a standard sinner's prayer but rather with knees and spirit bowed to the Lord; tears falling like rain. I acknowledged my need of a Savior; God provided the rest.

"That's absolutely super", Jerry responded to my testimony. "But what about since then? What's happened spiritually since then?"

"Well, I immediately bought a Bible and started reading it, remaining with the Catholic Church for about a year. Soon I could no longer agree with anything more than the Church's anti-abortion stance, so I left. Because I was still in the Air Force, I started attending the Protestant service in the base chapel. They were kind of generic in nature and not especially moving, except for the first time I heard the Doxology. I just about got raptured."

Jerry stopped me long enough to interject, "The rapture, now that's another story. I don't mean to cut you short but I do have a job to get to, and there is a different subject we were supposed to be discussing...you know, the radio station."

I finished my breakfast as Jerry completed the verbal picture of his immediate needs at WPFH and a quick outline of his goals. He then asked me what I needed from him to help make my decision process easier. I told him I was beginning to think God wanted me to join him at the station, but I felt He hadn't yet confirmed it in a way that satisfied me. I also told Jerry it was important in the decision process to know more about the station's history, his involvement, commitment, and the financial status of the station, as well as what he estimated I would be worth to him.

Jerry told me he would like me to spend some time with him at the station when we both would be free to discuss these topics. In fact, he pressured me into setting a date and time. My schedule was flexible but his was not. It was now Friday and I remembered Jerry's words from our previous conversation at my house, "...you will have your answer from God by Saturday..."

"Well Jerry," I said, "What's on your agenda for tomorrow? My Saturdays are always free."

"I have a lot of work to do. But if you can spend some time with me at the station tomorrow, then tomorrow it is."

We left the café together but turned in different directions. My office was

22

around the corner, two blocks down on Chaffin Street. The WPFH studios and offices were five blocks further down Washington Street. The transmitter site was about a mile away on the top of Signal Hill, which was the highest point in the county.

The rest of the day consisted of three portrait appointments with seniors from Ridgemont High School in the morning, and in the afternoon, darkroom work from the previous night's social shootings. It was while in the darkroom that I had time to think about the events of the past two days. Although I hadn't given hours on end to prayer and meditation on the subject, I did feel God had been closely guiding my life. I was still filled with wonder, especially at the call letters and the two unusual sentences I had experienced the day before.

Soon the thoughts and meditation led me to a time of prayer, asking God to let me keep photography as a part-time job or at least a hobby. It was as though I had already made up my mind. Such a strong, overwhelming peace came upon me in a way I had never experienced before. It could best be defined as confidence—a confidence in taking a new direction in life. Yet it was even more than that—as if I could make no mistake in this decision because no mistake was possible. That's what I was feeling—a confidence, an enthusiasm and a sense that I was moving in the direction God was leading. God was, for the first time since my salvation, involved in my life in a way that was tangible and real. He was providing a clear and definable purpose that made me aware I had simply been meandering though life. I concluded my prayer as the photo prints were coming out of the dryer. "...and with Your help in future, God, just as real and close as it is right now, I will be obedient to Your call. I know You won't let me down, but I pray Your guidance and strength so I don't let You down. This will not be an interim job or part-time calling. I fully expect, and rest my faith in the fact that You will use this as my life's calling. But more than that, God, place within me the burning desire to have souls saved that this job requires, and that has been lacking in my life. I ask it all in the precious name of Jesus, Your Son and my Savior. Amen."

As I came out of the darkroom someone was leaving a message on the answering machine. To avoid disruptions and accidents in the darkroom, I always turn it on when I'm in there. Although there is an extension phone in there, I refuse to answer it when I'm working with solutions or printing negatives. The last time I did, I ruined a batch of beautiful Mackinac Island nature scenes. Playing back the message, I was taken by surprise. It was the mayor's secretary.

"Mayor Tom O'Keefe wants to see you on an important matter. Please call his office at 448-9800."

I immediately returned the call. The city's official photographer, Mike Rogers, had accepted a job in the Detroit area. The vacancy was going to be filled by the mayor next week. If I wanted the job or at least an opportunity to be interviewed for the position, I needed to be at City Hall Monday morning at nine.

This meant rethinking my decision. Or did it? I had just committed to letting God direct my life and to giving Jerry an answer upon completion of our Saturday meeting. How could one phone call cause me to change my mind or rescind my heart's pledge to God? It couldn't, I confirmed with the thud of my fist on the desk, but I would go to City Hall on Monday just to see what the deal was.

The moment that thought resounded in my mind, my spirit rose up within me, causing me to feel uneasy. It was as though I had just betrayed God by even contemplating the Mayor's offer. Although I couldn't properly describe or define the rumblings in my spirit, I believed that what I was feeling was not of God. After all, God had left me feeling good, confident, at peace, and alive. This was leaving me with feelings of insecurity, guilt, and being out-of-sorts with God. That must have meant it was from the devil. I became more certain of that as the realization came to me that the city job would be out of God's will. I wanted no part of that scenario. I decided just as abruptly that I wouldn't even go to the mayor's office. Case closed! I felt better immediately.

I took the proofs of the social to Madame Francene DeVille's mansion, chatting with her over tea for the better part of two hours. She is a marvelous conversationalist, and quite well informed on most topics of discussion, even at her rumored age of 83. She didn't display the slightest concern with the gossip that purported her two grandsons, Charles and Milton, to be in a power struggle over the estate of her late husband. She was desperately, and hopelessly locked into the past as far as her role as matriarch of the family. Yet I found her to be as contemporary as the latest fad or fashion from New York or the west coast. By the time I bade farewell to Madame DeVille it was nearly five – still early enough for me to walk through the woods again, and I felt a compelling need to do so.

24

Tossing the day's mail on the sofa, I changed my clothes and set out for the woods. The majority of the morning's snow had melted, especially in the sunlit areas and along the roads. But the trail through the woods still held much of the beauty that is naturally a part of the season's first snowfall. Many of the trees were bent over under the weight of the heavy snow, while others had shed their covering, having been urged to do so by the strong breezes of the day. Visible through the shroud of lacy white snow crystals and transparent ice shards was the luscious red of some tempting late fall berries. Normally tasty morsels to the raucous and scrappy blue jays of the north, these treats had somehow escaped their foraging.

When I returned to the house I was greeted by friend and fellow photographer Cal Simmons. He had just arrived and was getting out of his car. His visit was triggered by his concern about the vacant city photographer job. I told Cal that the Mayor's office had contacted me but that I had pretty much dismissed it. His face immediately reflected a relieved look as he spoke.

"Apparently the mayor was considering just four of the county's 45 professional and semi-professional photographers. If you're not interested, then besides myself, only two others are in contention."

"I certainly wish you well, Cal," I responded as he turned to leave. If anyone could do a good job for Mayor O'Keefe, it would be you."

"Thanks for the encouragement, Dave." Cal said, while giving me a half wave and half salute as he departed

Once he left, I went inside to fix supper. My evening consisted of eating, watching the news and climbing in bed. I was anxiously looking forward to the next day's planned events. Surely, I supposed, God would finalize his answer tomorrow, just as Jerry had predicted. My human reasoning determined that God's undeniable answer would somehow come during the course of morning's discussion with Jerry. No matter how He decided to give me His confirmation, it wouldn't surprise me too much; I already knew the answer. As I saw it, it was just a formality. After all, peace had led me this far; peace I would continue to follow.

The phone rang about five in the morning. It was Jerry.

"We've had a fire at the station, Dave! Can you...." The sentence was temporarily left unfinished as he spoke to someone in the background, then continued, "...can you come over here right now?"

Because I was more asleep than awake, his frantic words fell chaotically on the floor rather than entering my ear and processing in my head. Suddenly

I caught their meaning and the reality of what Jerry had just said hit me. "You say the station's on fire?" I asked, trying to reconfirm his startling statement.

"Not now! It's out! They put it out about ten minutes ago. Please Dave, I'm going to be very busy for the next couple of days, if you're going to take the job, I need you to be here right now!"

The urgency of Jerry's voice demanded and got my answer. "I'll be right there," I responded. Without waiting for further instructions, I hung up and got dressed. Thank God the roads were clear of snow and ice. I drove much faster than I should have, arriving at the station in just over ten minutes. Jerry greeted me at the door as soon as I entered. He ushered me to where the fire had been. The smoky, choking smell apprehended me as we entered the AM studio.

Jerry started filling me in as we walked. "We've just lost the AM side. The fire started in some of the old equipment I was telling you about that needed to be replaced. The morning announcer, Dan Franklin, was just arriving for the start of his shift, sometime before four. The fire chief said he suspects that was about the time it started, but there was enough damage to take it out. As far as I can determine, we've lost four cart machines, two turntables, the modulation monitor and remote controller and of course all the cables, wires and patch cords...oh, yes, and the three brand new mikes and two compact disk players we had just installed."

"What does all that mean, Jerry," I asked. "How do we get the AM back on the air?"

"We don't!" Jerry asserted. "We get the FM up! If we took the new equipment from the FM side, using it to get the AM side back on the air, that would delay the FM start-up, and cause the loss of the FM license. We can't do that. Don't forget, we're talking about the Gospel of Jesus Christ and we know who it was that tried to do us in with the fire, don't we?"

I nodded.

"In fact," Jerry continued, "I wouldn't be a bit surprised if he did this not only to knock us off the air but to get you guessing about whether you should join the station. All things considered, I wouldn't be too surprised if you turned me down right now."

He stepped out of the AM studio and went down the hall and into his office. I followed. After a slight pause, Jerry continued, "Now would be a good time to start our scheduled conversation, Dave. You know, the one we were supposed to have today anyway. My problem is, I don't know where to start."

"Then let me start," I said, grabbing two Styrofoam cups and filling them with coffee. "Fill me in on your involvement with both WCDP and WPFH."

"All right. That's as good as any place to start," he replied, holding his face in his hands, elbows resting on the desk and looking as frazzled as expected under the trying circumstances. "WCDP was licensed back in the early sixties and had a format of contemporary music, rock and roll, as well as top forty: you know, Beatles, Turtles, Rolling Stones, Dion, Herman's Hermits. You get the idea. I joined the station on the graveyard shift, nine in the evening until sign off at one, initially in the traffic department and as a runner. My job was to get advertising and promotional tapes in and out as required as well as getting records for the D.J.'s from the library. You see, you can't possibly keep all those records in the studio, you have to store them where they can be retrieved easily when people call in on the request line. Then, once I graduated from Northern Michigan University, they moved me up to a position that included making promo's.

"The next step up was to make me an on-air position, reading news, sports and weather. That's when I went from part-time to full-time. The manager then, Steve Busadis, said I had a good radio voice and that I should develop it. I never got the opportunity because it was at that time that the station was sold to Mr. Gramswald—Jerome Gramswald. He still owns the station, but his first move back then was to switch formats from top forty to Christian. He's a very nice man; I've had several occasions to go to Chicago, where he lives, and visit with him, and he's been up here. You see, this is his personal missionary project. He doesn't do it for the profit. In fact, we don't need to make a profit; he subsidizes us. We get some donations and there's some income from the Christian programmers we air, but the fact is we get over ninety percent of our annual budget from him. Financially speaking, we're in good shape. That's why Satan used fire; he can't get to us through finances.

"Well, when Mr. Gramswald bought the station he had to apply for a new license. The call letters of course changed, as they usually do with the sale of a station; that's how we got the WPFH we use today. That was nearly five years ago. Two years ago, Mr. Gramswald told us he wanted to switch to the FM band, which is a much better media to broadcast on, but we told him that the broadcast distance would be greatly reduced. He still wanted an FM station. We, the Board of Governors and myself, flew to Chicago to try to persuade Mr. Gramswald to keep the AM and upgrade the equipment. The compromise that we worked out was to keep the AM for distance primarily and get the FM station to develop its own audience. I believe he still fully intends to do away with the AM side but we've bought some time, so to speak. Well the rest is history. We got the FM license roughly five months ago and the restrictive clause in the license is that it must be up and at full power, 50,000 watts, within eight months. We're nearly there as you know.

"As I said a few minutes ago, financially we are in good shape. All the big-ticket equipment for the FM is in and nearly all set up. It just needs to be set to specifications, speced if you will, and put in line. The transmitter site is prepared and ready to beam the word of God to the people living in a 65-mile radius. We were expecting to have it on the air by the middle of August, the end of August at the latest. That was, before we encountered a few major technical delays, all of which have been resolved. Now this fire hits. Although the fire didn't damage the FM side of the building, it could cause a delay or it could mean an earlier start up."

I immediately interjected my first question. "Explain that paradox to me, if you will."

"Sure," Jerry replied as he refilled our coffee cups. "If I drop the renovation and upgrading of the AM side, placing all our attention to the FM, we could be on the air by this time next week. But if I stop all work on the FM side, place the emphasis on getting the AM back on the air, then the FM falls as much as two months off the pace and right smack dab in the FCC's cancel zone. Remember what I told you the other day? I simply can't do both—at least not by myself.

"Now Dave, do you think you want to join me here and make your first decision? Which is it?"

"Hold on, who put me on the payroll? I'm certainly leaning toward joining you here, but let's finish the background information before you saddle me with any major decisions." My statement surprised the both of us with its directness, but Jerry smiled in agreement and proceeded with the history class.

"Shortly after Mr. Gramswald bought the station, he fired the station manager. I have no direct confirmation of this, but Steve Busadis wanted, as manager, to keep the top forty format and go to hard or acid rock in the evening hours. Keep in mind Dave, there were only three Christians here, receptionist and part-time D.J., Trish Ivey, who now works as a full-time air personality for WJOH, a middle of the road station in Castleton; a midday news anchor and fill-in disc jockey, Carl Worth, and myself; the rest of the staff were non-Christians. Mr. Gramswald laid it on the line saying, '...the format turns to Christian and it turns to Christian now. Turn with it or leave!' With that ultimatum, Steve left. That put me in charge temporarily until Mr. Gramswald came up from Chicago about a month later. At that time he spoke to me about being station manager on a permanent basis, which I accepted, and temporary president, which I also accepted. He signed power of attorney papers and gave me free rein with every aspect of running the AM, and getting the FM rolling. I make the purchases; he pays the bills."

By this time Jerry and I were about to polish off our fourth cup of coffee. The sun had risen over Lake Superior and was shining right into Jerry's office window.

"Okay so far," I started. "What about your future here?"

"I've moved up so fast I really haven't had time to think about that. But one thing's for sure; I'm really not a radioman. I don't have anywhere near the background or education needed for the position here. I'm trusting God for everything, and I do mean everything. I have no plans to leave the station. First of all, the Upper Peninsula of Michigan has become home for me. I may have been born and raised in Illinois, but this is home now. My wife, Carol, is from Munising, and her folks still live there. I've come to love and truly enjoy the atmosphere of the U.P. It's still clean, wholesome, safe, and in nearly the same shape it was when God created it. I don't anticipate any job offers or changes, nor have I solicited any. The bottom line is this, Dave, if you agree to come on board, you'll be stuck with me for the foreseeable future. Is that the answer you were looking for?"

"Yes it is Jerry," I replied. "But, I'm sorry to say, there is still one more question that I have to ask. Now please don't get me wrong, I know...."

Jerry didn't let me finish. He anticipated my next question. "Stop. Don't ask. Here's the package I'm offering you." He slid a legal size sheet of paper across the table he had retrieved from his inside coat pocket. It listed the compensation I would receive for joining him in the radio business.

On reviewing Jerry's offer, I found it to meet my needs so I asked Jerry one more question. "Do you have the authority to offer this proposal, or do you have to get Mr. Gramswald's okay on it?"

Jerry's reply took me by surprise. "That is Mr. Gramswald's offer, not mine. If you find it acceptable, you can sign it and start today. If you would like to renegotiate any portion of it, well, we would need to call him and discuss the changes. Is that fair enough?"

It had finally come to this. The time had finally arrived for me to make up my mind. "It's quite acceptable, and more than adequate. I'm getting more excited about this offer than I ever thought I would. It's just...well, just a difficult decision to make, you know, in the flesh. Spiritually I have absolutely no reservations. God hasn't spoken to me audibly. But what has transpired during this period, especially the call letters of the station...Oh, say, I didn't tell you about that did I? You see, Jerry, a question came to me while I first started seriously contemplating your offer. The question was simply, 'What problems face humanity?' I thought about that for some time. The answers that came to mind led me to the conclusion that the problems facing humanity – including the humanity that resides in this area – can only be resolved by Him; Him being the Lord Jesus. That line of reasoning led me to the second question, 'Where do people find Him?' That answer is as vast as each personal, life-changing encounter God has recorded in the Lamb's Book of Life. One of the ways people can find Christ is through the various broadcasts of Christian radio stations. As you can see, if you jot down 'what problems face humanity,' and 'where people find Him,' the first letter of each word can represent the station's call letters WPFH. I know that's not all that profound in and of its self. But the way God quickened my spirit as each of those revelations came to me was undeniably real. Jerry, I accept your offer. I'm working for you, effective right now."

Jerry straightened up in his chair, saying as he did. "David, don't ever discount the way God decided to work out His answer to you. He doesn't normally hit you upside the head to get your attention. Most of the time He gently taps you on the spiritual shoulder."

I retrieved a pen from my shirt pocket and inked the contract.

CHAPTER THREE

Closing my photo shop required immediate action so I left the station about ten o'clock. The first thing to be done was inform the owners of the building I rented that I would soon be vacating. I would work the remainder of my scheduled appointments from the house, and perform the darkroom operations there as well. The schedule was sure to be busy for the next several weeks, especially if I wanted to be out of the photography business by the end of September.

Inside the shop the answering machine took a message. I listened intently to the call without picking up the phone. It was the mayor. He was concerned about my apparent lack of interest in the vacant city photographer's job.

"Name your salary, Dave," he started. "I've interviewed three of the top four prospectives – all but you. I believe you're really the man I want. I know this is Saturday and you may not hear this until Monday, but I'll be here 'til six tonight. If you can't come in today give me a call. I believe we can arrive at agreeable terms right over the phone."

I didn't expect the job to be delivered on a silver platter, and certainly not on a Saturday morning. The mayor had even called me "Dave" and we'd only met twice. I assumed the reason he was so adamant about wanting me was because he had seen several of my photos in the paper or some of the local travel brochures I had been involved with. At any rate, I wasn't too thrilled about going through that decision routine again. After all, I had just accepted Jerry's offer a mere three hours earlier.

I quickly dialed the mayor's office and politely asked him to take me out of consideration. I also made a pitch for Cal Simmons, telling Mayor O'Keefe I thought Cal was an excellent candidate for the job. He took my recommendation under advisement and said good-bye. I could tell by his tone of voice he was either disappointed or angry, but it didn't matter to me.

My next call was to the home of my business attorney, Pat Harvey. We agreed to a Monday afternoon appointment. After we hung up I started on the next item on my ad hoc checklist; that being to prepare a letter to all my clients informing them of the closing. The letter would provide them an opportunity to buy their respective negatives and proofs, and thus reduce my otherwise hefty files while eliminating future return business.

While the computer was running in the PRINT mode, creating the nearly 400 letters, I searched for another station to replace the now vacant frequency of WPFH. The scanning brought in WJOH and a song I liked, so I left the dial there while slowly walking to the coffee pot. I was standing there, stirring in the creamer in when I heard the soft, gentle, and attractive voice of the lady announcer. She identified the station and then herself, Trish Ivey.

I immediately recalled what Jerry had told me earlier, that she had once been with WCDP, around the time it became WPFH, leaving for a job with WJOH. Soon my listening became more intent, discovering I liked her style of delivery. She seemed to be a no-nonsense, smooth, articulate announcer. She also seemed to work her on-air routines well, easily giving me the impression she was a master of live, fast-paced radio work.

"Just listen to me," I said aloud to myself. "Not even four hours in the broadcast business and already I'm a know-it-all on radio disc jockeys." But, I argued with myself, she revealed a lot of talent and that kind of talent should be on WPFH-FM. I got the yellow pages out and jotted down the phone number for WJOH. I punched the numbers quickly on my phone without giving myself a chance to chicken out.

"WJOH, your easy listening station in the north country. May I help you?"

While my call appeared to be answered by a secretary or receptionist I only wanted to talk to Trish. Although I didn't want to, I left a message for her to call me, leaving my office and home phone numbers.

What kind of chance could I have to sway her back to WPFH? It was a good thing I was just stuffing envelopes because that was just one of many questions that raced through my mind. I likewise went to mentally wandering over all sorts of other things; the radio station, the fire, the program format, announcers, DJ's, etc. After the lengthy program run the printer finally stopped spitting out letters. In just over an hour all the envelopes were stuffed and sealed, awaiting postage stamps. I would do that job at the house later.

Trish hadn't returned my call by the time I completed my work, so shortly after five I decided to go home. I was still mulling things over in my mind as I drove home. Normally I only schedule appointments on for photo shoots Saturdays, but for the next several weeks there would probably be other weekend photography work, if only amounting to a couple of hours. Tuning on the car radio as I drove home I located WJOH but Trish was no longer in the air-chair. I breathed a short prayer asking God to give me a chance to talk to her about coming back to WPFH.

The evening was spent sitting in the living room with my feet propped up on the coffee table, moistening stamps. I'd done that job enough times to know the right way; a damp sponge on a saucer of water. I attacked the mountain of envelopes and had the stack about half done when the phone rang. It was Jerry.

"Oh it's you Jerry," I responded.

"Hey, you sound a little disappointed. You aren't second guessing yourself now are you?" He asked.

"No, Jerry, I'm not. I was just expecting a call from Trish Ivey."

"Well, I know I'm no Trish Ivey," Jerry answered. "But will I do for the time being?"

After taking a swig of Coca-Cola, I answered him. "Of course. I only mentioned Trish because I left a message at WJOH for her to call me. Do you think she might come back to WPFH-FM?"

`My question must have taken him by surprise because his answer didn't come as quickly as I had expected. "Well," Jerry broke the silence. "She might. Then again, she might not. Why do you want her specifically?"

"I guess it's really just an impulse. I was at my shop, getting things in order to close the business. I turned on the radio and of course with no WPFH-AM I scanned the dial until I found WJOH. Trish was on the air at the time. If I remember correctly, you told me she was a receptionist and part time D.J. with you prior to leaving WPFH. Apparently she's working as an announcer, and doing a great job of it, I might add. You said she was one of the three Christians that were at WPFH. It's important that our FM staff be Christians, considering the purpose of the station." I paused for a moment as the thought hit me that I may have over stepped my area of responsibility. Then I cautiously continued. "Jerry, I'm sorry, I wasn't thinking right. Tell me if I did something I shouldn't have, you know, not consulting with you first."

This time Jerry was quick to reply. "No, Dave, that's not it at all. Listen, you're the boss of the FM. The only area you have to consult with me on is programming. Mr. Gramswald holds me personally responsible for the doctrinal considerations, like what can and can't be aired. The FM side is going to air some of the same programs as the AM was, but with considerably more music time. Who you hire to spin the discs or cue up the tapes is your area of responsibility. I've already turned that over to you. You'll also make the decisions on other things like program time slots, with the exception of those programmers with whom we've already contracted specific times. We'll get more into that on Monday. Yes, Monday– that's what I originally called you about–what time are we going to see you? I know you have to gradually get out of the photography business."

"I haven't given it much thought," I replied. "I guess about seven o'clock, is that okay with you?"

"Sure Dave. Now how about church tomorrow? Where do you attend? Would you like to visit my church?" Jerry had changed the subject and fired off those questions so fast he caught me by surprise. In the back of my mind I knew tomorrow was Sunday, but the thought of church hadn't come to me. It must have been because of all the recent distractions.

"I hadn't given that much thought either. I'd like to go with you to your church. Where and when should I meet you?" I asked.

Jerry seemed ready for my question. "Meet Carol and me at the corner of Washington and Hyte at say...8:45, you can follow us. I'm sure it'll be a pleasant surprise for you. But know this, you will be blessed. When was the last time you went to church and God showed up?"

I believed his question to be rhetorical. I wouldn't have known how to answer it anyway. Instead, I just confirmed the time and gave him something to think about. "Jerry, be prepared tomorrow to tell me all you can about Trish. Somehow I think you know more about her than you're telling me. If there's some reason, any reason, that you would think it better not to offer her a job, then let me know. But know this, if she calls me tonight, I am going to talk to her about it."

"Dave, I don't have any reason to hide anything from you. I've already told you to hire whoever you believe will meet the needs of the station. Trish is a very pleasant woman and she is very good on the air. I dated her some before I met and married Carol. She attends Lord of the Harvest Church, where we go. We may even see her tomorrow. If she's there, I'll be sure to point her out to you—introduce you if you'd like.

"But I don't have to wait until tomorrow to tell you what I know about her. She's a strong Christian who lives her faith. She would fit well into our format. Like I said, as a professional radio announcer, she's the best there is. And she's a joy to know and work with, but....."

The "but" told me to expect bad news.

"Trish was married once," his story continued. "In fact, it was while she was working at WPFH that she married a very nice guy, or so we all thought. To make a long story short, Frank, that's her ex, left her two years into the marriage. She hasn't remarried or even dated since. Part of her reason for leaving WPFH was because she felt uncomfortable working with people who knew the circumstances of her failed marriage. What made it so hard on her was Frank professed Christ. I mean, if you gave me the top twenty attributes of a solid Christian, I'd tell you Frank Ivey had them all.

"There were absolutely no warning signals. No financial problems, no arguments, nothing to make you think they were headed for divorce. It was almost as if he had another person living inside him, and that other person was...." Again there was another pause. "...he just took off with some younger gal from down-state. I'm not one to spread rumors or tell secrets, and to be honest, I'd just as soon not tell you this at all, but you do have a need to know. I'll tell you so you can handle the situation if it comes up in any conversation you might have with her. Frank had apparently been seeing the other girl all the time he and Trish were dating, engaged and through the entire two years of their marriage. In short, she left for the job at WJOH so she could be more comfortable in her work environment.

"She's just a real sweet gal, but she may still be coming to grips with all that. My guess is she's still hurting. I would estimate it's been about ten months, maybe, since the divorce and nearly a year and a half since the story first came to light."

I waited momentarily to make sure Jerry was finished, then said, "I don't know if I should thank you for that information or not. At any rate, I'll be able to sidestep or be tactful about certain questions if she calls me. She hasn't yet and maybe she won't. I asked God to at least give me a chance. That may have to wait until tomorrow at church. Maybe she didn't even get my message."

With that, Jerry and I said good-bye and hung up. I went over all he had talked about while I finished up the stamping job. I must have sat there in a daze, thinking for a long time. The phone rang again, jolting me back to reality. I quickly answered; it was a wrong number.

CHAPTER FOUR

I tossed and turned all night pondering the Trish Ivey story and thinking about the FM format. It was nearly 2:30 a.m. before I finally fell asleep only to be jarred back to consciousness by the alarm. Yielding to its insistent call, I got out of bed, grumbling under my breath. Stumbling groggily to the bottom of the stairs, I flipped the switch to the coffee maker. The sun was already edging above the horizon and the colors of the leaves were a delight. It wasn't long before the beauty of the morning's unfolding scene had transformed me into a better state of mind.

Anxious as I was for a cup of coffee, I was too busy to stop. My hands hurriedly mounted a camera on the tripod. The outdoor panorama was progressing much too fast. The hues of blue in the sky, the colors of the leaves and the constantly brightening sun were just too enticing a temptation for me. I quickly recorded the vivid, ever-changing colors of the panorama until three rolls of film were exposed; 36-shots each. But by now the aroma of the coffee overpowered my artistic creativity, so I poured and consumed two cups like an addict in need of a fix.

After putting the camera equipment away I dressed for church. I was really looking forward to attending services with Jerry and Carol. Church had, of late, become a routine; no, a struggle. In comparison I could get closer to God from my own Bible study and prayer time than in church attendance, but even that didn't meet my total need. Somehow I knew my spirit was ready to experience something new—something that would cause growth. There had to be a church somewhere that was capable of waking my spirit from the drowsy rituals and programmed traditions of men to which it had grown accustomed. It wasn't that I dreaded the thought of leaving the church I attended, or even that my leaving might hurt the pastor and the Christian friends I had there. There just had to be a place where joy—real, deep, complete joy in the Lord—was the motivator for living the Christian life, rather than stark obligation. An obligation I felt leading me to frustration, and frustration resulting in guilt. Over the past several months I had slowly come to realize it was time to move on. Although I may have realized it, I hadn't yet convinced myself sufficiently to start the search. In other words, I hadn't found the right time for a switch. The only certainty I knew was there had to be more of God available to me than what I now had. I wanted more of God and maybe, just maybe, Jerry's church would show me where more of

God might be found.

Jerry spotted me, motioning for me to follow them, which I did. We drove out of town about two miles and turned left into the parking lot. The church appeared to be new, and big enough to hold four, maybe five hundred. The sign out front proclaimed in large white letters, "Lord of the Harvest Church".

There were no indications of what denomination it was so I asked Jerry as he and Carol stepped from their car to greet me. "Say, Jerry, you never did tell me what kind of church this is."

"It's non-denominational, Dave. How are you feeling this morning?" Jerry replied with a question.

"I'm fine, even though I didn't sleep well last night. I guess I just had too much on my mind. But listen, every church is something. What kind of church is this, so I know what to expect?" I persisted.

Jerry opened the door, holding it for Carol and me to enter. "If you must put a name on it–and I would rather you didn't–it is a combination of Word & Faith, Pentecostal, Charismatic and Holiness. I guess you could say it's the best of the best, at least according to Jerry McFarland."

The front pews were already filled so we sat about a third of the way back. These people surprised me. Most churches I had attended normally filled from the back to the front. This one was doing it in the opposite manner. And there was something else different. Instead of having my choice of seats as late as five minutes before the service was to begin, this church was filling up with forty minutes remaining prior to worship.

Some of the musicians had stationed themselves on the platform and were tuning their instruments as I leaned over and whispered to Jerry. "Am I going to see some of those gifts of the Holy Ghost you were telling me about the other day? You know, speaking in tongues?" Without allowing Jerry time to answer with more than a nod of his head, I continued my line of questioning. "What are the services like? How long do they last? What's the preaching like? The pastor does preach from the Bible here, doesn't he, Jerry?"

Jerry overdosed on my questions, motioning to stop the interrogation long enough to answer. "We don't follow an order of service here. If you look at the bulletin the ushers handed you, you'll see there's a schedule of events for the upcoming week, but there's no order of service that we follow. You see, unless God tells us to print an order of service, we don't. We do generally start the service with a time of praise and worship. This may be in the form of singing songs, spiritual songs and hymns, just as the Bible says we should. This time of praise and worship may even lead into high praise where either the pastor or song leader will start praising God in a heavenly language while the congregation follows along in their Spirit-directed language. Obviously we worship God because of who He is, that just naturally leads us into high praise. Depending on what gifts God desires to operate under, we may then see the gift of tongues, interpretation of tongues, prophecy, healings, etc. I guess what I'm trying to say is we let God direct the service. We don't make Him fit our plans. You can rest assured that we'll be fed from the Word. And we will be given the opportunity to help spread the gospel with our tithes and offerings."

This sounded intriguing. I could barely wait for it to begin. All the musicians were in their places and the tuning of instruments ceased. The music they started playing I found to be very rich, full and most uplifting. The tempo, a bit faster than I was normally used to in a church, was done with a great atmosphere of respect and holiness. The choir started singing; I just sat there getting blessed. If this were all there was to the service I could have easily gone home saying that I had been in the presence of the Lord.

The song leader came forward at about five minutes to ten and started welcoming us to the church. He asked for raised hands of first time visitors and I obliged him and an ushers handed me a welcome packet. Then the service started and the songs that were offered up to God in praise just about raptured me. I had never heard such corporate singing and praise. It was the kind of music one might expect to hear in Heaven; I was sure of that. Looking around I discovered the church was filled to overflowing. Even folding chairs were being used in the back. There was no way the place could have held any more people. I was certain they were already violating fire code with a congregation I estimated at 700.

By the end of the service I had purposed in my heart this was where I belonged. I couldn't remember a time in my Christian life where I had been so close to the presence of God. At no time had I experienced such beauty, praise, peace, love, and unity. When it came time for the pastor to close the service, I looked at my watch. Over two hours had elapsed since the service started, yet I would have guessed it had been no more than 45 minutes. Although I had many more questions about this new experience, I knew if I opened my spirit to what God had just introduced to me, I would find myself moving closer to Him. And closer to Him meant I could have a relationship with Him resulting in a spiritually energized life. That was what I wanted. I felt confident, after just one service, that this was where I could obtain a walk with God that I hadn't yet achieved.

Jerry could tell too. He didn't ask anything but rather made a statement of fact. "You've had an encounter with God. I can tell; it's all over you. Praise God! I guess I don't need to ask this. Are you coming back for the evening service? It starts at seven o'clock. Get here early!"

On the way out of church Jerry introduced me to Trish Ivey. She immediately apologized for not returning my call. She had dismissed it as a sales pitch for pictures. Jerry told her I was the new FM station manager and that I just joined the staff on Saturday. I asked Trish to call me so we could discuss an important matter, assuring her it was not to sell her a portrait setting. She promised me she would first thing Monday morning.

I must admit I found Trish very attractive, yet I could also sense that the scars were not completely healed. It wasn't a lack of self-confidence, the way she talked, or even her mannerisms; there just seemed to be a hurt resident within her, evidenced by a cautiousness. Maybe she felt uncomfortable around Jerry. Maybe she felt uncomfortable around me or men in general. Whatever it was, I was not going to let it get in the way of a professional job offer. I wanted her at WPFH. I told her I would be expecting her call in the morning.

The seven o'clock service seemed better than the morning service, if that were possible. I went by myself and sat in the middle of the sanctuary, trying to get a better feel for how the worshipers responded to the leading of the music and the song director. The one thing that became apparent to me as the praise and worship progressed was the sincerity of and the unrestrained intensity and dedication the people around me put into their praise. Their worship helped me get over my inhibitions. I mean, raising my hands in my old church meant asking a question, or worse yet, trying to answer one. But with these believers it just felt like a natural, holy and spontaneous way to honor the God of our faith.

The praise reached its apex and then was brought to a reverent conclusion by Trent Jones, the worship leader. We were directed to return to our seats as the announcements were made and preparation was made to receive the evening's tithes and offerings.

Pastor Glen's sermon started at about the same point where he concluded the morning's service on the power, authority and meanings of God's Old Testament names. Trying to take notes was an exercise in futility; I simply couldn't keep up, missing many precious nuggets of truth while attempting to write one down. I decided to buy the cassette tape of the service. The pastor's captivating teaching style once again had its hold on me. After years of ho-hum sermons with little or no substance, or direction, Pastor Hershey's fact-filled, potent, Holy Ghost inspired teachings revealed truths that were exciting and practical. Before I realized it, nearly two hours had elapsed and an altar call for salvation was being made. I couldn't help but wonder, were today's services just two exciting ones I happened to attend, or were they the norm? Norm or not, God did indeed show up here, just as Jerry had said He would. The people had been blessed, and I would return. This was home.

Monday morning came and that meant my first full day at the station. I had one photo appointment in the evening but that wouldn't take more than forty-five minutes. Jerry and I went over many of the components that comprised the FM studio. He was careful to give me the names of the equipment and the short nicknames or jargon that was used in the business. Some of the equipment was in place, speced, and placed in line, which meant nearly ready to go on the air. Jerry explained that the few remaining pieces of equipment would be assembled and readied for service by the end of the week. Although we were awaiting receipt of one mounting rack and two long play tape decks, we could still go on the air, with or without them.

"While the electronics people are finishing the studio, you better spend the rest of the week getting your people hired. If you come up short you can use my AM people for a little while. That'll buy you some time." Jerry was already heading down the hall to his office as he finished his orders. I could tell he was under more pressure than he had let me know. Somehow the peace and joy of Sunday's two worship services seemed to be wearing off, so I offered up a short prayer.

I had no sooner finished the prayer than he stuck his head in my door and said, "Thanks, Dave, I needed that. Sometimes the stress won't let me be as happy..." He didn't finish the sentence, often his style, then continued, "...no, I won't make that negative confession. I will be happy; fire or no fire, FCC or no FCC, FM on the air or no FM on the air. Thanks for joining me and helping so much already. It's yours, run with it."

I wondered how he knew I had just prayed for him. The important thing was that his countenance had changed. The smile was back. I liked him better that way.

The stack of job applications looked as though they had been on file for nearly a decade. Some were yellow with the corners all dog-eared. Arranged in alphabetical order, I had just started looking through them when the voice of the station secretary, Susan Jacobs, came booming across the intercom.

"David, you've got a call on line 70, Trish Ivey. Can you take it now?"

I reached across the desk and pushed the talk button. "Yes, Susan, I'll take it, thanks."

"Hello Trish. How are you this morning?"

Trish displayed more enthusiasm in her voice than she did the day before at church as she responded to my opening question. "Really great, Dave; even though it's Monday, it's a great day. But you know I didn't call you for small talk. In fact I don't really know why I've called. Do you?"

"Yes I do. Let me say this first. I've never been the kind of person who beats around the bush; there's just too much military 'get to the facts' in my character. That comes from twenty-two years with the Air Force. This time, though, I'm having a hard time stating what's on my mind, but let me try. You know part of the story. Jerry hired me as manager of the FM side of WPFH, in fact, Saturday was my first day; the day of the fire. You have heard about our AM fire, haven't you?"

Trish quickly answered, "Yes. I hope it wasn't too bad."

"No, it wasn't, but it was serious enough to knock us off the air for at least two weeks, possibly more. At any rate, that was a trying first day on the job as you might imagine, but that's another story all together. My point is this, as a result of the fire Jerry has had to turn all his attention to getting the AM side back up. That leaves me with the full responsibility of getting the FM side operational, including staffing, before the FCC pulls the license. Simply stated, I would like to make you an offer to come to WPFH, full-time, on-air. You name the time slot; you call the shots for your own show, provided the main format is music. Would you be open to discussing an offer?"

Trish's response didn't come immediately, but I could hear her breathing and apparently forming a reply as she finally broke the silence by saying, "Yes, I believe I would consider what you have to offer. I haven't been away from WPFH all that long. I would entertain a discussion about the possibility of coming back. Okay, so what's next?"

My thoughts went crazy. I had expected to throw all my persuasive abilities at just trying to arrange an open discussion, so when she agreed so quickly to start a dialog, I was taken aback. Finally I mustered, "Could we get together for lunch, possibly today?"

"Sure, today would be nice, if you can make it at noon, say at the Villa Cantine." Trish replied immediately. "In fact, let's make it 11:30. Does that work for you?"

I agreed with the stipulated time, and we said our polite good-byes. It looked like a time for prayer to me.

After praying I returned to working on the job applications, hoping to arrange for interviews and find a broadcast staff somewhere from within the pile. Those I could not contact I stacked on one side of my desk, while those I had scheduled for interviews were placed on the other. By 10:30 I had filled most of the afternoon and all of the next day with interviews. With less than an hour until I was to meet Trish, I went down the hall with a fresh cup of coffee to see how the work in the studio was going.

Electronics is not my specialty. Whatever it was those engineers and installers were doing was difficult for me to say. I could plug something in or even flip a switch, but certainly not much more than that. I must admit that the studio was beginning to look a lot more like what I assumed it was supposed to be. In fact, the turntables were now installed and the workers had actually started playing records over the internal studio speakers, listening to music as they worked.

The intercom broke through the music with an announcement that a delivery truck was at the back door and I needed to sign for several packages. After greeting the delivery man, I signed for the shipment and checked to determine whether they were for AM or FM. They were mine; one mounting rack and the two long play tape decks. Receipt of that shipment made the FM studio complete as far as initial setup went, yet there hadn't been one person hired to operate it. Hopefully by the end of the week we would be staffed sufficiently for at least a 16-hour broadcast day.

After taking the packages to the studio I returned to my office for my coat. It was a quarter past eleven and time to meet with Trish. I grabbed her old personnel file from the front office and stuck my head in Jerry's office to see if he was in. He was. "Hey Jerry; I'm off to meet with Trish for lunch. How about a prayer for success?"

Jerry turned from the paperwork he was reading and smiled as he said, "You got it, Brother. God's speed."

Trish had already arrived and was at the table. "I've placed my order," she said as I approached. "I hope you don't mind."

"No, that's fine," I answered glad she hadn't felt obligated to wait for me. "Any recommendations, it's been a while since I've been here," I continued.

"Well, this is an Italian restaurant, all the pasta dishes are great." she replied. "I believe I've tried them all. There's really not a gourmet disaster on the menu."

Trish spoke in that pleasant voice I had so quickly come to appreciate and now desired for WPFH. I placed my order for the baked lasagna and got right to the business proposal. The word proposal somehow struck me funny. I had never made the other kind of proposal in my forty-four years of life. Now I sat just across the table from someone whom I barely knew, except that she was my sister in the Lord, and I mused how it would be if I had the other kind of proposal rather than a job offer. I retrieved Trish's personnel file and placed it on the table along with the job offer and contract. I was ready to begin when she held one finger to her closed lips, motioning not to say a word. What was the problem? I could only guess. Maybe she wanted to wait until after lunch. That was it. How inconsiderate of me, and then came the answer.

"David, I do want to discuss your job offer but not right away. First I would like to give you some background information. No doubt Jerry has told you of the circumstances surrounding my leaving WPFH. I hope you can understand that that was a very painful time in my life. Not a great deal of time has elapsed since then, but enough to know that three, possibly four months ago, I came to the conclusion it was time to get on with my life. I had sulked in self-pity as long as God would allow. He convicted me for leaving WPFH and not being stronger or toughing it out. I hadn't even consulted with Him or Jerry; I just left. After all, I should have known better. I had friends there, not the least of which was Jerry, my dearest friend and confidant during my tenure at WPFH. He always listened and shared his shoulder when I needed to unload.

"Am I making any sense to you Dave?"

She barely left me enough time to give a nod.

"For nearly three months I've wanted to come back to WPFH but didn't know how to swallow my pride or let Jerry know my desire to return. After confessing my lack of faith in God and my disobedience for leaving in the first place, I turned it over to Jesus. I didn't make any deals with Him or promise anything; I simply asked Him to make a way for me to come back. Apparently I wasn't looking very closely for an answer; if I had been, I would have returned your call. Looking for an answer or not, I really didn't expect God to respond quite this quickly, or for that matter, through a photographer. I hope you'll understand that failure and forgive me. While God's plan is never going to be halted by our disobedience or spiritual inattentiveness, those actions may complicate our lives. I suppose that's why we were introduced at church Sunday in spite of me almost deciding to stay home and have another pity party. So, even though I'm not concerned about what you are about to offer, as far as a job with WPFH goes, I'll take it because I know it's God's will for me and certainly the answer to my prayer. Thank you for being obedient where I was not."

As Trish finished she looked down at her salad plate, which had just arrived, then back up to me.

No words came to me as I looked at her. I could see her reddening eyes were only moments from brimming over with tears. "God," I breathed silently, "give me the right words to comfort this precious sister of mine."

Returning my attention to her I said, "Trish, I'm not in any position to judge, evaluate or even comment on your reasons for leaving the station. Yes, Jerry apprised me of the situation so I might not be so apt to say something I might regret. He also thought I'd be more prepared in the event you broached the subject. But that doesn't need to be part of this discussion. I'm here to spell out what WPFH will give you should you decide to join our staff. The fact that you've already stated you want to return has little bearing on the proposal; you'll still need an income. When you are ready to discuss that portion of it, we will."

I returned the papers to my briefcase and continued, "If you want to ask any specific questions, I'll answer them as best I can. Please keep in mind, though, this is all new to me. My answers are sure to reflect my inexperience. After all, it was just a couple of days ago Jerry was offering me a job, and now I'm offering one to you. And too, you've been in the radio business for a while, and you'll soon discover, if you haven't already, how uninformed I am."

Just then, the waitress arrived with my salad and Trish's spaghetti dinner. This looked like a good time to change the subject, so I did. "Would you like to say grace together?" just seemed like the right thing to say.

"Sure David, I'd like that. Go ahead."

Her voice had quickly returned to form, surprising me as she reached across the table to grasp my hand. We bowed our heads while I asked the Lord's blessing upon the food, thanking Him for it and for the successes and accomplishments of the morning's work.

I started eating my salad as Trish lifted her fork and then paused to speak. "David, I've really missed the Christian environment of WPFH. Please don't get me wrong; WJOH has some great, professional people both on air and off. For the most part we get along quite well, but I have to overlook the worldly influences that are there. You know, flirting, joking, and drinking at station parties, smoking and all that stuff. Fortunately it's a more mature group of folks; late thirties and up. But even with the good people at WJOH, there's nothing like working at a place where Jesus is Lord and where one is surrounded by Christian brothers and sisters. Even if they differ in some aspects of their beliefs, the love and fellowship of the Lord and other Christians just can't be beat. Don't you agree?"

Trish's question left a good opportunity for me to give her some background information on me so she might be more confident in my intentions and our future working relationship.

"To be perfectly honest, Trish, I haven't worked in a Christian environment other than my own photography studio, which I never really considered a Christian environment to begin with. I've probably thought of my studio as neutral territory. I have a feeling, though, that that might have been an oversight on my part; or maybe even neglectful. You see, I've been a Christian for eight years but the first six and a half were my final years in the Air Force. In the military you just tolerate the kind of things you just mentioned: the smoking, drinking, dirty jokes, cussing. I guess it comes with the territory. But when I retired I didn't have to associate with people who ascribe to that life style. I knew it was wrong for me, but the lack of good Christian teaching led me to accept or ignore their behavior. After opening my own studio, I was by myself most of the time. Oh to be sure, a customer might stop in or call on the phone, and occasionally they would use offensive language. There again, I've been guided by a church doctrine that merely goes through the motions of Christianity. I've never been taught how to live a victorious life, and it seems as though I've always been powerless to handle situations like that.

"Now don't get me wrong. I realize all too well I have my own failings. I'm more than aware of the scripture that says 'All have sinned and fallen short of the glory of God.' Although I try to avoid sin, that verse certainly includes me, and God lets me know when I fall. Actually I'm glad of that. But it's more difficult for me to live in an ever-present state of victory and joy than it should be. I just haven't attained that yet, nor the knowledge of how to attain it. You could say the radio business isn't the only thing I'm ignorant about."

Trish looked surprised at my statement asking, "You don't think Pastor Glen and Lord of the Harvest Church teaches you how to do that?"

"Oh Trish, I'm sorry. I didn't tell you. Sunday was my very first time at Lord of the Harvest. Jerry invited me and I was really blessed by both services, however I'm still on the church rolls at...."

Trish was quick to apologize, "I'm sorry too. I just assumed you were a member of Lord of the Harvest. I do hope you plan on attending again."

"Yes I do, Trish. Actually I've known for quite some time I wasn't being fed spiritually at my present church. It was just a matter of–kind of like your desire to get back to WPFH–waiting for God to show me where, when and how."

The lengthy conversation had given Trish's eyes time to clear. Looking deeply into them, they reflected an inner joy and peace that I attributed at least in part to her salvation. They sparkled even brighter as we talked about things that meant a lot to her. But yet there was something else deeper but visible there. There was warmth, sincerity, and a genuine concern for me to be a part of her church family.

"Well," Trish started the next conversation. "You were Jerry's guest at Sunday's services. I want you to be my guest on Wednesday for mid-week service. Or am I being too presumptuous?"

My reply came quickly. "Oh you're not at all presumptuous. I am going, and I'd love to be your guest. Maybe you might pray that I will receive the baptism of the Holy Ghost then."

Immediately all the questions I had for Jerry but hadn't yet asked, came to mind. Maybe Trish could answer some of them. After all she seemed to have a firm grip on her Christianity. I was beginning to enjoy our luncheon meeting far more than I had anticipated.

Soon the meal was finished and the conversation led back to the job offer. "Trish, when might you be able to come back to WPFH?" I asked.

Her reply was slow and thoughtful. "I really should give Sam Reichel, my station manager, a two week notice, but that doesn't meet your needs. Does it?"

"Not really," I responded. "If the electronics technicians finish sometime this week, as Jerry seems to think, he wants us on the air Sunday morning. I could handle Sunday by myself, especially with the arrival earlier today of two long-play tape decks. I could run prerecorded music all day. But Monday, I would like more than that. Could you prepare a six hour show for next Monday by working here in the evenings this week?"

Trish's eyes were glowing brighter as she thought through her reply. "I could if I had access to the music library, and if the studio is available in the evenings."

My next question summed up the entire conversation. "Does this mean you will join us at WPFH?"

The next several moments lingered like hours until Trish responded. Not because she was having second thoughts, but more from a desire to use just the right words.

"I believe I'll be obedient to Jesus by joining the staff of WPFH-FM."

I smiled, and then laughed as I responded to her statement, "You're not joining the WPFH-FM staff, you are the staff."

We laughed, enjoying the moment of emotional release shared in our obedience to the leading of God. For Trish that came in her agreeing to return to WPFH – an answer to prayer. For me it was the success in accomplishing my first major goal. Trish had been hired.

The next ten minutes I spent showing Trish the contract terms and financial package. She was satisfied and signed. I signed for the station and we shook hands.

Neither one of us wanted dessert so I paid the bill and we left the restaurant. I walked Trish to her car and asked her to let me know as soon as possible when she would be able to terminate employment with WJOH. She agreed to get back with me no later than Wednesday night at church. We agreed to meet there at 6:20. I shook her hand again and thanked her for making the switch. It was a toss-up as to which of us was rejoicing the most. We paused for a quick prayer of thanksgiving, and then said good-bye.

From the restaurant, I drove back to the station. I kept busy until it was time for my 2:30 appointment with attorney Pat Harvey.

The rest of the afternoon hours would be spent with the three scheduled applicants. I arrived back at the station in time for the 3:15 interview. All three looked good on paper but only one professed Christ as Savior. One thing was certain, if I was hiring people to work at a Christian radio station, then I should be relatively sure they were professing Christians; correction, professing born again Christians.

John Dwyer was one Christian applicant. He had just graduated from college and was presently unemployed. He was staying with relatives in Marquette while seeking employment. John related he wanted the job so he could stay in the Upper Peninsula. I was thoroughly convinced about his desire to remain here rather than return to the Detroit area where he had grown up. He agreed to work in any time slot so long as he could get forty hours per week. I assured him that I would let him know by Thursday. John was able to start on a moment's notice, which sounded like the kind of readiness I needed.

"Excuse me, Dave, are you there?" came Susan's voice across the intercom.

"Yes, Susan, what is it?" I asked.

"You've got a call on seven-one, Trish Ivey. And Jerry needs to see you stat."

"Okay Susan. Tell Jerry I'll be there in just a few minutes...Hello Trish. What's on your mind?"

"Sam, my boss, was very disappointed when I told him I had accepted a job with you."

Her uneasy voice told me she was nearly in tears again. I was willing to bet Sam had been more than just disappointed.

Trish continued, "He wasn't too happy about less than a two-week notice. I pleaded with him, but I've never seen him this way before; angry, verbally abusive to say the least. At any rate, he told me – expletives deleted – to clear out my desk. If you could use me in the morning, I'm yours."

"Oh my, Trish. I'm sorry it worked out so badly for you. Is there anything I can do to help?" My feeble offer, though sincere, seemed useless to me but Trish picked it up like it was just what she needed.

"Yes, can we...I mean, can I...I feel awkward asking this...can we talk somewhere this evening? I need to bounce a few ideas off someone I can trust. There doesn't seem to be a lot of people who fit that description in my life any more. Can I trust you, Dave? Please tell me I can trust you!"

"Trish, you know you can. Please believe me. Listen, I have an early evening appointment with Madame DeVille at the DeVille mansion on some photography business. If you would like, I can pick you up on my way, and then we can go somewhere afterwards. Is that okay?"

Trish agreed, giving me her address and acknowledging I could stop by her apartment shortly before eight. I assured her that the stop at Madame DeVille's wouldn't take more than forty minutes. After that she could talk for as long as she needed. Or so I thought.

CHAPTER FIVE

Time sped by the rest of the workday churning full speed through late afternoon and on into early evening. It was already dark when I finally left the station. I hurriedly drove home, remaining there only long enough to accomplish a few essential tasks. A quick shower and change of clothes were accomplished in record time. If I were going to keep this impossible schedule, supper would have to wait until later, maybe with Trish.

Her apartment was ten blocks north of the radio station and up hill from town. Trish was looking out her living room window, waiting for me as I parked in front. I met her halfway down the sidewalk and escorted her to the car. We hadn't said a word yet, each waiting for the other to start the conversation. Finally I broke the silence.

"As I said on the phone, I need to stop by the DeVille mansion. Madame's ready to place an order for some pictures I took for her. It shouldn't take me more than half an hour; forty minutes at the most. I'll make it cordial but quick. After this afternoon's situation, I hesitate to ask, but how are you feeling now? You sounded quite upset earlier."

"I was, and angry with Sam too as you might guess," Trish started. "I couldn't help thinking, here's another rough treatment by a man, but I knew that wasn't fair. Beside, God chastened me for it. Since leaving the station this afternoon I've been praying for peace. The kind of peace I felt earlier today when I was with you at the Villa Cantine. There I was making decisions about my job and the future, and all the time feeling the peace of Christ. Then, less than a half an hour later, I'm filled with boiling anger while rapidly slipping into another pity party. I'll bet you think I'm pretty messed up, don't you, Dave?"

I shifted gears, answering without looking at Trish, for fear of catching her crying. "No, you're not messed up. In fact it's quite the opposite—the smooth, tranquil, soothing voice of Trish Ivey over the radio—that led me to contact you. That pleasing voice just had to belong to a person who had something going for her. After talking to you I know what that something is. Or should I say, Who that someone is? It's the Holy Spirit of God."

"Thanks for the kind words. I need them. But let's not overdo it David. You seem to know I'm gullible for flattering words. Besides, I don't let my personal life affect what I do behind the microphone. But aren't there other things we should be talking about? You know, the station, the show, format, music?"

I could tell Trish's composure was returning. "You're right, while we're on our way to the DeVille mansion we should at least discuss your preference for a time slot. When do you want your six hours on the air?" I was certain that keeping the conversation on the right track would be important. To keep her mind on positive things, Trish needed complex questions– not yes or no questions.

She paused for a moment, and then answered, "I think I'd like the morning drive time, say six to noon. You didn't say if I would be doing any weekends. Will I?"

She surprised me with the question; a sure sign she had her emotions back under control. I figured if we kept talking two things would happen. One, I would get to know her better, and secondly, she wouldn't dwell on the upsetting events of the afternoon.

"As far as weekend duty goes, that depends on my success or failure at arriving at a full staff of announcers. I won't really know that until all the interviews are done, tomorrow night or early Wednesday. As for your show, I said just name the hours. Six to noon you want; six to noon is yours. How about format? What do you have in mind?"

Trish's mood had improved significantly. She was enthusiastic about making the transition to WPFH and with planning her show. The enthusiasm bubbled over from one sentence to the next, and from one topic to the next, using verbal side bar stories to describe her many ideas for a program she exuberantly called "The Good Morning Lord Show!"

"Dave, I think the best place to start is, of course, with prayer. There could be maybe five or ten minutes of soft background music with prayer. We could ask the listeners to send in prayer requests or we could pray for certain things of current concern; you know, the Country, peace, freedom. The concerns most believers have for our nation such as abortion, pornography, violence, etc. Things that listeners could relate to, joining in with our prayer as they get up, or while shuffling the kids off to school. Then maybe we could have a devotional with scripture verses of the day. About this time it would be nice for the weather, time, announcements like school closings, road conditions—those type of things. Gradually the music portion of the show would increase the closer the noon hour gets. News is important too. Will we have access to the same wire services the AM side has?"

I listened intently as Trish expressed her ideas, answering her questions as I turned up the long drive to the DeVille Mansion. The driveway was nearly a half-mile long and wound its way up a steep hillside. Because most of the leaves were still on the trees, we couldn't see the mansion until we were almost to the front door. When I rounded the last curve my heart sank. Flashing red lights on the top of the square silhouetted ambulance stopped our conversation in its tracks. The beam of light from my headlights illuminated the reflective letters that spelled "RESCUE SQUAD" across the side of the truck.

Trish saw the lights too and immediately went to praying in tongues. I couldn't. I didn't know how. But I prayed in English under my breath hoping that my praying wouldn't hinder or stop that beautiful language I heard proceed from Trish's spirit. I sped up to the front of the mansion. Madame DeVille's grandson Milton recognized my car and waved me up to the house. I got out of the car, ran up the steps of the front portico, and then into the large reception hall. Trish trailed cautiously behind, still praying softly in tongues as the EMT team wheeled Madame from the great room into the reception hall on their way out to the ambulance. Madame was conscious and motioned for the team to stop when she saw me.

"Come with me," she pleaded, grabbing my hand. "Please come with me." By this time Trish had caught up and was standing at my side. Madame pointed at Trish and said, "You too, honey. Come with me to the hospital." I looked to Trish for an answer. She nodded. I assured Madame that we would go with her.

After they positioned Madame in the ambulance we climbed in and sat next to her. With near lightning speed the driver skillfully maneuvered the emergency vehicle back to the main road while Charles and Milton followed in the family limousine. Trish and I sat praying at Madame's side as she held tightly to my hand. The medical technician worked feverishly at checking vital signs.

Up to this point we hadn't been told what the problem was. For a woman of her suspected 83 years she had always been in what I considered to be great looking shape. Now she lay semi-conscious, in pain and obviously hanging on to life with all the strength she had.

"Madame," I cautiously whispered, "Can you hear me?"

She nodded, letting me know she could.

"Do you know Jesus as your savior?" I couldn't believe I just asked her that. Where in the world did that question come from? I was more startled by the boldness that I felt course through me, than at the situation in which we had all unexpectedly found ourselves. I looked for Madame to answer but no words came. I could tell she was still breathing but apparently not able to answer.

"Madame, have you ever accepted Jesus Christ as Savior and Lord?"

She struggled to open her eyes looking straight at me and with all the strength and determination her self-pride could muster under the circumstances, said, "I didn't think I'd ever need to."

She squeezed my hand tighter. I didn't know if that was because she was scared, struggling to hold on to life, or prompting me on to lead her to the Lord. Trish was looking at me, still praying in her heavenly language. Her eyes flicked over to Madame and my eyes followed. Madame was looking right at me and started pulling me closer to her as if she had something to say. She did.

"Are you going to share your faith with me or is the young lady?"

The length of the question took her breath away. I knelt down close to her. "Madame, do you know that Jesus died to pay the price for our sins?"

She nodded in agreement.

"Do you understand that we are all sinners?"

Again she nodded.

"Do you admit that you are a sinner and in need of Jesus as your Savior?"

She spoke a quick, soft "Yes", so I continued.

"Jesus didn't stay in the grave; He was raised by God the Father to make complete the plan of salvation, and to show us we too shall rise if we place our faith in the name and the blood of His Son, Jesus. Do you understand and agree with all that I've said? Just nod if you do."

I could tell two things: Madame was getting weaker, and we were nearly to the hospital. I had to get her to salvation before she slipped into unconsciousness, or worse, passed away.

"Madame? Do you accept the death of Jesus as payment in full for your sins?"

She struggled to speak but couldn't, but I saw her lips form the word "Yes" as I asked the final question. "If you could right now, would you confess Jesus as Lord?"

Madame's eyes opened again. A smile pursed her lips as she said, "Oh yes."

Then just as quickly, her eyes closed, the smile faded, and the tight grip she had on my hand loosened.

The ambulance backed to the emergency entrance and the doors were swung noisily open by the ER technician. They had Madame out of the ambulance and into the emergency room faster than I could believe humanly possible. I sat for a moment quickly recapping what I had just done.

"Trish, did I say the right things? Do you think she really accepted Christ? No matter what, do you think it's well with her soul?"

Trish smiled and reached for my hand, the one Madame had just relinquished. "I'm sure she now belongs to Jesus. You did that just right. Don't tell me that was the first time."

I looked first at the spot where just moments ago Madame had lain, then out the open back of the ambulance at the now closed ER doors, and then finally back to Trish. "Okay, I won't tell you it was the first time but if I told you anything else I'd be a liar."

Mentally I regrouped, and then together we stepped out of the ambulance and went into the waiting room of the hospital. I checked with the nurse behind the desk to see if any report was available. It was as I suspected, too early for that. Charles and Milton had arrived from the front of the hospital, informing the emergency room administrative staff that they were there awaiting any report from the attending physician.

As I walked across the waiting room I spotted Trish hanging up the receiver to the pay phone. We walked across the room where two empty seats were. As we sat, she told me she had called the prayer line at church and prayer was being offered up for Madame. Trish also related to the prayer partner on the phone that Madame had accepted Christ as Savior just prior to slipping into unconsciousness.

I looked for a moment at the floor and then up at the clock. It was nearly nine. Next, I looked at Trish who was looking at me.

"This isn't exactly what you had in mind for this evening is it? You had something you wanted to talk about, and we haven't had the opportunity. Have we Trish?"

I can't explain the compassion I was feeling for her right then, knowing how life had gone so sour for her. She was nearly thirty-four and had been through a divorce, a job change, loneliness, guilt, and rejection. Who but God knew what other hurts were there. Though we had planned for her to just open up and relate her feelings and emotions, the turn of events, with a millionaire widow, had altered even those plans.

Trish replied in the only way I suspected she could–with caring and unselfishness. "Oh David, don't think about me, keep praying for Madame DeVille. She needs our prayers right now for healing. I'll be fine. There's plenty of time for us to talk."

Something kept me gazing at her face as she prayed. I had, over the course of my adult life, dated and shared many pleasant times with other women, but never one so captivating as Trish. I was beginning to see qualities in her that attracted me. I felt compelled to just watch her as she bowed her head and prayed quietly.

About a half-hour later, a nurse came out and related that Madame was in a coma but her vital signs had stabilized. According to the nurse, she had suffered a heart attack, but the severity of it could not be determined yet.

Milton and Charles soon appeared, and we chatted for a short time about Madame. I told them that she had accepted Jesus as her savior. It was obvious by their expressions they were unimpressed. They were pleasant but it was evident in their inattentiveness that what I said meant little to them. Although I was sure they loved their grandmother, it was rumored they would be joint heirs of an estate of over 25 million dollars should Madame die.

Trish and I decided to leave the hospital and get something to eat. We took a cab back to the mansion, got into my car, and headed for a restaurant. The evening was quickly eluding us and delaying our plans for an enjoyable and constructive conversation.

We stopped at the Kilner Highway Restaurant just outside of town for a light supper. It was nearly twenty to ten. As we waited I noticed Trish yawning.

"It has been a long day, hasn't it Trish?" I asked. "Do you still care to talk? If not, I understand. Maybe tomorrow after work would be better."

As soon as Trish heard the word 'work' she perked up. "Hey, that's right, I nearly forgot. Tomorrow I work for you. What time do I report?"

Trish's tiredness was quickly replaced by enthusiastic question.

"Well after the trying events of this day, I would guess if I were any kind of a boss, and I use the term loosely, I'd give you the day off. I just can't afford to do that, but I will give you a break the first day. How about nine o'clock?

"Sure Dave, but unless you're in a hurry to get home, I would like about fifteen more minutes of your time."

Whatever had been on Trish's mind earlier in the day was about to be revealed. "First, I want to know if it would be okay for the 'Good Morning Lord Show' to have an occasional guest. Secondly, I would like to know if it would be okay, especially considering the fact that we will be working together, for us to see each other again?"

I had already formed my answer to the first question and was about to speak when the impact of the second question hit me broadside. I stammered for a second or two and then stupidly asked, "What was the first question?"

Trish laughed and was once again radiating the joy I had come to expect from her.

I joined in her laughter and said, "Yes."

"Yes to which one?" Trish inquired.

"Both!"

CHAPTER SIX

With Trish back at her apartment, I headed home. The day's events had distracted me from nearly everything except autumn's encroachment. Even though it was only the 8th of September, I had noticed throughout the day that the leaves were changing colors fast. By my estimation they would be at full color in about a week, two at the most. We had already gotten the season's first snowfall, not an unusual occurrence in September for the Upper Peninsula where winter comes any month it wants to, except July. Looking at the moon for no apparent reason, I discovered a wide halo around it. An old wives' tale says that means snow is coming. I hoped not. There was just too much to do to have bad weather get in the way.

"Father, You have done so much in my life in just the past week. If you weren't with me through these changes, I doubt I would have made the right choices. But even now, especially after tonight, the peace of your Son, Jesus, which passes all understanding, has indeed kept my heart and mind as your word says in Philippines. I ask, dear God, that you continue to be with all of us at WPFH, as I know you are. Keep the staff, the facilities, and our decisions in your perfect will. In Jesus' name I pray. Amen." By the time I finished the prayer I was in the bed, exhausted but anxious for tomorrow's challenges.

I arrived at the station by 7 a.m. My slate was full of job interviews starting at ten o'clock. Jerry was already diligently at work when I poked my head in his office, asking if he had a minute to talk. He wasn't fully aware of the events surrounding Madame Deville's heart attack. Although he had heard she had been rushed to the hospital, he had no way of knowing that Trish and I were with her. When I got to the part about leading her to the Lord he let out a couple of "praise God's!" and some "hallelujah's!" too. He even stood up and shook my hand.

Because I wasn't exactly sure what Trish had in mind about seeing each other, I left that portion of the recap out.

Just as I was about to start discussing Trish's show with Jerry, the phone rang. Jerry answered it, and from his side of the conversation I could tell he was talking to Mr. Gramswald.

"...Sure thing, Mr. Gramswald...well, we're hoping for this Sunday morning...yes, Dave will probably run it the first day...I really haven't had an opportunity to talk all the details out with him. I've been keeping pretty busy these days with stripping out the damaged AM equipment...the insurance adjuster was here yesterday afternoon...he delivered a partial settlement check...Now we can purchase the replacements...Dave's here now, would you like to talk to him...sure, I can put you on the speaker...Okay."

Jerry cradled the phone and flipped a switch. The first thing I heard was "Good morning, David, Jerome Gramswald here. Let me start by saying not only thanks for accepting the job and getting with it so quickly, but let me welcome you to the staff of the station. I know you'll be freeing up Jerry to take care of the fire repairs."

Mr. Gramswald paused to hear my remarks so I jumped right in. "Well, you're quite welcome, Mr. Gramswald; I'm looking forward to the challenges ahead. I heard Jerry tell you we're shooting for a Sunday morning startup on the FM side. All the equipment is in. Hookup should be completed either late today or early Wednesday. Specing and signal readings should be completed on Thursday– Friday at the latest. We've got an extra day built in, Saturday, to work out any glitches. We also want to do a limited radius check. That's a time-consuming task, as you might know...."

"Listen, Dave," Mr. Gramswald inserted, cutting me off as he did. "Just call me Mr. G., it's quicker. How sure are you about broadcasting Sunday?"

I looked at Jerry who quickly wrote a note that read 90%. "Jerry estimates a ninety percent chance of making that schedule. Does that meet with your approval, Mr. G.?"

There was a short pause; then Mr. Gramswald came back across the monitor, answering, "That's sure enough for me. Which one of you can pick me up at the Marquette airport Saturday evening?" Jerry quickly frowned, shook his head while waving his arms, then he pointed at me.

"I will, Sir."

Mr. Gramswald then gave me his arrival time.

Jerry and Mr. Gramswald prayed a short prayer asking for God's blessing and success for the remaining tasks and said good-bye. Jerry said he was not surprised Mr. G. was flying up from Chicago. After all, the powering up and initial broadcast would complete this special missionary project and allow him to turn his attention to the final phase of his dream, a Christian television station in the U.P.

The morning sun, visible through my office window, was inching up from the horizon. Susan Jacobs came in to help me prepare much of the paperwork for the six interviews, after which I got a cup of coffee and strolled into the main studio. The installers were hard at work assembling the mounting rack for the two tape decks. With those assembled and ready, we could play several hours of non-stop, prerecorded Christian music. If I were to be the only one who would be in on Sunday, I would need to have my hands free for any situation that might come up. I certainly didn't want to be spinning records or plugging in cartridges all day long.

Wandering slowly back to my office down the quiet hallway, I once again started thinking about the baptism of the Holy Ghost. Although I didn't know much about it, I did know I wanted a prayer language like Trish's, and I wanted it now.

Trish stepped into the office and smiled, asking, "What do you want me to do first?"

"Tell me about the prayer language you used last night. I want to be able to do that. What do I do? Jerry started to explain it a couple of days ago but never finished."

"David, I don't know if there's a quick answer for all your questions; at least I don't have one in thirty words or less. Maybe we should go to the Christian bookstore in town. You can get some good books to read on the gifts of the Holy Ghost there. Or you can borrow some of mine. If you attend Lord of the Harvest regularly, you'll get a great deal of those questions answered there. Pastor Hershey is very anointed and operates under many of the gifts during services. Wednesday nights are just a good time for learning; you'll see that tomorrow night. For right now, though, know that I'll pray for you that God will answer the desire of your heart. Know this also that I'll help you study to find the answers as best I can. Just ask."

Trish's sincerity and Christian love filled the room. I hated to break the spirit of the moment, but I had to get her going on some important work. I looked into her eyes momentarily, finding the twinkling that seemed to always be there. "You look like you slept well in spite of last night's hectic situation. Are you always so bright-eyed and ready to go in the morning?" I asked.

"Of course! Especially when I get an extra two hours sleep."

"Well don't get used to it! The 'Good Morning Lord Show' starts in six days. Susan Jacobs, in the front office, needs to see you for some paperwork in your personnel file. Then in the next room down the hall to the right, is our yet unfinished and temporary Studio B. It's ready for you to work on your promos, spots, etc. There's a typewriter in there with plenty of paper for scripts or lists of music you want from the library. Give your music lists to Jimmy Thomas, the traffic manager. I assume you're still familiar with the facilities?"

Trish nodded, adding, "This wing, from your office back, was nearly finished prior to my leaving. If Jerry hasn't changed things too much, I believe I can find my way around. Thank you for getting things ready for me. Now, how about taping the spots and promos?"

"That's a good question, Trish," I answered. "It would have been nice if we had access to studio B on the AM side, but with the fire damage and repairs going on in their main studio, they'll need it. Jerry told me that doing those types of things are just going to have to wait until the main FM studio is ready. That means not sooner than Thursday afternoon. Can you still get everything ready in time for Monday if that plan holds up?"

"I believe so. I wish I had access to WJOH facilities, but what's done is done. Viva WPFH!"

Trish's bubbling personality, I thought to myself, just naturally showed up every time I was with her. How could all those sad things have happened to her? What ever could have caused her marriage to fail? Frank must have been a jerk!

Trish went to the front office while I returned to the task of composing a shift schedule on the computer. I built a calendar for the remainder of September as well as the final three months of the year. Trish's time slot was already blocked and the rest of the 16-hour broadcast days I hoped for were divided into two five-hour blocks. I felt confident the three interviews yesterday and the six today would result in the three announcers needed for full-time as well as the one part-time weekend position.

Time allowed for just a half-cup more of coffee and a stop at the temporary Studio B to see how Trish was doing. I peered through a small window in the closed door. She noticed me and gave me one of her smiles and a wave. I returned to my office and closed the door for prayer.

The first applicant, Ted Munson, arrived at the front office. Susan announced him over the intercom and escorted him back at my request.

"Hi Ted, I'm Dave Post. Have a seat. Let's get started, okay?"

I could tell Ted was nervous so I took off my suit coat and said, "Give me a brief description of yourself and what your goals are for employment here at WPFH-FM."

Ted told me he was 22 years old, a part-time college student, and was presently a sales clerk at Hankin's Drug Store. He was still living at home and hoped to get into radio broadcasting which would lead him toward the goal of someday being a station manager. Next, I asked him for his testimony which he gave immediately and without any reservation.

Ted had an encounter with Christ while a junior in high school. Although his parents were not Christian, they did not interfere with his faith. He explained further that it was while he was away on a high school band tour in Milwaukee, Wisconsin that he accepted Jesus as Savior. Many of the band members, he related, were smoking pot and drinking beer after their evening performances. They were living it up while away from home. Apparently the supervision left a lot to be desired. They had invited him to join them, which he did, but he added he didn't feel right about it. Mostly he just sat and watched the others while they got either stoned, drunk or both.

"I think the thing that convinced me what they were doing was leading them in the wrong direction was when the dirty jokes started. Both the guys and the girls were telling them; sometimes acting them out in pantomime as they told them. Then, some of the guys and girls went off to other parts of hotel. I got up and left. I must have walked nearly two miles just thinking about what the others were doing and how it could mess up the rest of their lives. I also thought about what I wanted for my life. I knew my decisions would have to be the right decisions if I didn't want unexpected problems to get in the way. I promised myself that if I didn't know the right choice in a given situation that I wouldn't make any choice. I hope you understand what I mean by that promise, Mr. Post." I assured Ted that I did and motioned for him to continue.

"About that time I happened upon some people who were street witnessing. They helped me sift through the things that I had just experienced. They made sense to me, you know, about eternal life, sin, hell, those kinds of things. I accepted Jesus right there at the corner of State Street and 16th."

After Ted's testimony, I asked him his preferences for working hours if he were hired, and if he would audition by reading a prepared script. He preferred either the late afternoons or evening shift.

Ted did a fine job with the script reading. His voice was deep and resonant, perfect for radio. Maybe he would work out. "Maybe he's quick to learn," I thought. I thanked him for the interest in WPFH and assured him I would call him one way or the other by Thursday afternoon.

The only drawback was that Ted had no experience. If I hired him, there would be very little training time available, and we would have to provide him a lot of on-the-job training before he would be ready. That was time I just couldn't afford to expend in that capacity; after all, I would be learning the equipment and studio procedures myself. I immediately recalled my words to Mr. Gramswald earlier in the day; "I am looking forward to the challenges ahead."

I knew getting experienced announcers hired was probably going to be impossible on such short notice. I also knew that getting an experienced Christian announcer would border on a miracle. And even if I found an experienced, Christian announcer, would he or she be available for Monday? I convinced myself that kind of a miracle only happened in the Old Testament, and besides, they didn't even need experienced, Christian radio announcers back then. I chuckled.

I pushed the button on the intercom to the front office and asked, "Susan, is Annette Chandler in for her interview?"

Susan escorted her to my office. Annette was from Escanaba, Michigan, and appeared eager for the interview. I followed the same format for Annette's interview as I had with Ted's. Annette was in her late thirties and married. She had just moved to the Ridgemont area about six weeks earlier. Her husband had been hired by the community college in the spring and he had been commuting back and forth on weekends since then. They had two children, both in grade school. One of them was a slow-learner and had just completed some summer school classes to improve his reading and math skills. That was the reason she had waited until late summer, just before the new school year, to move to Ridgemont.

Then came the surprise of the morning. Annette had been employed part-time by WCDF in the Escanaba area for over two years but she hadn't reflected that on her application under previous employment. I had overlooked it because it was listed it under other experience. Her part-time employment had provided the extra income her family needed. Here was a part of my miracle. Immediately I went on a hunt for more information.

"Annette, this is a Christian radio station; our purpose is different from most other stations." I stopped there to read the expression on her face, and allow time for a response if she desired to make one.

"I'm aware of that", Annette replied. "I am a Christian; at least I consider myself a Christian."

There was the tip-off I was looking for. I allowed her to continue.

"I was raised in a good Christian home. As a child I can remember we always went to church. My folks, they're both dead now, belonged to a small, independent missionary Baptist church where we lived back then, just outside St. Ignace. My husband and I don't go to church as often as we should, but

61

you know how it is raising a family don't you? Busy, busy, busy," she added.

"I can certainly appreciate that", I responded. "But you see, although being a Christian is not necessarily a prerequisite of the job, we would like to know where a person is in his or her spiritual life before we make any hiring decisions. Could you attest to the fact that you've had an encounter with the Lord Jesus Christ, Annette?"

Annette seemed to go on the defensive as soon as my words hit her ears. "I'll be honest here. I think you're asking me if I'm born again. I've heard that term just about all my life, though not certain if I know what it means. I know Jesus died for our sins and that He rose from the grave showing us that someday we too will arise. But frankly, religion doesn't cross my mind a great deal as I go through the day. Maybe it should, at least once in a while. I enjoy most of the music coming from contemporary Christian artists these days. Along with that I have valuable radio experience to offer. I would like to work here and hope my experience is of more benefit to you than my ability or inability to answer that question in the way you may have expected."

I leaned back in my chair a few moments and then came back to the upright position. "You're absolutely right, Annette. Your experience is a great plus for you and would be a great asset to us. Just how quickly would you be available to start work should we offer you a job?"

"My children are in school all day. We're all settled in as far as our new home is concerned, so I guess the answer would be as soon as you needed me." Annette's voice changed from defensive back to cordial.

I hated to admit it, but we were in desperate need of experience. Should none of the following interviews prove productive, it looked like Annette was going to be on our staff, even if I questioned her Christianity.

"My final two questions then, would be for you to tell me what your preferred hours would be, and if you would like full-time or part-time employment." I waited intently for her reply.

First Annette looked up at the ceiling, then down at the floor. Raising her head until her eyes caught mine, she said, "Whatever you needed most. My preference would, of course, be for full-time employment."

"With your experience being such a tremendous plus, should I offer you a full time position, would you be willing to train myself and others on studio procedures and techniques?"

Annette did a quick mental evaluation of the question, and then replied, "I could do that, but timing is important. Could I work afternoons or early evenings? My husband's hours at the college are nights, starting at ten p.m.

He's in security."

With that I concluded the interview informing Annette her desired hours would fit our needs. As I walked her to the door I assured her the results of the interview would be made known to her by Thursday. Along the way I invited her to Lord of the Harvest Church.

CHAPTER SEVEN

Slowly I turned the doorknob to Studio B to enter without disturbing Trish. The sound of the typewriter going at what I guessed was sixty words per minute greeted my ears. The door creaked slightly causing Trish to turn and catch me sneaking in.

"Remind me to oil that door," I said. "It's just after noon. Are you at a point where you can break for lunch, or do you want to wait until later?" I really wanted to go now for two reasons. First, I was hungry. My stomach growled through nearly the entirety of Annette's interview. Secondly, I wanted to be with Trish. She lifted her graceful, hands from the keyboard and stood.

"I can break now, but I have a question. Are there any spare tape recorders available for me to practice my promos and announcements? They won't be studio quality, but at least I can rehearse them until Thursday when the main studio is available. That will allow me to listen to them for tonal quality and voice control."

By now Trish had gotten her coat on and was nearly at my side as she abruptly changed the topic. "Where we going for lunch?"

"I don't know. What are you hungry for?" was my reply. I didn't give her time to respond. "And have Jimmy bring you anything you need. You don't have to ask. You know this business better than I do."

Trish smiled, stopping as she did midway down the hall as we walked, and then just looked at me. A small tear traced its way down her cheek as she broadened her smile. "Thank you for entering my life. Thank you for being so dependable. Thank you for being who it is you are. Isn't life great?"

"What did I do to prompt that?" I inquired.

She didn't reply. She just resumed walking down the hall, passing me by as she did so, yet going slow enough for me to catch up.

"How about a double-decker hamburger? I'm starved", I answered.

"That sounds like something I would say", Trish responded as we left the building.

I laughed out loud as I opened the car door for her.

While we were waiting for our lunch I described the results of the first two interviews. Trish stated that although she didn't know Annette personally, she had heard her on the radio several times, including the last time she was in the Escanaba area.

"She has superb voice control and can work the routines without any dead air or goofs. If I remember correctly, she went from one activity to the next smoothly. When you're in this business, you have a tendency to listen to other announcers to see how they handle what can be an often times stressful environment. I don't mean to scare you David, but depending on the program format it can get awfully hectic in the air chair, especially on commercial stations."

By the time we finished our meal we were exchanging testimonies. Trish asked me to share mine first, then came her turn. She accepted the Lord while in her first year of college. It wasn't that she was a bad person, as she put it, or had lived a sinful life style, but came to a realization that she needed the cleansing only Jesus' blood could supply. She had been raised in a Christian home with loving, caring parents with whom she had few differences of opinion. Trish avoided talking about Frank, and I didn't care to know anything more about him or the way he had treated her. I presumed he had not been a part of her born again experience, which, fortunately, allowed her to recall that portion of her life without displaying pain.

Trish continued, "I guess my first step in turning to the Lord was realizing that even though my life was relatively straight, I knew life inevitably leads toward a meeting with God. Sooner or later I knew I would stand before the Creator of the universe. That didn't bother me a great deal until I realized why I would be standing in front of Him. I felt uneasy, knowing I would have to give Him some kind of an account of my life, no matter how long or short that might be.

"While in college I was bombarded daily by secularly biased facts, figures, theories and isms. Everywhere I turned, it seemed, academia touted the greatness of mankind and how we were, by virtue of either imparting or obtaining an education, progressing to the eventual panacea of a humanly created utopia. In other words—mankind was the all in all impetus of human betterment. Because of that, I soon became confused. My life then seemed trapped in the preparations for some ambiguous goal. It was while pursuing that perceived goal, that the search for some kind of unalterable truth took place.

"I needed to know the purpose for going 60, 70, maybe 80 plus years, and then what? Looking at it from strictly a humanistic point of view, which was really all I had, a person's dead a lot longer than he's alive. My hunger for what life was all about was as strong as your hunger for that hamburger was ten minutes ago. David, dear friend, the desire for truth led me to the Bible. There I found four things: God's purpose, our need, God's plan, and our response. Because I wasn't sure about all that I was reading in the Bible, I sought out a church that could help me. Lord of the Harvest Church, with it's pastor Glen Hershey, was that place for me.

"Truth there not only becomes evident, it comes alive. It becomes something you can carry out of church on Sunday night and then keep with you all week. For me, I rely on it until I get another heaping dose on Wednesday night. Pastor Hershey's message one Sunday evening convicted me of my sins, convinced me of my need, carried me to the altar, and brought me to my knees. I wouldn't turn back now if...."

I don't know how she would have finished the sentence; she never did. I presumed it had something to do with Frank, or maybe her divorce.

It was time to get back to the station. There were four more interviews to do, and it looked as though it would be midnight before my work was accomplished. Wednesday night was church service, and Thursday night would be spent at my photo shop. On Friday it looked like late hours at the station again. Who knew what Saturday would bring? And of course, I was to pick up Mr. Gramswald at the Marquette County Airport Saturday evening. That didn't leave much time for Trish and me to get to see each other except while we worked. At least we would have that.

By 1:30 the next applicant had not arrived. That allowed me time to get Jerry's opinion on a few things and to check on the work progressing in the studio. All was nearly ready to start testing for proper hookup of equipment prior to actually applying power. Based upon what the technicians were telling me, signal testing could be accomplished on Thursday night as tentatively planned. I was surprised to see the two new tape decks had already been mounted and were now playing music over the studio speakers.

Much of the previous week's work had been thoroughly checked and readied for operation, including the two state-of-the-art turntables, CD players, frequency displays, signal enhancers, power meters, limiters and surge protectors. All those things had their respective proper names and applications but I certainly didn't feel adequate in my knowledge of them or their operation, at least not yet. That, I hoped, would come once we had some quick training sessions before the start of the weekend.

I usually tried to avoid conversation with the technical people to prevent my ignorance from showing, but on this visit I was unsuccessful in eluding the technical team leader, Jason Barnes. He was a tall, middle-aged, dark-haired fellow who always sported a Detroit Tiger's baseball cap and reminded me of the TV detective who did the same.. His wide leather belt, with deep pouches full of various tools, was always swinging back and forth, making clanking noises as he walked around the studio.

"We've done a lot of work in here over the past two weeks," Jason remarked, taking an unlit cigar out of his mouth. "Each piece of equipment has been unpacked, tested independently, and then placed in line with all the rest of the components, but we'll soon have to start testing the entire system as a whole. When that's done, we'll have to head up to Signal Hill for some transmitter site tests. My guess would be, on the air Saturday; early Saturday at that."

Jason talked matter-of-factly as he returned the cigar to his mouth and then stripped the insulation off a grounding wire while I watched and listened. He had obviously stripped many a wire in his job. So rapid and automatic were his hand movements I feared the knife might slip. My concern was unnecessary; the task was accomplished without incident.

As pleased as I was about the report from Jason, I still planned on sticking with the established schedule, if for no other reason than that Mr. Gramswald wouldn't be up until Saturday evening. And we weren't going on the air until he arrived. If we actually had any extra time we could spend it more wisely by getting familiar with studio procedures or other training.

Jim, the next applicant, was a retired gentleman with a firm, strong handshake. He could best be described as the 'grand-fatherly' type. I found it real easy to like him right off. According to his application, he was 61, and a long-time amateur radio enthusiast. His retirement had come early as a result of a minor back injury. His interests in radio had prompted him to apply for jobs at several other area stations, but apparently because of his age and disability, he had never been hired. His desire for employment at WPFH, he explained, was limited to part-time work. Jim had stipulated on his application he was interested in working weekends and holidays, when the schedule, as he put it, was more relaxed and less stressful. "Probably no more than 20 to 25 hours per week, Mr. Post. That's about all I would be able to work. You know, Social Security restrictions on income; it's not that I'm an invalid, as you can see; nor am I seriously handicapped. My disability limitations are in the amount of time I can stand up. And of course I can't run a three-minute mile either. Never could! But I can play records, tapes, read the news, give the weather and keep my eye on the equipment. With the exception of playing music and the talking, it would be a lot like my old job in the control room at the power plant where I used to work. What's more, I'll be doing a work unto the Lord. That's the best part. Do you think you can use me?"

"Well, to be perfectly honest, Mr. Osborne, I haven't finished all the interviews, but when I do, I'd like to think there would be a place here for you, if not on the air, then certainly in some other capacity. I just can't say until we've completed all the interviews."

I escorted Jim to the door and told him that I should be able to inform him of my decision no later than Thursday afternoon. There were just two more interviews remaining.

It was 3:15 p.m. and my energy levels were depleted. I stepped into the break room where I opened a cold can of soda and started nibbling on a chocolate-covered granola bar. Trish walked by, saw me sitting on the couch, and came in to join me and have a cola.

"How are the interviews going, Dave?" she asked as she fired several quarters into the pop machine.

"Fine", I replied. "If I don't even see the final two, I would feel fairly confident in hiring those that I have interviewed. There's one, Ted Munson; he may be a bit young and hasn't any experience, but I believe he has a lot of potential and a tremendous testimony. He didn't mince his words when describing how he came to the Lord. But how's your work going?"

Trish looked up from the can of pop and answered, "No problems here. Jimmy's pulled all the music I need for Monday's show and I've nearly completed the schedule for four of my six hours. I plan to have news on the hour with weather and time during each 15-minute segment until we see how that works out. Music fills the rest except announcements as needed. Oh yes, I've compiled a list of places to call to let them know they can announce closings or shift delays via WPFH. Is it okay if I start calling them?"

"Sure Trish, that's a good idea, especially as winter approaches, but maybe you ought to check with Jerry first. See if that might duplicate what he already has on the AM side. If so, we can use their information. Also ask him how he wants to coordinate this and other like actions so we don't waste time."

I paused for a moment at the doorway on my way out. "Trish, I'll be busy the rest of the afternoon. If I don't get to see you before you leave, have a nice evening. Maybe I can spend more time with you tomorrow, once I have the interviews done."

"Okay, Dave", she said, standing as she finished her drink. "There's probably not much chance of our getting together tonight for supper is there?"

I wanted to say yes. Somehow I wanted to make room for her. And I wanted to get to know her better so that I could determine if my interest in her was more than some kind of infatuation. "I wish we could, but I don't see how. Jerry and I will be here late tonight making our decisions on the interviews. I'll give you a call once I get home, if I get in before ten. Is that okay?"

She smiled. "I would appreciate that." She headed back to studio B, and I to my office for the remaining two interviews. I finished up at 5:45.

Jerry's intercom number was 33. I punched it up.

"Yes," Jerry responded.

"Dave here, Jerry. When do you want to discuss the interviews? They're all done." I waited for his answer for what seemed like a long time, and was about to redial his office again when he stepped into my office.

"I just love doing that," Jerry chuckled. "I haven't had an opportunity to pull that trick on you until now. Say, let's go get some Chinese food, then come back and go over your findings. Anyway, I need a break from here. It's been a long day. Oh, by the way, we've got a complete list of the damage to the AM and it's not as bad as we originally thought. We could be back up by the 21st. It all depends on the arrival of the replacement equipment I've ordered; it's on the way from California now. Cleaning and painting the studio plus repairs to the burned control panels will be finished about the same time the electronics gets here. In fact, the fire has really proved to be a blessing because it's allowed us to upgrade faster than anticipated. Good news, huh Dave?"

I smiled, sharing in Jerry's enthusiasm as we headed out the front door.

It was nearly seven when we got back. "The bottom line, Dave," Jerry offered in summation, "is just what I told you on Saturday. Hire whomever you like. I agree with your choice of Jim Osborne for the weekends and holidays. It's great that his wants fit our plan. I'm not trying to change your mind, but I'm just not sure about Ted Munson. You've slotted him in a time where he feels comfortable, and that's good, but I'm real uneasy with his lack of experience. Quite frankly, you're out there on that limb all by yourself. If you do hire him, get him in here tomorrow with Annette or Trish at his side, and start going over the console. He'll have to get acquainted with it in a hurry. I understand the installers will be out of there early tomorrow; maybe before noon. That'll allow him time to get somewhat familiar with board layout, practice some procedures and routines, work out the nerves some, and get as much time as possible with his trainer, whoever that ends up being. And while he's at it, have him make an hour-long audition tape for the files. I'd like to hear him before he's live. Have Annette make one too."

Jerry and I decided to quit for the day. It was nearly 9:30 and nothing more could be done until morning when I phoned Annette, Ted and Jim.

After picking up my business mail from the post office, I drove home. The air was cold but there wasn't any sign of snow. The sky was painted an impenetrable black; the stars sparkled against it with the clarity of diamonds. I casually tossed the mail on the coffee table, sat down on the sofa next to the phone, and propped up my tired feet. Carefully I dialed each of those numbers, 4-7-5-6-0-0-8 that wound their way through miles of wire to find Trish's apartment. I waited for the voice that just days ago belonged to an unknown announcer, but now seemed like a life-long friend.

"Hi, Trish. Did I catch you at a good time?" I asked. "I just got in. Jerry and I are finished. We made our choices."

"I'm glad you got in at a fairly early hour. I was afraid you might work too late and I'm definitely glad you called. Can you tell me whom you're going to hire?" she inquired.

"Sure, it's not a big secret. First, you've got the 6 a.m. to noon slot. We're going with Annette Chandler from one 'til seven and Ted Munson from seven to midnight. I'll handle the hour from noon to one for an expanded midday program consisting of news, weather, 'Manager Moments', and some other things I have tentatively in mind. The weekends, to answer one of your unanswered questions, will be handled by Jim Osborne who will also double as our resident grandfather. You'll love him right away. That will provide us eighteen broadcast hours Monday through Friday and eight hours on Saturday and Sunday for starters. I'd like to add at least one more part-time person on the weekend so we could broadcast sixteen hours, while easing up on Jim. All that can be worked out later, and it's all subject to change as we go along."

Trish listened intently and agreed we now had a staff nucleus. Then she asked, "Can I change the subject?" Without waiting for my reply she went on to say, "Do you remember when we were talking at the hospital and I asked you two questions that you answered with the word 'yes'. Do you remember that, Dave?"

"I sure do, Trish." My heart began to sink afraid she was about to withdraw one of her requests.

"Now don't get me wrong," she continued; my heart sank even further. "I know you've been busy with getting acclimated to radio work, as well as making some pretty important decisions in your life. I guess what I'm trying to say is that I've really enjoyed those few times we've been able to get away by ourselves. Even though we've only known each other a short time, I feel like I've gotten know you and can trust you. I know, too, you haven't had all your questions answered about spiritual matters you asked about; especially questions about the baptism of the Holy Spirit.

"I've said all that to say this, or ask this: Instead of meeting at church tomorrow night, could you come to my house for supper so we could spend some time talking the way I think both of us really want to talk? Maybe have a short Bible study? Then go to church together?"

My reply was slow and deliberate. I wanted to make sure I wasn't misunderstood. "Trish, you're right, we haven't had much time together, other than a couple of meals. I believe I would like to get to know you much better than what I do now. I find myself wondering about you and what...well, what the future might hold for us. Maybe a better way to say it would be what God might have for us. But you're also right when you mentioned my serious decisions of late; the most enjoyable was to contact you.

"Trish, I'm 44 years old, and in those 44 years I've learned to be alone rather well. That doesn't mean I enjoy it, only that I've learned to live that way. I find you most attractive but also find myself experiencing feelings and emotions that, quite frankly, I've never experienced before. I feel a need to be cautious, especially in areas I'm not familiar with. And yes, I agree, those few times with you have been most memorable, so I pray God will allow us to experience more time together. But—and there always seems to be a but—I would feel more comfortable, more in control, if we were to meet some place public, rather than at your apartment. Can you agree to that, at least for right now?"

Trish agreed, though she sounded disappointed. We decided on supper together prior to church.

"Good night, Trish", I said softly.

"God bless you with a peaceful, restful night's sleep, David", she replied.

My tired body beckoned for sleep. I obliged.

CHAPTER EIGHT

I awoke praising God for a restful night's sleep. Enveloped by a refreshing sense of alertness, I arose and showered. While preparing to shave, I was greeted by my own smiling reflection. After dressing and pausing for a light breakfast, I left for the office, anxious to meet the challenges of work and anticipating the evening church service. Last Sunday's services were a lifetime ago, and I was ready for the uplifting music and the inspired preaching of Pastor Glen. I had felt close to God there, and seen a fellowship of believers united in praise and worship. Of course I also wanted to spend more time with Trish other than at work.

Our lunch and supper times together, as special as they had been, were not the quality time we wanted. Likewise, time together in the ambulance or at the hospital was not what we would have planned. I had to admit, however, God had used those occasions to His glory and my spiritual growth. Still we hadn't even had a date. As I drove to the station I couldn't help thinking perhaps someone was placing obstacles in our path specifically to keep us from being together.

There wasn't a lot of traffic, but the light drizzle required a lighter touch on the accelerator. That, coupled with being stopped by each of the three slowest traffic lights in America, resulted in my arriving at work nearly fifteen minutes late. Trish was in the break room, steam rising from her cup of coffee.

"Can I join you for a cup?" I asked, acting like it was a matter of life or death to get to the coffee pot. "I need three or four cups before I'm ready to attack the new day. I only had one at the house.... I'm sorry Trish, how are you this morning? I've rambled on like I was talking to one of the boys. Please forgive me."

"I'm fine now that I know you're all right!" she answered. "But I started worrying when you weren't here when I arrived. Jerry said he thought you were coming in at 7:30. You didn't have car trouble, did you?" The concern Trish displayed was not so much in her words or tone of voice as it was in her facial expression and in the slow, deliberate walk across the break-room toward me. As she did, she held her cup gracefully, not spilling a drop though it was filled to the brim; all the while she never allowed her beautiful eyes to break contact with mine.

Those eyes, I thought, *I could honestly spend the rest of my life just gazing into them. Listen to yourself.* my thoughts continued at the speed of light,

You're acting like a schoolboy. Get real; you're 44 years old. Why, all of a sudden, is your heart racing like a locomotive?

"Yoo-hoo! Oh David, anybody in there?" Trish asked, now standing directly in front of me, the power of her perfume captivating me. She had switched her voice from normal to enchanting; whether intentionally or not, I didn't know.

"Ahh, yes. I'm sorry, Trish. That makes twice today that I've gotten distracted by my thoughts. Forgive me?" I pleaded melodramatically.

"Only if those thoughts were about me", she responded.

Now I could tell that the voice switch had been intentional and I couldn't help but wonder, was I...was she...were we...falling in love? Trying my best at a W. C. Fields impersonation I said, "I can assure you that I was indeed thinking about you, my dear. And you knew it all along, didn't you?"

"I was hoping so."

After taking another sip of coffee I headed for my office motioning for her to follow me. "I've got some things to start working on and I'll need your help with them. I want you to put this into a quick spot for station identification '101.9 FM, WPFH, Where People Find Him. Your Christian FM station, serving Christ, serving you, and completing the great commission in these final days.'"

"Hey, that's good; maybe a tad long though. Are you sure you haven't done radio before?" Trish joked.

As I got in the office I turned, facing her as she entered. "No. Don't you forget, I'm the rookie on the staff, that is until Ted gets my phone call this morning." I sat behind my desk while Trish occupied the casual chair in front. "Okay," I continued, "I've got those phone calls to make after nine o'clock and a few other odds and ends. What I'd like you to do is to periodically check on the work in the studio and as soon as the technicians leave, which should be this morning, probably by ten, you can get rolling in there. Make broadcast-ready copies of your promos, spots, etc., and please start recording a wide variety of music for me for Sunday. That should pretty much fill your day. While you're recording the music, you can work on anything else you need to finish for your 'Good Morning, Lord' program. Jerry told me last night that Jimmy is at your beck and call for equipment, supplies, blank reels, tape cartridges or whatever you might need. His intercom number is 35; mine is 32, Jerry's is 33. Well, never mind, here, make a copy of this list of IC numbers or have Susan get you a copy. Any questions?"

Trish could tell I was trying to keep my mind on business, but not very well. Her first question got me back on track.

"Yes, where's lunch?"

Surprised, I looked up from my desk. "Are you hungry already? You really should eat a better breakfast. You know that don't you?"

By now Trish was nearly to the door. She turned around and faced me saying, "Of course I know that. And no, I'm not hungry yet, but lunch is on me whenever you get the time. Just say when, okay?"

"You got it! Sounds great." I felt my heart start racing again.

Trish left the office and I turned my attention to the work piled on my desk. I would schedule more interviews for next week, and hoped they would result in hiring at least one more part-timer for the weekend, allowing us to expand those broadcast days. My only other option was to work seven days a week myself or divide the additional weekend time with Trish. "Annette might want more time, too", I thought aloud. "Overtime, that's always an option."

Jerry called me to his office at 8:30 to discuss in detail some of the events for Sunday. "I would like to be in a position to start the initial broadcast at 7 a.m.," Jerry started. "I think some appropriate scripture verses, then a prayer of dedication. I've already talked with Pastor Hershey and he's tentatively agreed to be with us. He'll confirm that tonight after service. By the way, that would be a good time for you to meet him, that is, if you haven't already. You're going to church tonight, aren't you, Dave?"

"I sure am, Jerry. Believe me, it seems like a month since I've been there. I really need to go to get another dose of 'joy unspeakable and full of glory.' Besides, Trish asked me to be her guest tonight!"

My voice must have reflected an excitement more than Jerry expected as he asked, "You're not seeing too much of each other right off the bat, are you Dave?" I could sense a genuine concern in his question.

"No, I don't believe so. We've had lunch a couple of times, and one late-night snack after Madame DeVille's heart attack. That reminds me, I should check on her to see how she's doing. Maybe during lunch today I can swing by the hospital. Oh well, what else do we need to discuss?" I asked, trying thoughtfully to get the discussion back on track.

Jerry spun around in his swivel chair, looking out his window. It was raining harder now, the drops streaking down the pane of glass. "Have you got a schedule for training sessions for Ted and Jim?"

"In my mind, but not on paper. It all hinges on the phone calls I'll be making to them a bit later. I'm going to call Annette first because Ted's training really depends on whether she can start tonight, tomorrow or Friday. Trish and I plan to work some Friday night because tomorrow night I need to be at the photo shop. I've got some work there and an appointment for a portrait shooting. Saturday we'll both be in, and Sunday I'll be in by myself once the dedication is over. On the surface it looks like there's not enough time, but I think we'll be ready. I know you're concerned about Ted, but if you had been there during the interview and heard that young man's testimony and his love for God, as well as the way he expressed himself, you might feel better about him."

"My next question then, would be; have you let Susan know who we're going to hire?" Jerry returned his chair to its original position and looked at his note pad as he spoke.

"Yes, I did, Jerry. Susan has the completed interview packets and is busy preparing the employment folders; all except Trish's. Hers is already done. I'll get them in to complete the employment forms with Susan right away, even if they can't start working until Friday. Is there anything I've forgotten?" Jerry made several notations on his notepad before answering.

"No, David. I think you've got everything under control. Just let me know the results of the phone calls. Remember this too Dan Franklin and Carl Worth are taking some vacation time while we get the AM side back up. They'll be back in next week if you need them, otherwise they'll help me paint the AM's main studio."

Jerry's mood hadn't returned to what I had grown accustomed to as normal; that was evident in the tone of his questioning.

"Is everything okay, Jerry?" I asked. "You just don't seem yourself today. Is the AM still going to be down for two weeks, or has it slipped?"

"Oh, say, Dave, don't worry. Sometimes I just get to thinking, and when I do that my countenance changes and folks assume I'm mad, sad, or down. Hey, we still expect to be back up in two weeks! You've got the FM in good shape. Things are really looking good. A lot better than they did last Saturday morning. Right?"

Jerry smiled as he stood up. He came along side me putting his arm across my shoulders, and walked me down to the front office. While there, I checked my mailbox, grabbed its contents, and headed back to my office. Among the envelopes was a note from Trish offering to work overtime whenever I needed help to get things ready for Sunday.

My phone calls to Annette, Ted, and Jim revealed that Annette would be in during the afternoon to complete her pre-employment paperwork and would

75

report for work on Thursday morning. Ted was available to come in today. However, Jim was not at home, so I left a message with his wife, Barbara.

Sometimes a workday seems to drag along and sometimes it flies. This happened to be one that flew by. I was working diligently on the training schedule and a task requirements listing using the AM operations book as my guide when the room filled with the sweet smell of Trish's perfume. I looked up to find her standing in the doorway. "It's noon, David. Should I get my coat?"

I looked up, and then back at the paper to continue my writing as I answered, "Can you give me five more minutes? I want to finish this task listing." Trish smiled, nodded, and went back into the newly completed studio. As I had requested, she returned in about five minutes with her coat.

"The rain stopped but I've got my umbrella just in case it wants to start up again. I made reservations at the Charming Woods Village Restaurant. Have you ever been there?" she asked.

"Can't say as I have," I answered, donning my coat. "Let's go. You can give me a synopsis of their menu on the way. I'll drive, but you tell me where, and how to get there."

"Okay!" Trish replied excitedly, looping her arm through mine. "They have steaks, roast beef, shrimp...."

The meal proved to be the most enjoyable one Trish and I shared to date. We laughed, talked, sampled each other's food and acknowledged the fact that we not only enjoyed the other's company but had also experienced a deep and growing care for each other. Admitting it made me feel as though I had been released from some form of imprisonment; not so much by telling Trish that I cared for her, but because I admitted it to myself. I hadn't expected this kind of thing to happen to me, not at my age, anyway.

When our meal was finished we still had time to talk about the upcoming evening's church service. There were still many unanswered questions in my spirit, so I started asking them.

"Trish, I love God. I have accepted His plan of salvation, I'm sure of that. Not because of a textbook study I've done, or even because I have all the right answers to those questions designed to evaluate one's spiritual state, but because I know that I know. But it's just not enough to have that knowledge. I want to know God better and be closer to Him. I'm not satisfied with getting goose bumps in church or at the sound of good praise and worship music. That's part of my emotions, and although that doesn't make them bad, it does make them suspect. What I want, what I really want to...to do...is...well, sit on His lap and talk to Him. That doesn't sound too corny, does it? Do you have any idea, Trish, what I'm trying to attain? Maybe a better question is, do you know how I can get what it is that I want?"

Trish didn't answer right away. She paused even before she began to ask for God's help in answering my questions. Then she proceeded.

"Every person who even gets to the point of accepting God's gift of salvation, David, has made a tremendously large step–kind of like jumping across The Grand Canyon. The blood of Jesus gets us across the vast canyon of certain destruction and safely to the other side, salvation. But what do we do once we're there? Some Christians wander about like the Israelites in the desert. Oh, they know God all right, but they just don't know where they're going, how long it will take to get there, or even what the place looks like so they'll recognize it when they get there.

"Whether we move forward in God or not, after salvation, depends on what we do with those very questions you are now asking. Some people may have those very same questions, but not seek the answers. They almost seem to be saying, 'Okay, I'm saved, now what? Oh well, until God sends me a letter I'll just live my life and wait for Him to contact me.' Kind of just marking time, as it were. But on the other hand, when those questions come to us, if we recognize they are the promptings of God Himself, by His Holy Spirit, leading us on, then answers and growth will follow, provided we look.

"Like in a game of checkers or chess it's now your move," she continued. "God responded to your confession and acceptance of His son, Jesus. Now He waits for you to tell him how much more of Him you want to experience. Notice I said EXPERIENCE. With salvation comes ALL of God there is. If you keep Him in your hip pocket, like I heard a preacher say once, '...as fire insurance...', that's all you're going to get. But if you diligently seek Him, through feeding on His Word, and you receive the baptism of the Holy Ghost, then you'll see the changes you seek in your life. Then you'll experience God in your life daily and not just at church. Then you'll learn how to use the power God gives us. And then you will be able to move from one level of glory to another, all the time gaining strength in your spiritual walk. This may be difficult for you right now but don't get frustrated or give up—first things first—the baptism in the Holy Ghost...."

Trish shared many things about that particular baptism, things I had read in the Book of Acts but hadn't understood. She led me in a short prayer asking God to reveal Himself and His truths to me. Then she wrote down a list of scripture verses for me to read and meditate upon which would further explain and support her answers.

We had taken nearly an hour and a half for lunch so we hastily headed back to the station. Training session number one was about to take place.

The three of us were in the studio at two o'clock, Trish, Ted and myself. Trish took charge of the training session and briefed us on the names and functions of the equipment and apparatus positioned within arm's reach of the air chair. With the introduction on nomenclature complete, including the shorter nicknames, Trish provided a demonstration of typical routines for an on-air segment.

I closed my eyes when she wasn't looking, listened to her voice, and pictured myself back at my photo shop tuning the dial and finding her voice on WJOH. So quickly had I become familiar with that voice and the kind, caring person to whom it belonged.

Soon Trish gave each of us an opportunity to sit down and take control of the business end of the mike. Ted was first and he did exceptionally well, so well in fact, I dreaded my turn. Trish guided each of us through the mechanics of cueing records and CDs; plugging in a tape cartridge; and all the time allowing no dead air to be transmitted. We realized we weren't actually transmitting but we were sending our voices and music over the studio monitor speakers.

Ted and I practiced for nearly an hour each under the gentle encouraging, prompting and correction Trish provided. I was surprised how easy it became once we learned the sequences and some of the repetitious items such as station identification, time, and weather. My handicap was determining if the cartridge tapes were at the right starting point or not; cueing records or starting CD's seemed much easier.

Just before four o'clock, Trish took control of the board, having us watch her run through a twenty-minute segment, complete with switch over to hourly news on the feeder line from the AM side. Apparently she felt right at home in the new surroundings, flowing from one task to the next, making her announcements, cueing and playing records; at times taking an occasional sip from a soft drink. Then she cued up a tape cartridge, motioning for me specifically to "listen up."

"101.9 FM, WPFH, Where People Find Him. Your Christian FM Station, serving Christ, serving you, and completing the great commission in these final days."

When the taped spot finished, Trish ejected it and turned a dial to amplify a record already spinning. With the musical selection playing in the background, she eased up to the microphone and softly said, "David, was that how you wanted the station ID to sound?"

I nodded and smiled. "Looks like a wrap to me", I mused, grinning.

"Quit showing off!" Trish quipped. "What's next?"

By now I was standing. I looked at Trish and then Ted and announced the end of the workday. Ted wanted to stay a few minutes more to get some more practice, so Trish and I walked to my office.

"We'll be on the air soon; then we can start getting our temporary studio B into an actual studio B. Then we'll be able to do interviews for the show, either live or tape delayed in there. I haven't discussed that with Jerry but I expect we can accomplish that by the end of October, if not before."

By the time I finished my statement Trish and I were sitting in my office. Jerry stepped in and asked if he could join us.

"Don't forget church tonight, you two. How did the first training session go?"

I defaulted to Trish even though Jerry was looking at me. She related it had gone well and Ted's attentiveness and ability to learn quickly were especially impressive.

"Coming from you Trish, puts me more at ease about him." Jerry was now standing just to the side of Trish and looked at her asking, "And what about him?" pointing at me with a teasing smirk on his face.

"Oh, I don't know. He's probably a better photographer than radio announcer but I like his style. We might be able to make a weekend disc jockey out of him but don't hold your breath," Trish said, joining in on the tease.

I stood up, walked to the coat tree and grabbed my coat. "I don't have to stay here and take that. Besides, if I'm going to church, I need to get home and change. Your place at 5:45, Trish?"

"Yes. I'll be ready. Care to join us, Jerry?"

"No," Jerry said as he headed for the hallway. "I'll be up front with the pastor. I want to be near the anointing tonight; any place further back than the fifth row just won't do. But I will see you after the service in Pastor Glen's study. Both of you ought to be there as we plan the initial broadcast."

Jerry left the building with Trish, talking softly so they couldn't be heard. Ted and I were on their heels.

CHAPTER NINE

As I drove up the winding road to my house I observed the deepening colors of the changing leaves. Several weeks had passed since the first touch of autumn's splendor. The fall festival was approaching its peak. Although the transition from green leaves to bare trees takes nearly the entire month of September, the climax of the spectacle is usually the second and third weeks of the month. We were entering that time period and if I had still been a full-time photographer, I would have been wandering through the woods behind the house during each moment of available daylight. But not now, though; there were obligations requiring my attention. Although I would certainly have enjoyed a slow trek in the woods with my camera, I had no regrets.

As I stepped up on the front porch I could hear my phone ringing. I hurried with my keys, fumbling clumsily as I tried desperately to get in to answer the call. My hand grabbed the receiver on the eighth ring. The voice at the other end sounded familiar but she wouldn't identify herself. Whoever it was sounded raspy-voiced and groggy, nearly incoherent. Then it dawned on me, it was Madame, Madame DeVille.

She wanted to see Trish and me as soon as possible. As soon as she hung up I dialed Trish's number, hoping she had made it home already. The phone rang, three, four, five...seven...nine...twelve times.

"Hello." Trish's eventual answer almost startled me.

"Trish," I began frantically, "I just got a call from Madame. She was very hard to understand but she wants to see both of us, as soon as possible. Can you go with me to the hospital or would you rather go on to church by yourself?"

"No, come by and pick me up; I'll be ready. Did she say what she wanted, Dave?" Trish asked with deep concern.

"I really can't say. She was very hard to understand. I'll tell you more about it when I pick you up. The fact that she was able to use the phone leads me to believe she's not in a life-threatening situation, but there was considerable urgency in her voice. She sounded just like she had the night of the heart attack. Listen, I'll be by in about fifteen minutes, okay?" I paused.

"Okay Dave, see you then. Bye."

Trish came out of her apartment on the fly. I reached across the seat to unlock the passenger side door as she lifted the handle. "I wasn't thinking very well", I started. "You could have just as easily taken your car and met me at the hospital. Oh well, it doesn't matter now."

Trish looked at me while fastening the shoulder belt. "Did she give you any clue as to what she wants?"

"She just said she wanted both of us up there as quickly as possible. Apparently she is conscious and well enough to make phone calls. I intended to call her today but just got too busy and didn't remember. After I called you I tried to remember all I could. She wanted to ask us about Jesus. It had something to do with His healing power. Now if there's anything I'm not too sure about, besides the baptism of the Holy Ghost, it would have to be healing. I mean, I can answer simple questions about the Ten Commandments, or Moses and the plagues on Egypt, even Joseph with his coat of many colors, but not healing. Trish, what if she prays for a healing and doesn't get it? Worse yet, what if she asks ME to pray for her healing and she doesn't get it?"

Trish could tell I was about to spiritually hyperventilate. She didn't hand me a paper bag to breath in, but she went into that beautiful prayer language for about thirty seconds. Then she said, "David, the Bible says to trust in God and lean not on your own understanding, in all your ways acknowledge Him and He shall direct your paths. Tell God, right now, in your own words, that you need His help when we get to the hospital in ministering to Madame. That's what I just did in the spirit. Go ahead, tell Him."

Quite frankly, I was lost for words. Trish and I hadn't had much time together for prayer other than blessing our food and private prayer for Madame at the hospital. Trish had prayed in tongues but I had always prayed silently in English. Now she wanted me to pray out loud, so I tried.

"God, even now I don't know what to say. Please help me to pray right now as I should, and then give me wisdom, and the courage to use that wisdom when we arrive at Madame's bedside. Dear God, I don't know what she needs or wants but be with me and empower me to be your ambassador to her. Keep your presence with us as we try to minister to her. And Lord, keep me aware of your presence as I speak. Be with Trish too so that together we might do your will in this situation. In Jesus' name I pray. Amen."

There was a long pause from Trish who was silently moving her lips while I prayed out loud. She turned to me, waiting patiently until I had safely parked the car. She unfastened her shoulder strap, reached across the seat, prayed out loud in her prayer language while resting her hand against my forehead. I believe I slumped back in the seat and thought I had passed out, yet I felt such a wonderful peace. I was, for the moment, content to stay just that way; all urgency left me and I wanted to say something but was afraid to break the peace of the moment. When I finally opened my eyes several seconds later, I discovered that Trish was still praying with her hand still resting on my forehead.

I slowly straightened up in the seat. "What was that? Did I faint? What happened, Trish? Tell me!"

She opened her eyes, stopped praying and took her hand from my head. Smiling in a way that only she could, she said, "You've been slain in the spirit, David. I can see I'm going to have to give you a crash course on the basics of Pentecost at the earliest opportunity. How do you feel right now?"

"Fine, shouldn't I? I really do feel fine. Let's go see what Madame needs." My concern about Madame returned as I went for my door handle.

"Then let's go, David. Let's go minister to her."

When we reached the doorway to Madame's room we were intercepted by her grandson, Milton. He escorted us back out into the hall even before we were fully in the room.

"Listen," he said, "I don't know why she called you. She's weak; stable but weak. Don't upset her or do any of that loud praying or whatever it is you people do. If I had my way you wouldn't even get in there, but I don't want to upset her either. The doctors seem to think she may not make it out of the hospital. One more attack and the damage to the heart could be fatal. So whatever you do, don't upset her. Okay?"

"Milton, we came because she called us. Apparently we have something she wants," I countered. "If she wants me to pray, I'll pray. If she wants me to shout, I'll shout, and if she asks me to dance, I'll dance." I surprised myself with my answer. *Where did that boldness come from?* I silently asked myself. I took Trish by the hand and we entered Madame's room.

"Come close so I can talk", Madame whispered. "Don't pay no mind to Milton. He's waiting for me to go; I can see the dollar signs in his eyes." Madame was smiling now as she held my hand and reached out for Trish's. "But I got news for Milton and his brother, and excuse my poor English but, I ain't goin' nowhere. This won't take long but I have to let you know about it. I'm 83 years old. I know I don't have long to go, but I wasn't always this rich and high society lady I've come to be. If you can believe it, I was twelve years old once. That was when I visited a friend in Atlanta for the summer. My folks saved up so I could go. She and I used to be the closest of friends while we were young children but then her family moved to Georgia. It was while I was down there for nearly three months that I first heard about your

Jesus–correction, our Jesus. You see, I really did accept Him Monday night, in case you were wondering. There seems to be a deeper kind of faith down south, or at least there was when I was just a young girl because twice on Sunday and once at mid-week, I would sit next to her and her parents, on those hard wooden pews and hear of a Jesus who went about healing people. You know, making blind men see, and stopping a bleeding discharge, and curing the palsy.

"Well, there was one thing that the preacher used to say that just stuck with me over the many years, even when I wasn't attending church or praying as I knew I should. I can still hear 'He's the same yesterday, today and forever.' If that's the case, if that's true, then 71 years later shouldn't change anything, should it?"

I believed her question was rhetorical so I didn't answer. I glanced at Trish then back to Madame.

"That's okay, you don't have to answer", she said. "Just listen to me for a couple more minutes. I believe Jesus can heal me and give me a new heart, and as a result, maybe a couple more years. There are some things I've thought about since Monday that I would like to do before those boys get their greedy hands on my money. That's why I called you two to come up here. Please pray for my healing. I won't share with you now what my plans are, but when I accepted Christ the other night I really thought I was about to meet Him for judgment. Now I'm convinced He's got just a little bit more work for this old lady to do. Believe that with me, will you?

"Trish, honey, come here." She let go of my hand and pulled Trish down close to her face. "Two things," she whispered. "Men won't understand this so it's just between you and me. I know you. I've heard you over the past couple of years, both at the Christian radio station and over at WJOH. Your problems during that time might have made your heart ache, and rightly so, but don't miss this chance for happiness. Help him all you can to grow into the person you need. Secondly, I know you will understand when I say Jesus was in here with me today. He just walked in. We talked; well He talked mostly. He said you would know how to do it because you're a mature Christian. Show me His healing. Do you feel His anointing right now?"

Trish nodded, and then softly said, "It came on me in the car while we were on our way here."

"Good," Madame continued. "Then pray for me like He said you would."

Trish stood up and placed her hand over Madame's heart and prayed for the healing power of Jesus to restore her heart and health, claiming that healing by the stripes He received at His scourging, prior to His crucifixion.

Madame sighed, letting Trish stand up and step back from the bed. Then she looked at me and said, "David, I know you are a fine man, take good care of this lovely girl. She might make you a fine wife someday—that is, if you play your cards right. Now you two get along. I'll be fine."

Trish and I made our way down the hall to the elevators. As the doors slid open we met Milton again. We related our visit with his grandmother was enjoyable and that she was now resting easy. He made a face that reflected his disdain for our even being there at all, and then spoke.

"She's not going to make it. Why can't you people just accept what's going to happen? Always so pie-in-the-sky happy and optimistic. Well don't get too chummy. Once she's gone, you won't even get a DeVille order for a snapshot, you hotshot!" He sidestepped out of our way and went down the corridor. Trish and I entered the elevator, smiles still in place, and undaunted by his barrage of words.

I pushed the "G" for ground level, stepped back further into the elevator and asked, "What did Madame tell you?"

Trish said coyly, "Oh just girl talk. Nothing you would be interested in, at least not now."

"Now what's that supposed to mean?" I challenged, as the doors slid open and we made our way through the lobby and out to the parking lot. She didn't answer. "Come on, are you going to keep me in suspense?" I persisted, "Tell me!"

She smiled as I unlocked her door. "Not yet, David."

As I got in the car I asked, "You know you call me Dave when you want something or have something to say. But you call me David when you want distance or are playing a game. Which do you want now, distance or a game?" I finished the statement with a chuckle to let her know it was just part of a tease, then continued. "We've still got time to get in for the last part of church, if that's okay with you, Trish."

"Yes, by all means, let's get to church. By the way, Madame said, in not these exact words, she thought we made a pretty nice looking couple and that I should make sure we continue seeing each other. What do you think?"

Now Trish was teasing me, I was sure of it. "Ummmm, I think I like her advice. What about you? Ball's in your court now, Honey!" I mused.

"Is this going to be a mind game tonight? Don't answer that. I think Madame's advice ought not to be taken lightly, but would you mind if we discussed it further at a later date?" By now Trish was laying it on heavy, successfully employing the voice switch again. I melted.

"Hurry!" I said. "Let's get into church, back pew if you don't mind."

CHAPTER TEN

We quietly entered the sanctuary and slipped into the last pew. Pastor Glen was preaching on the healing power of Jesus. Trish and I looked at each other and smiled. I presumed our spirits had done the same thing–retraced our steps back to Madame's hospital room.

After the service, we found Jerry, and the three of us left the sanctuary and walked through the speaker's lounge into the office area. Jerry, who knew his way around, led us to Pastor Hershey's office. Once inside we seated ourselves and waited for the pastor to arrive.

"Hi, Jerry! How's the station doing? We sure miss it," the pastor inquired as he entered the office, stopping to shake Jerry's hand, Trish's, and then mine.

"We're slowly but surely getting things back under control, Pastor. It's not been near as difficult as we first thought it would be. Thank God for that. Let me do the introductions. This is Trish Ivey, one of our new FM announcers; you may already know her, she attends here. And this is David Post, my newly hired FM manager.

"We're here, as you know, to discuss the opening day broadcast of the FM side, scheduled for this Sunday morning at 7 a.m., and as I mentioned over the phone, we would like you to be a part of that dedication service."

We sat down as Pastor Glen replied, "Well that'll be an honor I certainly wouldn't want to miss. What specifically do you have in mind?"

"I'll start by announcing the station's call sign and then read a few scripture verses. We would like you to offer a prayer of dedication and make any comments you feel led to make. Trish will read a poem she has written, and Mr. Gramswald, who will be up from Chicago, may want to say a few words. I'll read the station's charter and purpose for being, and then go right into the day's musical programming. We wouldn't keep you long. We know you'll need to get back here for the morning service, but if you can join us in this capacity, we would be most appreciative."

Pastor Hershey agreed to be with us for the dedication, and we rose to leave. He escorted us to the front door of the church offices as the small talk diminished, but before leaving the building we joined hands and prayed for God's blessing upon each of us. We also prayed for His help in completing our work in the days ahead. I felt awkward when the others made the transition to praying in the Holy Ghost while I continued to pray in English. But I was confident that God hears English prayers too.

That portion of an event-filled day was now completed. Event-filled–now that was an understatement if ever there was one. As Trish and I got into my car, I started mentally recounting the major accomplishments of the past fourteen hours. There were the important phone calls to Ted, Annette and Jim. I paused momentarily wondering why Jim hadn't gotten back to me. There was lunch with Trish; our first training session; Madame's phone call; that wonderful time slain in the spirit in my car; our visit with Madame; Pastor Glen's message on healing; and finalizing the plans for the first FM broadcast. That would be quite a day in anyone's estimation.

"Just one thing missing," I said aloud.

Trish looked at me as if I was nuts and asked, "What's missing and who in the world are you talking to? It sounded as if you were communicating with someone way out in deep space."

"I guess I need to apologize again. I've been doing that a lot lately–thinking out loud and forgetting where I'm at or who it is that's with me. I sure hope that isn't old age setting in! After recapping today's events in my mind, the only thing I could think of that was missing was supper. When Madame called, I was about to change clothes so you and I could go eat. If you're real quiet, you can hear my stomach doing impersonations of a big, black, grizzly bear. I don't mean to wear out my welcome, but do you want to get something to eat?"

"That's what I was just about to ask you. Let's get a pizza at the Pizza Barn. We'll order a large and I'll take the left-overs home for breakfast." She laughed as she finished the thought.

"You'll have to fight me for any leftover pizza," I responded. "Cold pizza in the morning is the '...breakfast of champions.'"

While we waited for our pizza, Trish explained being slain in the spirit. Although I grasped what she said, and although I had experienced it for myself, I not so much doubted as wondered why God would do something like that. I must admit it was a truly enjoyable and educational experience, but it was a prayer language I wanted. And I wanted it now!

"Trish," I began, "tell me how you speak in tongues, and how you know when you can, and how you start, and how it feels, and...."

"Hold on, David", she said, holding up her hand like a traffic cop. "Cut me some slack. We'll get to all those questions, but first let's pray. Remember this David, my dear brother in the Lord, whenever you are filled with questions, seek God through prayer, to enlighten you and give you wisdom in all areas of life, but especially in the area you find yourself questioning. Let's pray.

"Father God," she began, lightly resting her hands on mine. "We ask for the blessing of wisdom at this moment as we discuss Your signs and wonders. All that we are we owe to You, Lord. It was You who created us and formed us, and it is You who sustains us. It was Your Holy Spirit who opened our spirits to the offer of salvation through the shed blood of Your Son, Jesus. Help me now as I try to help David in his walk with You and in his knowledge of You and the gifts You have given unto men. Be with him powerfully, God, as he receives Your truths. Make them plain to him and let them settle down deep into his spirit to become the foundations for more and more of Your truths. In Jesus' name we pray. Amen."

"That was beautiful, Trish. Oh if I could only pray that way. Lead me closer to God, Trish. Share your faith and beliefs with me so that I may have faith and believe as well." I reached up to my eyes as I spoke and touched the napkin to my face, softly wiping the tears, while gazing at her.

She promised to help me in any way that she could but explained growth, especially spiritual growth, depends on how much self-effort and desire one puts forth independently. Certainly she could help me, as would the preaching and teaching of Pastor Glen, but the results would be directly proportional to my desire to seek after the things of God.

As we ate the pizza I would ask Trish questions and she would answer as best she could, trying to avoid what she called "experiential theology." As she put it, a theology professed by some that simply states everyone's spiritual experiences should be the same as theirs.

"We really need a structured Bible study, David", she said. "But for the time being, let's start nearly at the beginning. I say nearly, because I know, and my spirit bears witness with your spirit, that you have accepted Christ as Savior and Lord. In that respect, we can skip the salvation preliminaries. Tell me what you guess, know or believe about the Bible, itself."

Setting my slice of pizza down, I started. "Well, I've heard it called, and I guess I believe it to be the inerrant, infallible word of God. Words that were inspired by the Holy Ghost and written by men who were known as prophets in the Old Testament. I believe the New Testament was written by people of that day who had either seen or received first-hand accounts of the events of Jesus' life. And too by those who saw the start of the church after Christ's ascension, right?

"For the time being that's accurate enough. The Bible, both Old and New

Testaments, is indeed the infallible word of God. But it's really more than that description implies. The Word of God is alive. That can best be dramatized by example. Have you ever heard an unsaved person say, 'I tried reading the Bible but couldn't follow it. It just didn't make any sense to me?' I'm sure you have. Likewise, you have undoubtedly read a verse and had it jump off the page. That's because your spirit-man is alive, while the unsaved person's spirit is literally dead, and as such, incapable of grasping the Bible's living truth.

"When you read a verse that takes on a different or more significant meaning than it had in the past, it's probably because through your daily living, your spirit has encountered new circumstances. It's in response to those new circumstances, and by the Word of God being processed by your spirit, that they take on their new meaning. This may happen many times with the same scripture.

"Even at that point, if we are truly seeking God, we must go at least one step further – asking for God's revelation. And it's that revelation that enables the spirit-man living inside of us, to be guided by that new truth, rather than living under the influence of what the flesh perceives. I don't mean all that the flesh perceives is false, but if we rely only on the flesh for our truth, it will be distorted at its best."

I could see Trish was gradually taking me deeper than I previously thought spiritual truth could go. She could see she was taking me deeper than I might be ready to go as she backed off a bit to regroup and approach the subject from a different perspective.

"If we can agree that the Bible is God's word to us then we can start making it applicable in daily living. By feeding on it with a hungry spirit we draw those truths into us. The truth becomes part of us, enabling us to rely more on God than what our physical man can know or even detect. Are you with me, David?"

I nodded, so she continued.

"The next thing that is vitally important for a sustained and powerful walk with God, is the baptism of the Holy Ghost. A lot of people seem to think it's just the emotional imagination of certain groups of Pentecostals, but God's word bears the truth of its existence. Seeking it, desiring it, and asking God for it, brings about the personal reality of it. Let me put it this way. We see with our eyes, and the eyes work in conjunction with the brain to actually accomplish the visual process. If either part is missing or malfunctioning there is no vision. We may still have eyes that wink, blink, water, and even let in light, but sight doesn't happen because the brain malfunctions or the connection is faulty. Many people are Christians, connected to God on a daily basis through prayer and fellowship in His Word, but they don't have the power to keep up, let alone win the battle against temptation or the inevitable trials of this Earthly life. This is because they have undernourished, underdeveloped, undersized spirits. All the connections are made, but the power to make moment-by-moment application is not there.

"The baptism of the Holy Ghost doesn't give you more of God than you received at the time of your spiritual birth, it activates your spirit so you can see and respond more powerfully and successfully than you ever thought possible. Maybe a better analogy would be a newborn baby. Yes, it's alive and breathing, growing, taking in nourishment and doing all those precious things that babies do. But has that newborn really experienced all of life there is for it? All the potential is there, but certainly not the ability yet to accomplish much of it except to grow and mature into the capability. So it is in receiving the Holy Spirit. Our spirits are indeed alive as promised with salvation but our natural reasoning, flawed as it is, will only make so much headway in our Christian walk through life. The hope of maturing into the capability of living a God centered life is greatly enhanced by this very special baptism. Have I lost you in any of this?"

"Trish," I replied, "I think I see what you're saying, but I'm not certain I've got it with the understanding necessary to apply it. Tell me about the application."

By now the pizza had grown cold and the place was nearly empty except for us and one other customer on the other side of the room. Trish began explaining while I finished my soft drink.

"Okay, you're a Christian. You've accepted Christ. You read the Bible and pray. You don't drink, cuss, smoke, steal, kill, tell dirty jokes or gamble. Great, keep it up! Your improved lifestyle is just one of the results of salvation. You now have a strong desire to stay clean before God, but each day you find yourself confessing that you've failed. It may be an impure thought, an unkind word, or an ugly feeling toward the guy who ran a stop sign and nearly hit you. Maybe you felt jealousy toward someone who got something you felt should have been yours. God knows what our individual sins are, and if we're truthful, we know them too. We also know they get in the way of a closer walk with Jesus. They get in the way of living pure, holy and powerfully the way our spirit wants to live. That's the flesh warring against the spirit: something that's going to happen all the rest of our natural lives. So how, in this world, do we ever become victorious; or is that even possible? Yes it is possible! But you won't get the formula from a textbook. You won't get it listening to the world's best preacher. And you won't get it from trying with all your human strength to live above circumstances and temptation. Sooner or later all of us falter because of our sinful nature. If we didn't, Jesus might not have had to die. He could have just shown us how to live a perfect life. Once we learned how He lived a sinless life, then we could. In reality, that's just exactly what He did, and throughout the New Testament we find the truths that reveal that reality.

Trish continued, "If we can't be victorious on our own, why didn't He stay on earth to help us? The Bible answers that question, in fact Jesus, Himself, answers that question. John 14:16-18 states that Jesus promised not to leave us comfortless and that He will be with us in the person of the Holy Ghost. But just like the eye, which cannot see unless it is connected completely to the brain, Christians cannot be victorious unless they are connected COMPLETELY to God, our source of power, via the Holy Ghost.

"Now to answer a more specific question of yours, 'How?' Ask God right now, if you truly desire this power, to baptize you in the Holy Ghost. He'll do it; it's part of the Bible we just agreed was His Word and incapable of error."

"Right here in the restaurant Trish?" I asked.

"Yes, right here. The Holy Ghost is a gentleman. He won't cause you any embarrassment or take control of you or run you like a robot. He will fill you with a power you may or may not detect physically, but honor your request He will."

Trish's reply was more intense than anything I had heard her say before. I couldn't help but believe every word she said, and I really did want to be more powerful and victorious in my daily walk.

"Father God, in the name of Your Son Jesus, I ask to be baptized with the Holy Ghost, not for a personal gratification or to think I'm any better than anybody else, but because Your Word says we can be so baptized. I need to be empowered by You to live a life more like Jesus. I want that kind of life. I want to be able to live by the spirit rather than be dominated by my flesh and the circumstances of life that confront and surround me. I don't believe I need to beg You, so I simply ask that You baptize me now in the power of the Holy Ghost. Amen."

I looked up at Trish. Although there was no difference I could detect in my natural being, I did feel different spiritually. "Trish, can I speak in a heavenly language like you now? I would like to be able to do that."

"You now have the ability, whether you do or not is up to you. I'll explain that to you on the way home. Let's go, okay? It's getting late."

Trish's comment reminded me that the day was indeed nearly over and the time had come to get some rest. There were just three busy training and preparation days left until the dedication and initial broadcast.

I paid for the pizza and we headed out to the car. As I drove Trish home she told me to practice speaking in tongues after I dropped her off. That way I would be less likely to feel uncomfortable. Eventually, she said that self-consciousness would diminish and I would be praying and praising God in tongues anywhere and everywhere. Then she gave me a strong warning I hadn't anticipated, cautioning me that the devil would immediately start fighting against me as soon as I uttered one word in the language God had enabled me to speak. She told me he would try to prevent me from obtaining and using this formidable weapon against him by any number of methods and that I should be aware of the certainty of the attack.

By the time I finished thanking Trish for all her help we were at her apartment. "Trish, I've really enjoyed your company tonight. I can't begin to tell you how blessed I am knowing you and counting you a very dear friend."

"The feeling is very much mutual," Trish responded as she leaned over and kissed my cheek. "Normal hours tomorrow?" she asked.

"Yes," I replied. "Except I'll be leaving about 3:30 for my photo shop. I've got some work to do there. I must start moving out so I can give the keys to the Realtor by the end of the month. I'll have a lot of work at the station tomorrow, so you and Annette take turns working with Ted and Jim. Gosh, that reminds me, I haven't heard from Jim. I wonder if he's been trying to get in touch with me or if anything's wrong."

Trish reached for the car's door handle and said, "I'll see myself up to the house, and I'll see you at 7:30 tomorrow morning. God bless you, David, with a peaceful, restful night's sleep. Pleasant dreams."

"Only if they're about you!" I said before I realized what words were coming out of my mouth.

She smiled for a moment. I looked deeply into her eyes, seeing a precious sparkle and the joy that was part of Trish's delightful personality. I kissed her.

CHAPTER ELEVEN

My mind just wouldn't shut off, even though my body cried out for sleep. It wasn't that long ago that I was a free-lance photographer and content to stay that way the rest of my life. Only a short period of time had elapsed since Jerry told me of his dilemma at the station and asked for my help. A short seven days ago I was living my own life and calling all the shots, no pun intended; not needing anyone. But now I was a radio station manager and, admit it or not, finding myself attracted to Trish in a way I didn't think was possible at my age. God was indeed doing a quick work.

Deciding not to fight my mind's incessant call for activity, I got up. It must have been close to two in the morning. With the coffee pot brewing, I sat on the couch next to the fireplace, savoring the solitude. Thoughts of Trish, the station, my prayer life and personal Bible study came to mind. Weaving through the countless pieces of data being processed in my mind came the urge to pray. Grabbing my head, I prayed out loud, "God, please give me peace. Ease my mind and let Your Spirit take control. Sort all this out, God. Give me clear direction, wisdom and understanding to all that's going on in my life. Let me know only that which You are a part of and root out all the confusion Satan has planted in my mind. Fill me with Your Spirit, and let me know Your will. Fill me, Oh God. Draw me closer to You now, more than I've ever been in my life. Renew my mind. Fill me with Your Spirit...."

As I fell back on the couch my arms went limp just as they had earlier in the evening at the hospital parking lot. But this time something else happened. I knew I was praying as intently as I ever had in my life, but my prayer changed from English to, well, to something else. The realization and certainty of what had just happened hit me with power, yet with peace and tranquility as well. I was nearly consumed with what had happened as I stopped speaking and silently evaluated the event. *David*, I thought, *you've just prayed in tongues. God has answered your prayer and given you a heavenly language. Just continue lying here and enjoy this peace that truly does pass all understanding. No, I want to speak more in tongues. I wonder if I can. How will I know what to say? Trish said to just try.* So I tried.

It worked! I did it! All I had to do was try. Immediately the words came rolling up, not out of my head, but from somewhere inside me, like down in my stomach area. Each syllable amazed me as faster and faster they came. I felt strong, refreshed, revived and ready to kick some devil, any devil, back to hell. Then it happened, just as Trish said it would. The thought came to me that what I was doing was nothing more than baby talk; gibberish. I stopped speaking in my new language long enough to yell out one sentence in English. "It's my prayer language from God, and Devil, you can't have it!"

Before I knew it the room was filling with the first streams of daylight from the rising sun. I had prayed nearly four hours and felt such sweet release in my spirit. The fire was nearly out and the full, untouched cup of coffee was cold. I checked the clock on the wall–6:35 a.m. I was about to be late for work again, but I wasn't worried or concerned. I showered, shaved, drank a glass of orange juice and headed out to the car, all the time praying in tongues and praising God in English for His most recent gift.

Trish greeted me at the door with a cup of coffee. "If you're going to do this to me so often–cause me to worry about you that is–then please call to tell me you're going to be late." Her concern was deep; I could tell, and I wondered why. I apologized for my being so inconsiderate.

"I promise, I'll call you next time, but if you only knew why I'm late this morning you would rejoice with me." I smiled as I took the coffee from her, took a sip, and started walking down the hall. "Uhmm, needs more sugar," I quipped as I detoured into the break room. "Go ahead, guess what happened to me after I got home last night."

Trish was standing at my side as I stirred in the sugar. Looking at me she said, "Well, the last thing we were talking about was how you were going to try speaking in tongues. But that was while you were on your way home. You just said 'at home', right?"

"Yep, at home, last night! In fact, all last night, well, nearly all last night!" I proudly announced.

We had arrived at my office. I took my position at the desk, wrapping my hands around the Styrofoam cup in an effort to warm them, while Trish sat opposite me looking intently at my face for clues.

"I can't even begin to guess. Come on, give me a hint," she pleaded.

"Okay," I said, "here's a hint..." and I proceeded to pray in tongues.

The joy Trish displayed was exuberant, yet refined. I could tell she was sharing in my spiritual celebration as she joined me in praising our God the best way we can, in the special language gift He provides.

Jerry was passing by, heard our celebration, and entered the office to join in, followed by Susan. Before long, most of the staff was in my office rejoicing and praising God. After about five minutes the jubilation subsided and everyone went back to their' respective work stations. I couldn't remember starting a new day any better than that.

Once alone in my office, the first thing I did was to make a phone call to Jim's house and again Barbara answered the phone.

"Yes, Mr. Post, Jim's here. He's been waiting for your call. I'll put him on, just a moment please." Barbara sounded very pleasant so early in the morning. By the sound of her voice, I pictured her as a short, gray-haired lady with wire glasses; kind of like a Mrs. Santa Claus.

"Hello Mr. Post," Jim began. "I was beginning to think I wasn't going to hear from you again. I left a message on your home answering machine." Jim's deliberate manner of speech came through clearly.

"No, Jim, that's my fault," I said. "I didn't check my machine for calls. I'm sorry. Can you come in for training today?" I asked.

"Why sure! Does that mean I'm hired? What time would you like me to come in? I can be ready and over there in less than fifteen minutes! If that's okay."

"It sure is, Jim, the sooner the better. You'll begin at Susan Jacobs' desk in the reception office. She'll start your personnel and payroll files. Then you'll be working with Trish Ivey in the main FM studio. Have Susan help you find Trish or me when she's done with your paperwork, Okay? Any questions?"

Jim came back in a loud voice that led me to believe he'd just had his own personal Christmas, three months early. He seemed proud, pleased, and ready to get to work. "No questions right now. Give me a couple of hours and I'll probably have more than you can handle. Thank you, Mr. Post, for letting me have a part in your station."

"No 'thank you' required, Jim. I know you'll work as unto the Lord. And by the way, it's His station, not mine. See you in a little while."

Trish was busy in the studio, so I took a few minutes to stroll through the rest of the station's facilities, stopping to observe the restoration work on the AM's main studio. I ended up in the unfinished FM studio B, picturing how it would look when finished.

I caught Jimmy Thomas coming out of studio A with an armful of albums and tapes. "Say Jimmy, when you get a minute I've got a list of things I would like to listen to for the Sunday dedication. No rush, though, just sometime this morning."

"Sure thing, Mr. Post," he responded, continuing down the hallway.

Upon returning to my office I started thumbing through the job applications once more.

"The mayor's on line three, David," Susan announced over the intercom.

"Thanks, Susan. Hello, Mayor O'Keefe. What can I do for you?"

"You're a hard person to get hold of, Post," the mayor grumbled. "Listen, Cal Simmons is sitting in front of me right now. He's about to get the job, you know the one I called you about? He knows he's my second choice. So don't worry about how you answer this question. Have you reconsidered? I really want you to take the city photographer's job."

I could tell the mayor was upset. Having to settle for his second choice, but there wasn't any changing directions now.

"Well, sir, I hate to disappoint you, and I know this is going to make Cal's day, but I just don't want the job. In fact, by the end of the month I'll be nothing more than a casual hobbyist as far as photography goes."

"Okay," Mayor O'Keefe grumbled once more, "I just wanted to give you one more chance. Remember, next year I'll need some work done for my re-election campaign. Cal won't be able to do that once he takes the city job. Give me a call then if you're back in the business."

"There's not too much chance of that, Mayor, but thank you for your interest. God bless you sir. Bye."

As I hung up the phone I looked up and saw Jerry out of the corner of my eye.

"What was that all about? A news tip from the mayor?" Jerry asked.

"Oh I wish it were that simple," I answered. "The mayor wanted me for the city photographer's job. He even gave me two chances to take it, but I don't want it, too cushy for me, no challenge, at least not like this one." Jerry smiled as I finished my reply.

"I'm glad you're with us, Dave. I know Trish is, too."

"Oh yeah," I responded, intrigued by his matter-of-fact statement. "How do you know that?"

"I know Trish pretty well. Remember, I said we dated some before I met Carol? She still confides in me, when the opportunity is right, that is. Let's just say the opportunity was right this morning in the break room. I noticed the way she was pacing in there this morning. She would sit down for a moment, take a sip of coffee, look at the door, get up, walk to the door, then return to her spot on the couch. That happened ten, maybe twelve times before I finally asked her what was bothering her. Suffice it to say she confided in me. And don't ask what she said, because I won't tell you. By the way, your pay will be docked the fifteen minutes you were late this morning. Jerry turned as he finished and walked out. I could tell he was chuckling under his breath and having a hard time keeping a straight face. I hoped it was an indication he was kidding.

The distractions finally stopped, allowing me to return to the applications. Things at the station were falling into place and if I could get two more part-timers or one more full-time person for the weekends we would be set for the time being. There were four applications that looked good enough to check into. I made phone calls and arranged for three of them to come in for interviews on Friday. The telephone number of the fourth one had since been disconnected.

Jim was completing his employment file in Susan's office when I spotted him. I took a moment to greet him, and to tell him he would be getting instruction and hands-on-practice with Trish and Annette. He smiled like a Cheshire cat and was eager to start.

On my return to the office I found Trish waiting for me. "What's on your mind, Trish?" I asked.

"Everything's ready in the studio for Jim's training session," she answered, "but I wanted to check with you to see if there's anything in particular you wanted me to give extra emphasis."

"Gee Trish?" I responded, unsure of how to reply. "You should be able to tell me that after this morning's session. But now that you mentioned it, maybe you should pay close attention to his slow, deliberate speech; it might be too slow through the news and weather. Otherwise, you let me know what you notice. Is Ted in yet, or Annette?" Trish was about to answer, when Jerry's voice came booming across the intercom.

"David, my office, right now!"

As I started for the door I looked back at Trish saying, "The last time he was that excited the station was on fire!" I hit the hallway flying and entered Jerry's office without knocking. "What's the matter, Jerry?" I asked, nearly out of breath.

"No practical joke this time, buddy! I just got off the phone with Mr. Gramswald. He's at the Marquette County Airport, two days early and unannounced! I should have guessed he'd do something like this. He's been known to go off on a whim at times. I'm at a critical point with the AM repairs; I just can't leave. Can you go get him? If Annette's in and can handle the training take Trish with you. It'll take you roughly an hour to get there. Take him to lunch while you're in Marquette. He loves Presque Isle, so drive him through there too. Better yet, stop at the public fishing pier, he likes walking out to the end of it. Then stop by the zoo. Trish can help you keep him occupied. I really can't afford to have him in here yet. He's great over the phone but in person, well, he just gets into everything. Kind of like a kid at the end of summer vacation. Do you know what I mean?"

I nodded.

"Good. Then go! Take the company station wagon."

I jogged back to my office only to find it abandoned, grabbed my coat and stepped into the studio. There I found my entire staff: Trish, Annette, Jim and Ted. "Hi, gang. I'm sorry for the interruption. Trish, can I speak to you for a moment out in the hall. Annette, can you pick up with Ted and Jim where Trish stopped? Thanks."

We barely got into the hall when Trish asked, "What's the crisis?"

"Oh Trish, you're not going to believe this. Get your coat, we're driving to Marquette!" She quickly retrieved her coat from the front office while I got the keys to the car and we hurried out of the building. "Mr. Gramswald's waiting at the airport," I started explaining as we were adjusting the seat belts. Before finishing the explanation we were heading southeast out of Ridgemont on US 41.

"I thought he wasn't arriving until Saturday?" Trish interjected.

"That's right, in fact he wasn't due in until Saturday evening. Jerry didn't say it in so many words, but made it clear he would just as soon not have him around the station for two whole days. I guess he just gets in the way, putting it about as nicely as Jerry did. Have you ever met him when you were with WPFH before?" I inquired.

"No, I never had the opportunity; nor did I ever pick up vibes that Jerry didn't want Mr. Gramswald around. There were just two times when he came up from Chicago while I was still with the station. Once while I was on vacation, the other—." She paused and squirmed in the seat. I could tell she was either going to say something painful or not finish the sentence at all. "The other was when I was on my honeymoon with Frank. I wish I could just erase that part of my life! I get feeling so spiritually strong and able to face anything life throws at me, or should I say Satan throws at me. Then something comes to remind me of that...that...well I'll never be able to...." Her pause lengthened.

"Never be able to what, Trish?" I asked.

She didn't answer.

"If you would rather not continue that topic of discussion I think I can read between the lines and leave it at that."

"No, I need to confront it. And really, I need to do so with you. My faith in God is strong. I believe He will eventually, when I've grown from the experience, help me overcome the bad memories and of course the pain. But it still hurts when I think of my marriage and the divorce. David, I think you already know I'm especially fond of you. Even in the short time that we've known each other I can sense your kindness, and understanding. And too, I can tell you care about our relationship. My hesitancy to finish expressing that one painful thought is something I would rather share with you at a more appropriate time. For right now though, I'm very happy to have this time with you. Did Jerry say anything else about Mr. Gramswald's early arrival?"

"No, nothing at all. He had just hung up the phone when he called me over the intercom. I was supposed to pick Mr. G. up Saturday evening. He was going to be here for the dedication on Sunday and meet with a real estate agent on Monday about some possible building sites for the television station. My guess is he would probably fly back to Chicago Monday night or early Tuesday. He has a private jet so there's no airlines schedule to meet. Why he's arrived this early is anybody's guess."

I glanced across to Trish and caught her wiping tears from her cheek. When it comes to being the strong male type, I fail miserably, especially when I see a woman crying. "Trish, is there anything I can do?" I offered. *What a dumb question*, I thought to myself. *Of course there was nothing I could do.* I wanted to kick myself for asking.

"Yes, there is, David," She replied, much to my surprise. "Just continue to be there for me. There are a lot of things that I would like to say but now is just not the time. Maybe later when we're both under less stress, that is of course, if I can hold on till then. At the right time I want to share with you the things on my heart. Things I want you to know but that can't be said right now. Would you be willing to do that?"

"Trish, you know I would, but without getting pushy, I never liked general invitations. Do you think we could set aside a date and time, like next Thursday, after work? Or is that too soon for what you had in mind?"

"That'll be fine David. But where?" she asked, now able to face me, the tears having stopped.

"I think I'd like to show you my woods. It would be perfect, you should feel comfortable there, but yet it's private enough to know there would just be the three of us."

"The three of us?" Trish said raising her eyebrows.

"Yes," I responded smugly, "You, me and God. What did you think I meant?"

"To be honest," she answered, "I didn't know what to think. I guess I wasn't on the same spiritual wavelength, no pun intended."

"What pun?" I quickly asked.

"Oh David, I keep forgetting you don't have a background in radio. Wavelength is a radio term. Forget it, it's just not as funny when you have to explain it. Besides, we were talking about Mr. Gramswald. Do you have any specific instructions from Jerry about the visit?"

"As a matter of fact I do. Jerry would like us to keep him busy in Marquette all day. He told me some of places we were to take him." I handed Trish the list I had jotted down as Jerry fired them off.

As she read the list aloud she added, "I'm glad he likes that roast beef sandwich place, I'm hungry."

"You're always hungry," I teased. "When was the last time you weren't hungry? Don't answer that. How do you burn off the calories, or shouldn't a guy ask that question?"

"Oh, I have my ways. I do aerobic dancing and I have an exercise bicycle in my apartment," she answered.

The casual conversation concluded as we neared the western side of the airport. The scenery, with it's mix of trees, was especially beautiful as we wove our way over and around the hills of the Marquette Range and through the little communities that begged us to stop and take in their postcard perfect landscape.

"The airport's up here on the left, David," Trish reminded me. "At the flashing caution light."

"That's right!" I acknowledged. "It's been awhile but I remember flying out of here one October day on my way to Korea, my only overseas assignment. Although certainly not to be compared...."

"Why didn't you finish that thought?" Trish asked.

"Because I was about to put my foot in my mouth, and I'd just as soon not do that at all, let alone while being with you. Let's see, parking is on the right. Yes, well here we are. Are you ready?" I asked rhetorically. "Let's go meet Jerry's infamous Mr. Gramswald."

CHAPTER TWELVE

Neither Trish nor I knew what Mr. Gramswald looked like. We spotted an older looking man in the snack bar drinking a glass of orange juice while reading the morning paper. At the time there weren't many people fitting the description of what we assumed a Mr. Gramswald would look like. We walked up to the distinguished looking gentleman and asked if he was Mr. Jerome Gramswald. Meticulously he folded the newspaper while studying us. Then, after finishing his juice, he stood up.

"Yes, and I presume you are David Post. I will not be so bold as to presume the young lady's name; I'll wait for a proper introduction." He shook my hand, then reached for and held Trish's while awaiting my compliance.

"Trish, this is Mr. Jerome Gramswald. Mr. Gramswald, this is Trish Ivey, our morning announcer. He leaned over slightly and placed a friendly kiss on the back of her hand.

"I'm pleased to meet you, Mr. Gramswald," she responded, giving me a quick glance. As she waited for him to release her hand, her expressive face telegraphed, "What an eccentric fruitcake!"

"Please," Mr. Gramswald asked, as he stood erect. "Call me Jerome or Mr. G. It's easier that way. Listen, I know you are surprised at my early arrival so let me explain as we go. I'll get my bags; maybe you can help me, David. And Trish, honey..." he looked at her and then back to me. "She really is a lovely lady, isn't she? Trish, dear, you can get the car."

She responded with a smile, a nod, and took the keys from me. Then Mr. Gramswald pointed to the three suitcases sitting beside the wall, within full view, just outside the snack bar entrance. "Those are mine, David. Tell me, how's Jerry doing with the repairs?"

"He's coming along fine. In fact that's why he sent Trish and me to meet you. He's at a crucial point and couldn't break away, although he did give me specific instructions as to what you like to do when you're here in the Upper Peninsula." I paused long enough to see if he wanted to interject anything. I didn't want to make a bad first impression or hog the conversation.

"Go ahead, David, tell me how Jerry wants you to keep me busy and out of his hair." A large smile sprawled across Mr. G's face that lit up his eyes.

As my recently acquired habit dictated, I didn't answer the challenge Mr. G. issued. I found myself entranced with evaluating the expression on his face. "Excuse me, sir, I wasn't, or didn't mean to stare. I was just wondering why you said that." My eyes traced the deep age lines that spread out from the corners of Mr. G's mouth; his smile deepened them dramatically.

"Listen, I know Jerry McFarland pretty well. I've been up here before, and he's pulled the same tactics time and time again. He's a good manager and a super worker; that's why I offered him the job as president. But one thing he's not—and I'm glad of it—he's not a fake, character-wise. The person you see is the person you get, except maybe in one area. I know I get in his way. I'm just nosy that way. I know he knows I'm on to his game. It's just something we play. We don't mean any harm by it and we don't let it get in the way of the job or our Christian love for each other. If he ever did, he'd be gone and he knows it. But you see, the station, and that includes the FM too, are part of my three-fold missionary vision for this part of the country.

"That brings me to why I arrived early." We stood just inside the door until Trish pulled the station wagon up to the curb. She quickly got out of the car and unlocked the back hatch.

"Shall we load the car and be on our way?" I asked, stooping to pick up the two large suitcases while Mr. G. picked up the smaller one.

"Yes, let's get out of here. First stop; let's make it the restaurant of your choice for lunch. It's not too early, is it?" He chuckled.

"Are you serious?" I responded. "Why Trish here, can eat 24 hours a day, no specific time required."

"David!" she fought back teasingly while gently landing a mock punch to my left arm. "Why did you say that in front of Mr. G.? He'll get the wrong idea about me."

"Not a chance of that happening," Mr. G. interjected. "I've got you figured out already, honey. I wouldn't believe anything he said about you unless it was flattering."

"It's nearly eleven-thirty. Do you want one of those famous roast beef sandwiches or a pasty while we're here in Marquette, Mr. G.?" I asked as I shut the hatch door. Before he answered we were all inside the car.

"Hey, both sound good, but I was thinking about that roast beef place on the way up. That'll do nicely, but you can forget the diversion to Presque Isle and the zoo."

Trish, who was now sitting in the back seat behind Mr. G., glanced at me as I turned my head back to look at her.

"I didn't say anything to him about that," I pleaded.

"Well I certainly didn't either," Trish whispered. Then we both laughed loudly.

102

Then I added, "I guess you know 'Dirty Tricks Jerry' pretty well. Right, Mr. G.?"

"Yes, I suppose I do," he replied while adjusting his head against the headrest. "And probably a lot better than what you think!"

We left the airport parking lot, and headed to Marquette, slightly more than a ten-minute drive. Mr. Gramswald rested his eyes and I adjusted the rear view mirror so I could see Trish. She caught me looking at her and made a funny face at me, so I smiled back.

I turned my attention back to driving, while thoughts of Trish raced through my mind. How was it that God had undeniably placed her in my life's path? What if my choices had been different during the past few years? I could have left the Upper Peninsula after my Air Force career. But because of the beauty of the area I had decided to stay, moving only seventy miles to the northwest.

What would life be like if Jerry hadn't been so obedient to God's prompting? For that matter, what if I hadn't accepted Jerry's offer? What if I hadn't tuned the radio to WJOH that particular morning and heard Trish's voice? What if there was no fire knocking WPFH-AM off the air? All those questions didn't require answers. God had ordered my steps and had caused Trish's path and mine to intersect. If nothing more than a lovely friendship resulted from that meeting, then certainly my life was richer for it. I looked again into the mirror catching the sparkle of her eyes and the warmth of her smile. Suddenly I was interrupted from my inattentive driving by the front tire drifting onto the rough shoulder of the road. After regaining control of my driving I found myself fighting the desire to continue gazing upon her face in the mirror. I disciplined myself to keep my attention on the road.

"Mr. G., we're here. Let's have some lunch." Cautiously I nudged him to wake him from his dozing.

"Oh, I'm all for that," he eagerly responded, reaching for the safety belt release.

"Me too!" Trish added.

Once inside Mr. G. began explaining his early arrival.

"Let me know if any of this is news to you. In case Jerry hasn't told you, my goal is to establish Christian television here in the U.P. My original plan for this trip was to meet with a real estate agent friend on Monday and look at a parcel of land that's coming available between Marquette and Ridgemont. The main disadvantage is that it's not close enough to the broadcast audience of Marquette proper. Nor is it convenient to Ridgemont where I'd like to keep all three stations, the AM, FM, and TV.

"On the other side of the coin, if I get land in the immediate vicinity of Ridgemont, the broadcast signal would be ineffective because of the sparse population. That would require us to rely totally on the cable systems for retransmission and distribution.

"Well, that finally brings me to the reason for my getting up here today, and for that matter, not having time to call Jerry in advance. There's a small but adequate plot of land available, just listed on the market, right here in Marquette County. It's about six miles south of here and I want to take a close look at it. Although it will not allow for co-location with the radio stations, it might otherwise meet our needs. And with it we could have the largest northern Michigan broadcast audience short of Sault Saint Marie. It's also close to a microwave site for distribution to distant cable companies in both the U.P. and northern Wisconsin."

Trish and I listened intently as Mr. Gramswald spoke. We could sense his enthusiasm for the project, and rightly so. He was, by the grace and help of God, fulfilling his late-life's missionary call. As I watched his eyes, seeing the story they told, and studied his mannerisms, Madame DeVille came to mind but for the life of me I couldn't figure the connection. What caused the thought of Madame to cross my mind while listening to Mr. G., I couldn't guess. There was no connection, I assured myself, and discounted the coincidence.

"If you two are finished eating," Mr. G. began, "then maybe you can drop me off at the Soumi Hotel; that's where I'll be staying until Saturday. You can come for me at noon on Saturday; better yet, send Jerry. I really need to talk to that boy!" He chuckled out loud as he finished the sentence. What the chuckle meant, I could only guess.

"May I ask a dumb question, Mr. G.?" I asked.

"Sure son. If it's your intention to reveal your mental prowess, then ask away."

"If you intended all along to stay in Marquette Thursday and Friday, why didn't you take a taxi from the airport to the hotel? Why did you call Jerry, and then wait over an hour at the airport for us? I'm pretty sure he expects you to come back with us."

Trish listened intently to my questioning, turning to Mr. Gramswald and chiming in, "I agree. Why did you have us come all the way from Ridgemont to pick you up?"

"I'm impressed, David. I was wondering if you would get around to asking me that. I did it for a couple of reasons. First, I wanted to give you information about the television station to take back to Jerry, including architectural plans for the building. I didn't want to get into a long telephone conversation with him. Secondly, he told me the two of you had been working hard and hadn't had much time together. He seems to think there's something going on between the two of you, strictly on the up and up. I wouldn't know what this beautiful young lady sees in an old coot like you, David, but if she does, and I did say IF, this would give you a couple of hours alone.

"There's one other thing that prompted my actions, that being I wanted to meet you by yourself, without Jerry around. I like Jerry a great deal, please don't get me wrong. In situations like that he tends to be domineering, if you catch my drift. I wasn't sure I'd get to know the real David Post unless I did so. Any other questions?"

I shook my head and looked at Trish. She also responded in the negative.

"Then let's get going," Mr. G. said, terminating the conversation.

We drove him to the hotel, said good-bye, and started the drive back to Ridgemont. "It would be nice if the station was on the air," I said trying to get a conversation going. "You know Trish, we're obviously going to get back sooner than Jerry expected. Maybe we ought to stop by the hospital to check in on Madame."

"That's a good idea, David. Let's do that." Trish smiled and then settled in for the hour-long drive by adjusting her seat and headrest.

"We'll have a staff meeting tomorrow afternoon so I can go over the training agenda and production restrictions. It would also be good, especially for you and Annette, to give me your ideas on setting up studio B for production work and live programming. Oh yes, while it's on my mind, remember I'll be leaving the station at about 3:30 this afternoon. I have some work that absolutely has to get done at the shop. I'll probably work late into the night, so be ready for Grumpy in the morning. Tell Ted, Annette and Jim about the staff meeting if I forget, okay?"

"Sure, Dave," Trish responded. "I have some ideas for that staff meeting, too: things we should all go over. Annette and I will identify to Ted, Jim and you, some of the annoying things that can show up as verbal mannerisms – audio 'tics', if you will. In our training sessions, we'll demonstrate how to avoid them with voice control. Experienced announcers know they'll happen from time to time, and how to listen for them. A good radio personality will often use self-evaluating techniques to preclude them from becoming habitual. It may sound funny, but we must listen to ourselves. If we don't, habits set in, and that's just bound to annoy and distract the audience.

"Will you be needing any help this evening at the photo shop? I would like to spend some time with you. It seems like I know you and yet I don't. Did that make any sense to you, David?"

"Yes, it did," I replied. "It's really the only way to describe it. I've had the same feeling."

"My only real knowledge of you seems to be at mealtime," Trish laughingly remarked. "I mean, I know you hold your fork funny but I don't even know your shoe size."

"Well, Trish, if you can believe this, it's an eleven, and that's the most exciting fact about me you'll ever know. The rest is pure boredom."

Trish leaned across the front seat. "Why don't you let me be the judge of that? Where's your hometown? When's your birthday? How long were you in the Air Force? Where, besides Korea, have you been stationed? Where did you attend college? What did you major in?" Trish fired off one salvo after another, without waiting for an answer.

Finally I jumped in, "Hold on, that's the kind of stuff you'll find in boring novels. There's nothing in that line of questioning that will ever reveal the true me. That was long before I accepted Jesus as savior. In those days there was a lot of wasted time. I feel like I was just marking time in worldly pursuits, and certainly nothing very noteworthy. Trish, to be honest, prior to my encounter with the Lord, my life was about as pointless as it could get. It's a history of things I would just as soon forget, let alone tell you.

"To be sure, I wasn't involved in those things associated with a criminal life; after all, I was pursuing my military career. I retired as a Senior Master Sergeant. To put it in laymen's terms, I was second from the top of the enlisted ranks. That doesn't come easy. My assignments were Korea, Mississippi, Ohio, Texas, and here in Michigan. In fact, I had three tours here in Michigan– twice at K. I. Sawyer and one at Paul B. Wurtsmith Air Force Base, in Oscoda, down state.

"You know that I've never married. You also know I had, for just over eighteen months, a photography business of my own; a legitimate photography business, none of that pornography stuff. Now I'm with WPFH. In nearly all that time, until eight years ago that is, I was lost and knew virtually nothing of God or spiritual truths. I thank God often for allowing me to live long enough to come to the saving knowledge of His Son, Jesus.

"That, in a nutshell, brings you up to date. As for your question of whether I need help tonight, I'll leave that up to you. I'd love your company, and there are some packing chores I could use help in accomplishing. You're free to join me if you want to, but it's more important that you get a good night's sleep and are well rested for the remainder of the week. It's going to get rough with long training sessions, plus the early Sunday dedication. Annette will share the training work with you, to be sure, but I don't know her well enough to give her responsibility for things I want to place specifically under your control, like production. I planned on turning that over to you during the staff meeting tomorrow, but you may as well know it now."

The conversation then turned to spiritual matters. Trish started explaining the other gifts of the Holy Ghost as listed in I Corinthians 12, beside speaking in tongues. I was amazed not only at what God had provided; His recording in the Bible the gifts He designed for our learning and use, but also at Trish's ability to explain them so well to a beginner. I could tell a lot of Pastor Hershey's teaching ability had been imparted to her. She had a strong grasp of the gifts, their definitions and applications.

"Trish, how does one obtain these gifts, and how many of them can one expect to experience?" I asked.

"That's not an easy two-part question, Dave, so let me start with the first part. You seek the gifts at their source. God gave gifts unto men, and you must ask God to show you those He has given to you. Remember in one of our earlier conversations I said that at the new birth one gets all of God there is to get?"

I nodded that I remembered.

"Well, that's true, but in I Corinthians 12 we see that God's gifts are given as He wills. That means that through salvation you have access to all of God there is, but you may not have all nine gifts of the Holy Ghost. In fact, very few people have ever had all nine, and most seem to have only one. The fact that a person has one or more gifts doesn't mean they'll use them. Some use these gifts, some don't. Just like we have been given the opportunity to accept Christ and His salvation, we are also invited to have the gifts of the Holy Ghost. Even the ability to use those gifts has been given. Whether or not they are used is strictly up to the person. Are you still with me?"

Again I nodded.

"Good!" she continued. "You have recently experienced speaking in tongues. This is the gift that all people receive and that's because it's the initial evidence of the Holy Ghost and one that people need most. As you can already attest, once you start praying in tongues you feel bolder and stronger. Your faith gets stirred up and active. And what's more, your spiritual man starts taking his rightful place as the dominant part of your tri-part being."

"Come again?" I quickly interrupted. "What's that about my 'tri-part being?'"

Trish sat up straight, lifted her head from the headrest and turned to face me directly. "We really need to get you a couple of tape series by Pastor Glen, one entitled 'The Spirit Man', and the other, 'Just Who Am I?' Those will get you well grounded in that area. In fact, if you've got a tape player at the photo shop, I'll bring a tape or two with me tonight. Do you have one?"

"Yes I do, Trish, it's built in with the radio."

"Good, but for right now let me say it this way. You are a spirit who possesses a soul and you live in a body. The spirit is the part of you that will live forever; your soul is your mind, will and emotions, and you know what your body is."

"Yes, forty-four years old and hopefully on hold," I said.

Trish laughed and then continued. "That's another subject, walking in divine health and healing; we'll get into that later. For right now though, if you want to know what other gifts God has given you, then you must seek them. Ask God to give you knowledge of them and to let you know by application. It's not spooky, or out of control. In fact it's no different than when you started speaking in tongues this morning in your office. You take the first step; God responds to your faith and provides the words to speak forth. And so it is with the rest of the gifts: interpretation of tongues; the gift of prophecy; a word of knowledge, etceteras. First and foremost, ask God by praying about it and reading the Bible for guidance and instruction. And by all means, remember this, don't be in a hurry. Patience is a gift too, though not listed in 1st Corinthians 12."

Trish had no sooner finished than I realized we were approaching Ridgemont and the hospital. I drove into the parking lot, and found a space close to the sidewalk. As we got out of the car I looked up to the row of windows on the fourth floor. Surprised, I yelled to Trish and pointed, "Look, up there, fourth floor, third window from the right, it's Madame. She's out of bed and waving to us! Wave to her, Trish; it's a miracle!"

CHAPTER THIRTEEN

We hurried into the hospital, catching the first available elevator. We reached the fourth floor barely able to wait for the door to open. As it did, we saw Madame standing right in front of us, dressed and waiting to greet us, and looking her radiant self. "Madame, what happened to you?" I asked, puzzled.

"Just what do you think happened, David? Jesus healed me, just like Trish prayed yesterday. Isn't it wonderful? About five this morning the nurse woke me up for medication, so I told her I didn't need any more pills. I threw off the covers, swung my legs over the edge of the bed and instructed her to get my clothes. If she were going to wake me up at that ridiculous hour of the morning for pills I didn't need, then I would use the opportunity to pack my things and go home. Well they wouldn't hear of it, calling in every intern, doctor and specialist in a twenty-mile radius to evaluate my sudden return to health."

Madame paused long enough to step back about three steps and held up her arms, revealing the fullness of an elegant, flowing dress. Her elegance was heightened with a beautiful strand of pearls, recently applied makeup, and a fresh hairdo. She asked, "How do I look?"

"Just like a princess," Trish answered.

"Do Charles and Milton know of your miraculous recovery?" I asked.

"Oh, dear me, no," she responded. "Those boys are probably still in the bank vault studying account balances right now. I'll bet they even have my casket picked out. This will knock their argyle socks off, won't it, honey?" she asked, putting her arm around Trish's waist and walking down the hallway to her private room. "Praised be God for His blessing of health," Madame continued. "If I can talk that doctor of mine into signing the release, I'll be out of here today. Would you be so kind as to take me home, David, once they release me?" She didn't get through to me so she asked again, this time more sternly. "David Post, can you drive me home?"

"Oh, sure, Madame, can you go now?" I asked.

"You haven't heard a word I said, did you, David?" she inquired.

"I'm sorry, Madame, I'm still back wandering around in yesterday's visit, trying to remember the exact words Trish prayed, because they got God's attention. Don't get me wrong, I'm just as elated as you are Madame, about your recovery, but I'm likewise intrigued by the method."

109

Trish joined the conversation. "David, remember a little while ago, on our way back from Marquette, we mentioned divine health and healing?"

I acknowledged Trish's leading question with a nod.

"And remember," she continued, "how I said we would get into that subject later?"

Again I nodded.

"Well, the Lord's not going to let the opportunity escape. The prayer isn't so important, nor the fact that I laid my hands on Madame as I prayed it. To be truthful, it didn't even matter who had prayed. The healing comes from Jesus; He's the healer. He can heal someone, with or without people getting involved.

"You see, when Jesus was nearing the end of his earthly life, He did something very, very important– nearly as important as His death, burial and resurrection. During the course of His mock trial, and its sentence of death by crucifixion, He fulfilled a prophecy of Isaiah. He bore the stripes of a scourging across His back and it's those stripes that purchased our healing. The New Testament also states it by saying '...and by His stripes we ARE healed....'

"We know that His death paid the price for our sins. His resurrection showed us that we too will be resurrected, but just what does the word healed mean in the verse '...by His stripes we ARE healed...'? If our salvation is assured by His death, then the only possible healing that remains needed, or unmet if you will, would be for our physical bodies. Jesus purchased our physical healing by bearing the whipping at the hands of the Roman soldiers. Now, David, watch closely: if sickness is limited death, then the opposite, divine health, must be the epitome of a healthy physical life. There's just no scripture that says you have to be sick. There are plenty who say, "You will be attacked by Satan." But none that say, "He wins." Walking in divine health should be as natural and expected a thing to a Christian as praying and expecting God to answer.

"Madame's health was restored not necessarily because of the prayer or because I was the one who prayed it. Nor can we say that she would have been healed if we hadn't prayed. Actually, the prayer might have been only important for us. The prayer could have been a preparatory move on God's part for this very conversation and learning situation. Madame may have been restored to health because of her faith and because Jesus honored that faith. Madame told us yesterday that Jesus had visited her. That visit caused her young faith, her unblemished, childlike faith— not altered by the opinions or doctrines of men—to activate the healing power of Jesus in her life. Isn't that right, Madame?"

"It must be, Trish. Here I am, standing here, feeling the best I've felt in years! I believe Jesus gave me a new heart. I don't even care if the doctors are able to confirm that or not. All I know is Jesus said He would heal me and I rested on that promise until it happened. Besides, I wanted to be at the radio station Sunday for the dedication. I have a little something for WPFH as a gift to help in its operational needs. That is, if I'm not overstepping by inviting myself where I'm not supposed to be."

Her words were spoken as gracefully as I had come to expect, and as graceful as was her stroll over to the window.

"Madame," I started, placing my hand gently on hers, "I'm growing spiritually by leaps and bounds. Trish has helped me a great deal in that area, in such a short time. And even though I've a long way to go, when it comes to the radio station, and specifically WPFH-FM, I can speak as an authority. If you're out of here, able, and feel up to it, we want you there for the dedication, by all means."

"Well, David, rest assured, there's no IF involved. I'll be out of here and at the dedication with bells on. Now, where's that doctor of mine?"

Madame's doctor arrived just as she finished the question. "It's about time you got here! Tell me I'm free to go home. See my ride is already here. Let's not keep them waiting!"

"Now Madame," Doctor Gerrard started his reply, "You know I'm not going to let the town's leading lady out of here until the hospital gets another $500 out of her for this room. Just kidding. Seriously, let me do a few more tests later this afternoon. If you pass them with flying colors, then I'll let you go home. Is it a deal?"

"It's a deal, but let's make it snappy, sonny!" Then she turned to me saying, "Now you two get along. I hate to do it, but I'll call Milton to come get me." She escorted us to the elevators, and while doing so, said, "Some doctors hate to admit it when they get outdone by God. They'll run tests, check the results, and then shrug their shoulders as they always do when God gets involved. But we know, don't we? Have a nice afternoon, you two."

Trish and I said good-bye to her and entered the elevator. Soon we were waving to her from the parking lot. It was nearly 2:30 and that left about an hour of work at the station. As we drove, Trish asked, "David, are you going to go straight to your photo shop after work?"

"Yes."

"Then I'll bring something to eat when I come. I know where your studio is, but I'm not sure where to park."

"If you come after 5:30, parking on the street is free, and there's plenty of it available by that time. There's some right out in front. The door will be locked, but just knock and I'll let you in."

"Okay. Anything special you're hungry for?"

By now I was like Pavlov's dogs. I had been conditioned by Trish to respond to the word hungry. I immediately started salivating.

"Yes," I announced. "Bring me a bacon cheeseburger with everything, fries, onion rings and a large chocolate shake. You need some money?"

"No," Trish answered. "I'm buying, but no onions or onion rings."

"You know, Trish, I hate to be the bearer of bad news, but I'm the kind of man who always gets in the last word. So if I want onion rings, and you said 'no', then I must have the last word: yes, dear!" We laughed heartily as we arrived at WPFH.

Trish went straight to the studio to see how the training was going, while I reported to Jerry. "What are you doing back here so soon?" he asked, shrugging his shoulders and then running to the door, peeking out of his office to see if Mr. Gramswald was there. "I thought you were going to keep him occupied until later! Where is he any way?" Jerry asked as he continued looking up and down the hall.

"Oh don't worry, Jerry," I answered, amused by his actions and considering whether to let him continue entertaining me or to remedy his precarious state. In a moment of compassion, I opted to end his anxiety. "He's still in Marquette and he's onto your game. I hope you know that."

Jerry slowly returned to his desk, looking perplexed as he sat down. "What do you mean he's still in Marquette? He's not here?"

"Nope," I quickly replied. "And what's more, he won't be here until Saturday afternoon. By the way, he wants YOU to pick him up at the Soumi Hotel. I believe his exact words were, 'I really need to talk to that boy'. Does that mean you're in hot water, Jerry? You know the man better than I do. I mean, he was a perfect gentleman; ask Trish, she'll agree." I was thoroughly enjoying pulling Jerry's leg.

"Just what happened when you met him at the airport?" Jerry asked looking more puzzled than ever.

"Well, let's see, we got there; parked the car; met him in the snack bar; I carried his suitcases to the car; Trish pulled the car up to the curb; then..."

Jerry interrupted, "Cut the nonsense! You know what I mean. Why is he staying in Marquette, and why did he come up here two days early?"

"Okay Jerry, I'll quit teasing. He came up early because he has an opportunity to look at some land in Marquette for the television station. Here's a copy of the preliminary plans for it. He asked me to give them to you and to let you know that he would be at the Soumi, room 246, if you needed to reach him. Apparently the land, some six miles south of Marquette, had just been placed on the market and might be suitable for building the television station. He said if the price were low enough, it would certainly offset the 65-mile distance factor. As you know, he really does want both the radio and TV to be located in Ridgemont, if at all possible. That's really about all he said, other than...." I paused for one more tease.

"Other than what?" he bit.

"Other than the cupid act you laid on him about Trish and me."

"Oh, David," Jerry turned to pleading whimsically, "you've got it all wrong on that count. I was sincere about that. I know you and Trish have started hanging around together. I also know what she's told me in confidence, a confidence I'm still not about to break. And while we're on the subject, let's get judgment day honest. If you don't have love and romance written all over your countenance, then I'm one of Santa's elves. I just figured you wouldn't want that drive all by yourself. Besides that, you and Trish haven't had a formal date or a good evening to sit and talk. What's wrong with a brother in the Lord working the schedule a little in your favor while making the most of an opportunity?"

I pondered Jerry's words as I surveyed his face for the slightest crack of a smile, certain he was pulling one of his shenanigans, but found no evidence of it. He sported a perfect poker face. "Okay, I'll buy that, for the time being, but that could have been a costly amount of productive training time for Trish to be working with Ted and Jim. Didn't you feel you were taking a chance there?" I asked.

"Well, if you remember, David, I made sure before you left that Annette was in. She's an experienced announcer; certainly for such an honorable motive she could work the training session while you two were out. You have any more questions Inspector Cluefinder?"

As I turned to leave Jerry's office I smiled and answered, "Not right now. I really need to get some work done before 3:30, so I'll head back to my office. But if I think of something, I'll be sure to ask." I left Jerry's office smug because I had gotten the last word, yet uneasy that Jerry was waiting for the right opportunity to play his winning hand.

When I got to my office Trish was at my desk, crying. I hurried over to her. "What could possibly be the matter so quickly after getting back?"

She hesitated to look at me, tears flowing nearly uncontrollably. Her hand, trembling, was still resting on the receiver of the telephone now back in its place. "That was...was...oh David, it doesn't really matter and it doesn't concern you...I should never have left WPFH in the first place."

I slid a chair next to her and tried to soothe her by putting my arm around her shoulders. "Please tell me what's caused you to be so upset. If it concerns you, then it concerns me. You asked me to be there for you. Here I am." At first it didn't appear that my pleading would coax her into confiding in me, but then she checked the tears, grabbed a tissue from the desktop dispenser and faced me with her eyes swollen and red.

"David that call was from John Fairbanks, the late afternoon/early evening announcer, at WJOH. He's always been the jerk, you know, a womanizer. Well when I first got to WJOH he...he, aaah...."

"Hit on you, Trish?" I asked.

"Uh-huh," she slowly replied, wiping more tears, then her nose. "He somehow knew I was at WJOH because of the divorce. Although he didn't have all the particulars, he did know my marriage was over and that I had filed for divorce. He may have thought it was my fault. Maybe he figured I would be an easy...I really don't know what he thought. I do know he...well his reputation wasn't exactly saintly. I guess he was intending to add me to his list of adventures, so to speak. I let him know, in no uncertain terms, I wouldn't be a part of his plans. He didn't handle the rejection very well. To make a long story short, he never totally gave up. One of the main reasons for my asking God to get be back here was because of his constant...constant...just what do you call that?"

"It's probably sexual harassment, Trish. You could hang him for that if you wanted to," I answered.

"No, thank you!" Trish quickly responded. "I don't want any part of another courtroom. Thanks, but no thanks!"

Trish seemed to relax and open up to further discussion, so I asked her another question. "What, then, was the phone call about?"

"He had apparently just found out I was back at WPFH. I think the others were protecting me; telling him I was sick or something. Somehow he found out and called. Susan had no way of knowing who or what the call was; she buzzed me in the studio and I had her switch the call to your phone. When I discovered who it was, I wanted to hang up, but I'm tired of running from things. Do you understand that, David?"

I nodded and motioned for her to continue.

"The long and the short of what he said was, 'I see you're back at that religious station. What's the matter, ANGEL, can't you take the heat here on earth either, you frigid holy roller?'"

I could feel my emotions swirling inside; they were nearly out of control! I didn't know which way to go or what to do yet somehow I managed to ask another question. "What else did he say, Trish?"

"Nothing after that. He just waited to hear my response. When I didn't say anything, he hung up. Maybe that's the last of him."

"Boy, I'd like to make it the last of him," I announced, standing abruptly and slamming my fist into my other palm, hurting myself as I did.

"No, David. That's not the way Jesus would handle the situation. It might hurt, it might be hard, but I'm going to forgive him right now, just like I did each time he...."

"Say it Trish; every time he hit on you!" my anger still in hot pursuit of someone I didn't even know.

"No again, David. I won't say that. He's sick. He needs help or he'll be in trouble some day. But for right now I need to forgive him or it will fester inside me and rob me of my joy. That's a deliberate choice on my part, David. I can choose to be bitter, hateful, and vengeful or I can forgive him and then it's out of my life. Either way, I'm the one in charge, not John. I choose to forgive."

"Okay, Trish," I said, more subdued, though still pacing the floor. "That may make sense and I know you're right, scripturally and emotionally, but that's just no way to treat a lady! And not just any lady! My lady!" My voice rose in excitement as I spoke but then rapidly faded after realizing what I was saying.

Trish looked up at me, stood to her feet, and pulled me gently to within perfume range and asked, "Do you mean that, David?"

"Well, I said it, didn't I, Trish?" I answered.

"You sounded unsure of yourself, and that's not what I asked you, David." She was not going to let the remark slide by as she stood there looking at me, not moving from her established position. I felt uneasy. Yes, I had said it, but was it what I really felt, or was it just a protective statement by someone who cared for her? I really didn't know: both reasons seemed to be right, but I knew I had better say something.

"The Bible says, 'out of the heart the mouth speaks' or something like that, right, Trish? I guess I meant it and I don't apologize for having said it."

"So who asked you to apologize?" she asked, rhetorically. "I just wanted you to stand by what you said. Am I your lady?"

I carefully moved sideways to get free from the aroma of her perfume, knowing I wouldn't be able to carry on a factual or unbiased conversation under the hypnotic influence of its fragrance.

I really wanted to sidestep the question, too. My motives may have been pure in stating 'my lady', but the responsibility for saying it was something that made me feel uncomfortable. My apprehension certainly wasn't because I didn't care for Trish; I knew I did. Still, after forty-four years of not making that kind of verbal declaration, making it a second time in the lone strength of my mental reasoning, and without the previous emotional impetus, was difficult, especially at this stage. Yet I had to admit, there were some pretty strong feelings of attraction, care, and yes, love.

"I'm still waiting," Trish reiterated.

"I know you are. Can I be honest and say this is difficult. Can you understand that I'm torn between coming right out with it and being cautious? Maybe saying those words again would be the best thing for me, or maybe I need more time."

"I can understand that," she replied, "but I'll pray that whatever is hindering you will be overcome. If it's still okay, I'll see you later tonight, but for right now I better get back to the studio to help Annette with Jim and Ted's training."

She turned and headed for the door, with her composure nearly restored. I hurt for her deeply as I watched her leave my office. She had reached out to me, at my invitation, but I didn't measure up to the call. My guts screamed out that I had betrayed my promise to her. What could I do? There was one thing I couldn't do. I couldn't wait until six tonight to answer her question.

"Trish!" I called.

She turned and looked at me through her still reddened eyes, kindness and beauty showing through, even in her sadness. "Yes, David?" she inquired, softly.

"I love you too much to let it go unsaid. And I love you too much to let you walk away from me while you're still hurting. Yes, I meant what I said, you know, '...my lady...' that is, of course, if you would like to be?" I finished the statement hoping she would understand it to be a question. She did.

"Thank you, David, I would indeed. Thank you too, Jesus," she added, looking upward while slowly moving toward me. She had almost returned to the exact location where the conversation had started. The last two steps brought her right in front of me. She placed a gentle kiss on my cheek, then without a word, headed back to the studio.

I stood there in my empty office for a moment trying desperately to recall all the words we had just shared. Although it had happened much faster than I would have envisioned, I liked what had transpired. I returned to the desk and the unfinished work but just wasn't able to keep my mind on it. My wristwatch alarm alerted me to the fact it was 3:30. I closed my office and headed for the photo shop.

CHAPTER FOURTEEN

I stopped at a local moving company to pick up several empty boxes, tape, cushion paper and plastic foam peanut shells, arriving at the shop just after 4:30. I unlocked the door and set the packing materials against an inside wall. The first order of business was to empty the mixed darkroom chemicals I didn't want to transport. Getting the darkroom equipment dismantled and home was the most important task to be accomplished. There were several photo sessions on the schedule including a portrait shooting in about a half an hour, so the lighting equipment would remain. The film processing and printing operations, however, could be done at home.

I paused few moments with a cup of coffee, surveying the studio. It seemed strange, moving out so soon when I had originally intended to be in the business for the foreseeable future. During the cursory inventory I noted those things to be included in this first moving session. The rest would be removed later in the month. The computer, furniture, lights, props, screens and backgrounds would stay until the lease was up at the end of the month.

The front door opening took me by surprise. In came the young engaged couple for their five o'clock portrait sitting. They were an attractive pair, both in their mid-twenties. As I directed them into a casual yet complementary pose, I couldn't help but join them in the joy of their love and upcoming wedding. She was all aglow and flitted about like a small sparrow searching for seeds, causing me countless adjustments to their pose. He, a tall, slender, dark-haired man, was an engineer with the city.

Life seemed to be different now for young people when compared to the stress and trauma of the age I had grown up in. The draft and the Vietnam War seemed to tear young couples apart in those days. This couple, though, hadn't experienced anything like that. How lucky they were, I thought. Then I chastened myself for using the word luck instead of blessed.

Almost before it had started, the session was over and they were gone. The fragrance of their bliss and excitement continued to fill my mind as I returned to my work. Finishing the last gulp of the now-cold coffee, I returned to the darkroom. I had it nearly dismantled and ready for packing when I heard Trish's knock on the door. "I'll be right there!" I yelled, loud enough for her to hear. I set the top section of the enlarger on the floor, resting it against the wall and the side of a chair, and went to let her in. "I believe this is the first time I've seen you in jeans." I said as she entered the studio.

"Well, I came to work," was her reply. "Where do I start?" She walked by me and turned gracefully back in my direction, glancing around as she did so, to size up the chore. When her eyes finally met mine I perceived a genuine eagerness to help me surmount my monumental packing job.

"What a blessing you are! You can start," I replied, "by telling me how the afternoon training session ended. Are Jim and Ted any closer to being radio announcers now?"

"Ted's really good. But then you knew he would be. Jim is, just as you said, very deliberate in his delivery, but we'll work on speeding him up tomorrow. With some practice he'll be okay. As far as grasping a working knowledge of the control board and all its aspects, both were initially awkward as you might expect. We worked on that until just before quitting time. The CD players seemed the easiest for both of them."

"They're awkward? Wait until you get a good look at me!" I interrupted.

"I have," she said, smiling intently while looking into my eyes. "And I like what I see."

She paused long enough to see if I were going to show some kind of reaction to her flirting. I knew what she was doing so I decided to play her game. So trying to get the conversation back on the subject would, I reasoned, reveal her true intentions.

"How about Annette?" I continued the inquisition.

"As I told you the other day," she capitulated, "I had heard her several times when I was in Escanaba. When I got back in the studio this afternoon, she had Ted and Jim going over the cueing procedures on tapes and albums and reading the cartridge markings for spots and how to annotate the air-time in the log."

"I sure hope somebody goes over all those things with me or everyone in the place will know more than the boss," I whined.

"David, I don't want you to worry about your training or Sunday's broadcast day. I'll be there all day with you; that can be your personal training session. Okay?"

I looked at Trish, surprised that she would be willing to give up her day off. "Are you sure, Trish? I mean missing morning church and all?"

"I'm sure NOW David," she replied.

"'NOW'? What does the heavy on the 'NOW' mean?" I quickly asked.

"I mean right now. Earlier today, when the thought first crossed my mind, I didn't have much hope of making that offer to you. You see, you've come to mean a lot to me, David, and I didn't know exactly how you felt about me.

We've been kind of coy about our feelings on that subject, using innuendo or double-meaning remarks and such. I didn't know if I could spend eight straight hours or more with you, not knowing how you felt about me, yet knowing how I feel about you. Do you understand what I'm trying to say?"

I stopped my packing routine long enough to smile, nodding my head to confirm my understanding. "I believe I do, Trish."

"Then there was that very important conversation in your office this afternoon, you know, when you called me your 'lady'. I guess the shoe is now on the other foot; that foot being mine. I had better admit, right here and now, that you're special to me too. If we're going to be perfectly honest with each other, we might as well do so right from the start.

"Being honest," Trish continued, "would also include explaining that small 'thank you, Jesus' prayer in your office. The best way would be to say you are, I believe, the answer to the third part of a three-part prayer. A prayer sent heavenward many times over the past several months."

I stood up from the box I was packing, certain that what Trish was about to explain was of the utmost importance to her and thus important to me. Intrigued, I asked, "Third? Refresh my memory on the other two."

"The first was to get away from WJOH, and more specifically, back to WPFH. The second was to remove the bitterness from my heart and get on with my life."

"And third?" I asked again.

"Third was asking God to put His choice of a godly man in my life to help me overcome the pain of the divorce, be able to forgive Frank, and heal the trauma that had penetrated my being."

I was, by now, feeling warm inside. Gazing intently into Trish's eyes always did that to me. I didn't know if she knew what kind of effect she had on me, but if she didn't, I had a feeling it was going to become more than evident to her very soon. Slowly and deliberately I asked, "Do you think I'm that man?"

"Yes," she said confidently. "If you look at how we got together you would have to admit, God has had something to do with it. I'm also looking for Him to confirm this belief again. In the meantime, I just can't help but believe He has something grand for us," she reasoned.

"Well, if I'm a 'godly' man, or even hope to be, it will be because you've helped me. I'm sure of one thing though, I'm not there yet."

Trish returned her attention to the carton she was taping shut. "None of us are where God wants us to be. Hopefully though, we are working on that.

Philippians 2, verse 12 mentions '...working out your salvation....' That doesn't mean working to earn your salvation; it means working with your salvation. To put it another way, let's compare it to a doctor. After he's completed his medical schooling, internship and all, he's ready to hang up his diploma and practice medicine. Although the degree looks great on the wall, he's not doing anything with it until he starts working with the knowledge and skills he has studied to develop. Once he does, he can then say he's working out his degree. Likewise, as we go about life in ways the Bible has shown us, we will be working out our salvation. That will undoubtedly bring about a forward walk with God. Based on what I've seen, you're going forward, David."

"It looks like you got everything on your wish list, doesn't it?" I asked, not really expecting a reply.

"What do you mean, 'wish list', David?" she quickly asked me, setting the sealed box down on the floor near the door.

"Well, you asked God for three things and it appears you've received all three," I replied, feeling rather proud of my deductive reasoning.

"David, I'm surprised at you," she chastened. "You don't make wish lists to God like a child would to Santa Claus. I shared with Him the desires of my heart, relinquishing their outcome to His perfect will. The Bible says God will give you the desires of your heart. So who is it that puts the desires in there in the first place? I believe it's Him. What I've just shared with you is one of the major aspects of my Christian growth lately. Pastor Glen had been preaching on that topic, 'God's Will For You', for nearly two months. It was about that same time when I first recognized leaving WPFH was a mistake, and my prayer was to somehow get back. Then, as Pastor Glen continued the series, I realized my heart was filled with bitterness and animosity. Animosity especially toward Frank, and I guess, all men. Although God heard my prayers, He apparently had no intention of answering until all the ugliness was out of my heart. Soon my prayer expanded to include asking for God's forgiveness as I forgave Frank. Finally the prayer evolved into a request for someone to fill the void in my life. By the time the sermon series was completed, about four months ago, the third part of my prayer had grown even more to include getting out of my self-inflicted, private pity party. I've listened to that tape series many, many times since then, especially when I experienced doubts and fears about the future and where my life was heading.

"David, even though I presented these things to the Lord, I didn't do it as a petition of wants. I would pray in English first, then switch to my prayer language, trusting God to form a prayer through me that would meet the need of the situation."

"I think you just lost me Trish," I responded. "Could you expound please?"

"Sure, David," she said, settling into one of the customer chairs. "Let me start by saying the Bible makes it clear, when we pray in tongues we are praying in a manner that our minds do not understand. I believe the Bible says '...our minds are unfruitful....' When we pray in English it is possible and probable that we are praying amiss. But when we change to our heavenly language, our prayer aligns with how God wants it, matching His will. Does that make it clearer to you, David?"

I had to admit it did.

Trish sauntered over to her purse, retrieved an audiocassette and slipped it into the tape player near my desk. After starting the tape she returned to boxing the smaller pieces of equipment and supplies. I listened quietly and intently. We had nearly finished the evening's packing chore around 7:30 and paused to eat the burgers Trish had brought. As she warmed them in the microwave I spread some brown wrapping paper on the desk.

On the tape, Pastor Hershey was defining our purpose in life and the relationship we should have to God, as our Father. When the first side of the tape was done Trish and I discussed several points of the teaching.

Soon our conversation changed back to the radio station as we finished the packing. Trish expressed several ideas she had for airing guest interviews on her show. When the small talk ended, we filled the back of my station wagon with the boxes. All that remained unpacked could be moved in one or two more evenings at the end of the month. The evening's work was completed, and it was time for Trish and me to say goodnight—something I didn't want to do.

I locked the shop and we each headed home. I didn't like being without her. Contrary to Jerry's notion that we hadn't had much time together, I felt the exact opposite was true. Because of the circumstances of the past several days, we had spent a great deal of time together. Under more normal circumstances, we might not have known each other nearly well enough to express ourselves as openly as we had.

When I got home I unpacked the car. Although it was only ten o'clock, I was convinced it was a good opportunity to get to bed early, and sure enough, the Lord blessed me with a restful night's sleep.

Friday morning was cold and rainy. The forecast called for a whole day of the same. Blahhhhh, those dreary September days make me wish for summer to return or for winter to just get on with it. But no amount of wishing was going to change the weather, so I decided to attack the area of my responsibility: getting ready for and going to work. I arrived at the station at quarter to seven in an attempt to make up for my two late arrivals.

Jerry was in the break room making the coffee. "Just how early do you get here, Jerry?" I asked.

Jerry turned to greet me with a handshake, answering, "I just got here. The coffee will be ready in about five minutes. Normally I don't get here until 7:00 or so. I'm a bit early today."

"I hope you made that stuff strong enough to give my pacemaker a jump-start," I joked, laughing out loud.

Jerry joined in with a chuckle and said, "I believe I did. Not to change the subject, but how did the work at your shop go last night?"

"Pretty well," I replied, rubbing my eyes and fighting off a yawn. "Trish helped me, and we managed to get the darkroom equipment packed and out to the house."

"Oh, did Trish go out to your place?" he asked, showing an interest now that distracted his attention from the brewing coffee.

"No, she left for her apartment right from my studio. We sat and talked until 8:30. Then we loaded the car. I plan on being out of the building by the end of the month, and totally out of the business by the end of the year, if at all possible.

"You know something, Jerry? I forgot to tell you about Madame DeVille's total recovery. Trish and I stopped in to see her on our way back from Marquette yesterday. She was waving to us from her window. When we got to her floor we found her dressed, walking around and ready to go home as soon as her doctor finished some tests. Can you believe, from cardiac to Cadillac in just a few short hours." Jerry jubilantly praised God for His healing power and I joined him in the spontaneous worship.

"What a great God we serve, David. Don't ever take His healing power for granted nor fail to apply it."

"Amen to that, Jerry," I smiled. "That reminds me, Madame asked if she could be present for the FM dedication, and I told her she could. I believe she wants to make a presentation to the station. She didn't say what it was but did say it would be something for the 'operational needs', as she put it. I was sure you wouldn't mind."

"That's great!" Jerry quickly responded, grinning ear to ear. "She's more than welcome to be at the dedication."

"Since I've started being around you and Trish and the others here at the station, and since I've been to a couple of the services at Lord of the Harvest Church, I feel different, somehow. It's like I've been experiencing a God I didn't know before, and I'm really enjoying the learning process. Is it possible that I'm learning so much or growing so quickly that my mind can't keep up with my spirit?"

Jerry looked at me, leaning forward toward me in his chair and said, "David, that may be part of it, but what I think is happening is that your spiritual man is awakening. You're probably noticing the starving status of your spirit being changed; built up by the nourishment of real food. It's no longer a spirit suffering from malnutrition. But don't worry you won't overdose. Just take all that God provides. He'll be faithful to keep the supply coming at the right rate."

"That certainly makes a great deal of sense, Jerry, but can I get back to the photography business for a moment? I don't want closing the shop to get in the way of my job performance, or keep me from attending those important training sessions here at the station. I do appreciate you being so understanding and liberal in giving me time off as I need it to meet my scheduled obligations."

"No problem," Jerry said putting one arm around my shoulder and handing me a plastic cup with the other. "But we don't use the 'L' word here, you know—liberal. It's just about done," he said, pointing to the nearly full carafe resting under the hood of the drip coffee maker.

"You get yours first, Jerry," I remarked while motioning to him to get the first cup. "After all, you made it."

Jerry turned slightly away from me glancing toward the door as if something caught his attention and then said, "No, ladies first." The statement confirming what I had just surmised. I turned to look at the door. But instead of Trish, it was Susan Jacobs.

"No way, Jerry!" she chided, wagging her finger in his direction. You take the first cup. If you survive, then I'll get mine. Better yet, if you survive, I'll let David get his. If you both survive, then I'll get mine."

Susan's words were teasing, that was clear, but her actions verified her cautious attitude by watching us consume some before filling her blue ceramic cup. Slowly she stirred in the creamer while fixing her gaze on us, as if expecting either one or both to keel over at any moment. Jerry and I were at a disadvantage because our backs were to the door. Susan used the situation to continue the ploy.

"No wait, Trish is here now. I'll wait to see how the coffee affects her. Trish, Jerry made the coffee this morning."

Trish cautiously continued walking into the break room. She smiled, took off her coat and draped it over the arm of the couch saying, "What's the matter Jerry, your coffee still the worst in the Upper Peninsula?"

"It sure takes a long time to lose a bad reputation around here," Jerry responded. "You see, David," he continued, "what the gals are alluding to, is one day, over two years ago, we were out of coffee filters, so I made the first pot using the one from the day before. No one knew what I had done, but they all made ugly faces when they tasted it, and even uglier noises when they found out why it tasted so bad. My coffee-making abilities have been challenged ever since. They all fight to get here before me so they can make it."

"What coffee-making abilities?" Susan uncorked.

"Once you're in the management business for a while," Jerry said, "you'll learn little tricks like that for getting your people to work on time. It's been quite successful here." Jerry was now grinning smugly in a pompous fashion.

With that, everyone left the break room except Trish and me. We waited a moment and then sat down on the couch to talk. "I want to thank you for helping me last night, Trish, and to apologize for not saying so before this. I'm sorry."

"No apology needed, David," she replied. "I enjoyed the time together. What I need to do is thank you for being so open and honest with me. Mutual admiration society games are okay for some and they might be fun for teenagers in puppy love, but we're adults, and as such ought to be able to relate our feelings openly, without any apprehension. Don't you agree?"

I sat poised on the edge of the cushion, listening to every word she spoke. "I can certainly agree with that," I responded. "And what's more, I simply can't wait for us to have more time like that, today. What's on your agenda or am I being presumptuous?"

"Well, as far as work goes," she answered, "I have the training session for the three of you this morning while Annette prepares her Monday show. This afternoon she'll do Jim and Ted's training while I prepare for my Tuesday and Wednesday airtime. It's getting exciting, isn't it, David?"

"Scary is more what I'd call it. I suppose we ought to get to work; every minute's going to prove critical at first, but what about our getting together sometime today? I've got to work at my shop tonight but I can't expect you to meet me there all the time. How about lunch?" I asked.

Trish looked at me a moment, pondered, and then asked, "Now? You're getting as bad as I am."

"Not now," I replied, "at lunch time!"

"Okay, David. Let me know when you're ready."

As Trish stood to leave, I said, "I wonder if Jim and Ted are in yet. I haven't seen them pass by the break room."

"I'll let you know if they're in the studio in a minute," she said, slipping past the door and into the hallway. I took a moment longer to refill my cup, then walked slowly to my office, organizing my thoughts.

Trish buzzed me on the intercom to inform me that Jim and Ted hadn't yet arrived, so I joined her in the main studio. Not wasting any time she immediately started quizzing me on the equipment to refresh my memory on the different names, functions and operating procedures. She led me through all of it once and was about to start through it again when the others arrived. Jerry came in with them to let us know the equipment installers might be in and out during the afternoon, performing some additional checks. He also informed us they were planning to apply power and send out a signal later in the afternoon or early evening and that our training would be temporarily sidelined if that happened.

"What are your plans for tonight, David?" Jerry asked.

"I was going to do some computer work at the shop tonight, mostly billing and mailings, maybe some phone calls, that's about it. Why?"

"Oh, that's okay" Jerry responded. "I'll see if Carl can cut his vacation short by one day to do some checks this evening. Trish, could you pull some overtime this evening with the technicians?"

"Sure, Jerry," she answered. "I had planned on working some anyway this evening after supper. Will that meet your needs?"

My heart sank as Jerry accepted her offer. I was hoping she would want to be with me at the photo shop. So much for that, I guessed.

CHAPTER FIFTEEN

Just before noon the four of us came out of the studio after completing the morning training session. Ted and Jim went to the break room for lunch. Trish and I walked slowly down the hall to the main office to check the morning's mail.

"I have to say, Trish, Ted is really good. It seems he's able to understand things the first time through and retain them. To me, and of course mine is an untrained evaluation, he worked very professionally and smoothly. Would you agree with that?"

As we entered the office, she began, "You're absolutely right. He has a natural talent for this profession. I don't believe I've seen anyone catch on so quickly. To be sure, he has a couple of weak spots, but they'll work their way out in time. Jim was much better today too. He deliberately tried to speed up, and that tends to make the delivery somewhat unnatural at first. But there again, that should work itself out over a period of time. In his case though, with just weekend duty, it might take a little longer. Can I make a suggestion about Jim?"

I stopped flipping through the mail long enough to answer her. "Sure. What is it?"

"If the budget allows, maybe he could come in next week for five days of intensified training before putting him on the air by himself. We can make a temporary mock-up in studio B using some of the old AM equipment."

"That sounds okay to me. Could you handle the added workload by yourself and still get your programming ready, or would you need Annette's help?" I asked.

"It'll probably take the two of us. Work like that would be a drain on just one person."

"Okay, we'll bring that up in the staff meeting this afternoon. That reminds me: I posted the staff meeting notice on the employee board in the break room, but I don't know if everyone saw it. Maybe after lunch, before the afternoon session, you can make sure they're all aware of the three o'clock meeting and point out the need for them to check the employee board daily. Would you do that for me, Love?"

"Seeing as how you put it that way, LOVE. How could I refuse you?" she answered, sweetly.

We headed back towards my office where I aimlessly shuffled again through the twenty or so envelopes that constituted the mail.

"Is this a good time for you to break for lunch, Trish?" I inquired.

"It is and it isn't," she coyly replied.

"Explain por favor?"

"Don't mix English with Spanish," she quickly reprimanded, grinning.

"Okay! I stand corrected."

"What I meant," she started, "was this would be a good time for lunch if I were eating lunch, but I'm fasting breakfast and lunch today. But I'd still like to go with you, wherever you're going. I'll just get something to drink."

"I thought you were charismatic, not Catholic," I said.

"I'm not Catholic, but they're not the only ones who fast. Sometimes it's just a good practice to say 'no' to the flesh. A great way to do that is by fasting." Trish had retrieved her coat from the coat tree in my office while I placed the mail on my desk.

"Tell me more!" I was intrigued.

"I will as we go. You see, it's our flesh that gets us into spiritual trouble. Our flesh cries out for all kinds of gratification, not necessarily sinful gratification, but gratification just the same. If we continually give our flesh all that it demands, we'll soon find that it demands things that ARE sinful. If we've grown accustomed to responding to the flesh without thinking, then giving in to those sinful calls soon becomes inevitable.

"When we fast, however, our body, specifically our stomach, calls out for food, which when supplied, is a form of gratification. By not complying with the call for food, whatever the specific spiritual reasons, we determine to allow the spirit-man to rule. Without getting into an area known as experiential theology—which is the belief and teaching that what a person experiences in their Christian life, is the only way that God works—the fasting causes at least two things to happen. One, we strengthen the resolve and ability of our spirit-person to be the dominant person of our—here it comes again—tri-part being. Secondly, at least for me, when I feel the hunger it reminds me to call upon the Lord who shall renew my strength. It serves as a good reminder to pray in the spirit; something we can't do too much of. After all, what better way can we be reminded to realistically 'pray without ceasing'?"

"Good question. I guess I never really thought about that biblical command. Speak on, oh wise one!" I mused as we got into my car. She laughed heartily at my comment.

"David, you make me so very happy. Just being with you is nearly as fulfilling as communing with God and as important to me as breathing. Can

128

we have our walk in the woods at suppertime? Just for a little while, before you head to your photo studio and I work some overtime for Jerry; okay?"

All of a sudden I wasn't hungry anymore. Spotting a small grocery store, I pulled into the parking lot and set the brake. "I've just changed my mind about eating. I'll be right back. Hold that last thought."

I quickly purchased two cans of cola and returned to the car. "Here, you wanted a soft drink, right? Would you open mine too, please? Now, did I hear you right? Did you say you wanted to take a walk in my back woods this afternoon?"

"Yes," she answered, handing me an opened can. "I believe now's the time to talk to you about something that I've put off several times before, including last night. Can we get to your place, eat, have a short walk and be back in an hour and a half?"

"Sure! It's only about fifteen minutes to my house from the station. Round trip, half an hour," I answered.

I started the car and drove into town, stopping at the city park. "Coming here at lunch time is a habit of mine," I told Trish. "Especially during the spring and summer months. These silly squirrels put on a real show. Have you ever watched them?"

"No, David. I'm not into watching squirrels, but I do have a toy stuffed squirrel that's part of my stuffed animal collection; would you like to have it?"

"Sure, Trish, but I don't want to take a valuable part of your collection. How many do you have?"

"I started collecting them when I was twelve. Over the years I've given many of them away but I still have probably thirty-five or forty. Many have some sentimental value, but no intrinsic value. Besides that, you're not taking it, I want to give it to you as a token of my friendship. Do you want it?"

"I would love it! Thank you."

We enjoyed the squirrel show a few minutes, but all too soon it was time for us to get back to work. Trish said, "My apartment is only four blocks away, why not stop by and I'll get you the squirrel?" I agreed, drove to her apartment, and waited out front.

She seemed thrilled handing me the toy, beaming as bright a smile as I had seen her display. "I accept this gift in the love in which it is given, but you must tell me its history. Why don't you introduce us?" Trish took the squirrel from my hand as I started driving.

"David, this is Nutsy, my silent pet squirrel. Nutsy, this is David, my favorite pet person. Now David, don't laugh, Nutsy's history is quite simple. He is the only stuffed animal I've ever won at the U. P. State Fair. In fact, the only one I've won anywhere. It was five years ago and I did it by throwing three darts to break a balloon. When I burst one, realizing I had won, I went crazy. I jumped up and down, clapped my hands and shrieked. The man behind the counter told me to pick out a prize, so I picked this squirrel. He said it was an appropriate prize for someone as nutsy as me. What else could I possibly name him?"

"I'd be the dumbest man on the face of the earth if I argued with that logic. I'll take Nutsy home with me tonight and set him on my coffee table, no, better yet, on the dresser in my bedroom, where I can see him first thing every morning."

Trish laughed.

We arrived back at WPFH parking lot just as the clouds burst open. We waited for the downpour to subside, at first saying nothing, while looking intently into each other's eyes with a growing love.

"Trish?" I asked, breaking the silence of the moment.

"Yes, David," she softly responded.

"Would you mind terribly if I asked you to pose for me at my studio. You're beauty just begs to be captured on film."

"David, you're so kind, but I'm not..."

I stopped her with a kiss. "Don't you dare say what you were about to say. You are radiantly beautiful, and as an artist I want to record that beauty for all to see. Would you please give me the honor of a portrait session?"

I figured she didn't intend to refuse, but waited a moment to reply.

"Yes, David, I'll do that for you, but when? I'd like to get my hair fixed."

"Isn't that just like a woman? You just tell her she's the most beautiful woman on the face of God's creation and she wants to get a hairdo before she has her picture taken. Trish, your hair is fine, better than fine, it's exquisite. How about tomorrow night?"

"Aren't you going to work tomorrow night?" she inquired.

"I might, and if I do, it won't be right away, probably after dinner and some R & R."

Trish looked puzzled for a moment, and then said, "R & R means rest and recreation. Right?"

I nodded, saying, "the rain's let up, let's make a dash for it."

We paused just inside the door long enough to shake the rain from the umbrella and our coats. Trish caught her breath from the run up the sidewalk and said, "Let's talk about the portrait later; there's tons of work to do right now."

I silently acquiesced to her logic.

Trish went immediately to studio B to work on her Tuesday and Wednesday shows while I checked with Annette to see how she was doing with Ted and Jim. They were recording some practice sessions to play back and critique. Annette was also making a demonstration tape for Jerry's file as I had requested earlier in the week. With everyone busy on various projects I figured it was time for me get busy with my project, hiring some additional part-timers.

To date, my efforts in that quest had resulted in two scheduled interviews for Monday: George Sinclair and Holly Carlson. George, a high school speech and drama teacher at Ridgemont High, had previous experience in television. His resume reflected voice dubbing and spot and commercial announcement production. Holly was a part-time sales clerk at a local department store and didn't have any broadcast experience but was seeking higher-paying part-time employment. I was hoping one or both would have the abilities we desired and meet the need for additional weekend coverage. I prepared their interview packages praying over them as I did.

Three o'clock was drawing close, so I started jotting down things to be covered during our first staff meeting. During the assembly I officially appointed Trish as production control chief and air staff representative. Annette was, as our pre-employment agreement stipulated, to be in charge of all training pertaining to studio procedures. Jimmy Thomas, traffic manager, was present to coordinate the increased demands of providing assistance to both the AM and FM staffs. Eventual plans called for our own traffic manager as money, time and need dictated. I explained the station's policy for activities within the studio, break room and other facilities as well as outlining employee benefits. We discussed the plans for Sunday's dedication, and they all indicated they would be present for it. All were asked to submit ideas or suggestions for the station to me in writing, and I would take them to Jerry for discussion and subsequent approval or disapproval. The last item I wanted to cover was the plans for finishing studio B.

Trish handed out work schedules, a policy letter covering production standards along with the latest edition of the WPFH AM-FM announcer's handbook. Annette gave each of us a training schedule and stipulated that although we were about to commence broadcasting, training would continue during off-air times, either through self-study or on the simulated broadcast booth that was to be built. I asked everyone to work on Saturday; no one objected.

All in all, I felt the staff meeting went well. Each employee was provided an opportunity to ask questions or give input. I asked Jim and Annette to remain after the meeting so I could explain our plan for some intensified training for him next week.

The technicians arrived to perform the final studio equipment tests as Jerry had said they might. That temporarily pre-empted the afternoon training session. Jerry was with them and asked me to tag along as they went about their business.

"You may be able to pick up a term or two," he related. "Or ask a question about something you hear. This evening, when Trish is here, we'll have her run various voice and music checks and then again when we're up at the transmitter site. Those checks, for modulation, power and distortion, should take about two hours Dave. What time did the two of you have in mind for breaking for supper?"

"We hadn't really discussed when, just that we were going up to my place for about an hour and a half. If you would like, I can check with her for the exact time now."

Jerry handed the technician a large metering device and then returned his attention to me, saying, "Why don't you do that. I'd like to be able to tell these guys when to be back after their supper break."

Trish was in Jimmy's office selecting some music when I found her. "Hi, kid, Jerry wants to know when you intend to break for supper and when you'll be back to work with the technicians. I know we planned to go to my place; is that still on?" I asked.

"Let's see," she answered, "it's nearly 4:30 now. Why don't we break at five o'clock? That way I can be back around 6:30. Maybe we can pick up some Chinese on the way to your place. Does that sound okay to you, David?"

"What, the Chinese or the itinerary?" I asked.

"Both, silly!" she replied.

"Okay, I'll go tell Jerry, and I'll see you in about a half hour." As I turned to go, Trish went back to studying the shelves of music.

Jerry agreed with the plan for the evening, asking me, "Are you sure you can't make it tonight?"

"I would if I could, Jerry, you know that, but I absolutely must get some work done at the shop. What time do you plan on being finished here?" I inquired.

"Oh, I really can't say. If all goes well, the tests could be done by nine, provided we don't need to tear anything apart or need to do too much tweaking."

"I didn't know you were into snack food, Jerry," I stated, apparently showing my ignorance. Jerry looked at me kind of funny while the technician, who had been under the control table, rolled on the floor laughing. "What are you shaking your head for, Jerry? And what did I say that was so funny?" I asked, puzzled. By now Jerry had started laughing too and couldn't answer me.

The technician stood to his feet and said, "Jerry said tweaking, not 'Twinkie'. Tweaking the equipment means getting it to operate at peak or optimum levels and ranges by adjusting it as needed. 'Twinkies' are more fun, though."

Jerry was now laughing harder, nearly uncontrollably. "Maybe I'm not cut out for this line of work," I said, hanging my head while displaying an exaggerated pout. He put his arm around me, escorting me back to my office while the technician returned to his work under the control table, still snickering loud enough for me to hear.

"We'll get you up to speed on the jargon, I promise, Dave. But for now, why don't you stick to the office work. Better yet," he added, fighting hard to hold back another round of uncontrolled laughter, "Why don't you take the rest of the day off?"

"Oh sure, thanks a lot. I planned on leaving at five anyway. Looky here," I said, pointing to my watch. "It's seven minutes till; big deal."

Jerry succumbed to the urge to laugh again turning back toward the studio in retreat. I watched as he disappeared through the doorway still finding no humor in my ignorance. Before the door closed completely, I heard his remark to the technician, "Wait until I tell that one to Trish."

"You'd better not!" I yelled back, knowing he hadn't heard me. But someone else had.

"'You'd better not' what?" came that pleasing, familiar voice from behind me. "You're not in a tiff with Jerry are you, David?"

"Oh its nothing like that. Let's just say we had some words and leave it at that." I carefully chose my reply trying to pique her interest.

"I have a feeling I better leave well enough alone," she said tentatively. "Let's go. I'll ride with you, but you'll need to drop me off back here after supper, before you head uptown. I just made a takeout order for Chinese at

The Wok Inn. If you swing by, I'll go in and get it, then we can head out to your house. Oh, David, I'm so excited to see your place. Jerry tried to describe it to me, but he said he'd only been there once."

"Well, I call it home. Is the food good at that Chinese place you just mentioned?" I asked as we got into the car.

"Yes, but more than that, you don't ever need reservations. When you get hungry for Chinese food you just wok in."

"Oh, Trish, that's terrible! That's the worst one liner I've heard in years, and I wish I had thought of it."

The vivid colorama of fall escorted us on the drive to my house. Trish didn't speak, but rather quietly drank in the gorgeous gold of the maple trees, punctuated occasionally by an isolated white birch.

I led Trish on a quick once through of the house, pausing to put Nutsy on top of my dresser. We warmed up the shrimp-fried rice in the microwave and ate. As soon as we had finished we headed out the back door. The late-afternoon light was diminished by the overcast sky, but at least the rain had stopped. Trish stepped through the doorway and spied the three large, fully-grown maple trees that contended for nearly all my back yard. Two of the maples had reached their peak color and were ablaze.

"Oh, David, they're beautiful. How did you get God to put some of His paradise right here in your back yard?"

"He put it here long before I bought the land, Trish, but to put it in the words of a song from the mid-seventies, 'You ain't seen nothin' yet!'" I led Trish to the start of the wooded pathway, not knowing which captivated me more, the splendor of nature's beauty or the beauty of the Trish's splendor. It seemed time for a rapture drill.

"I'm nervous, David," Trish shyly admitted.

"Well let's just cast that lie of Satan out," I asserted.

She stopped, turned toward me, and looked intently into my eyes before speaking. "You're learning aren't you David?"

"I think so Trish. At least I'm trying to."

"I can see you are. You must keep it up, seek knowledge, wisdom and revelation. The spirit world is our battleground. If we can win there, and we can, then the victory will just naturally spill over into the physical world. But that's not what I'm nervous about. You know what it is, don't you, dear?"

"I don't believe I'm certain, Trish. All I do know is if you're uncomfortable, we can go back to the house or somewhere else. I would understand if you're not ready to trust me one hundred percent yet."

Trish resumed the slow deliberate walk, looking straight down the path. "That's not what I meant. I trust you explicitly. It's not you that's causing me to be nervous. Right now my heart is pounding, but I would rather say what I'm about to, and risk losing you, than not say it and be less than honest with you."

I squeezed her hand gently and said, "I doubt you could tell me anything that would cause me to withdraw my feelings for you, Trish. Please believe me."

"David, what I'm feeling right now; what's causing me mental and emotional discomfort; what I need to tell you; and what I need to work and pray through is...is the fact that ever since my divorce I have wondered about not being able to give myself to any man the way I did to Frank. Also, not knowing if I could be, or allow myself to get that close to a man again. For that matter, I've wondered if I could ever marry again—once these mental blocks were overcome. Do you understand that? Maybe it's unfair to expect you or any man to understand my dilemma."

She waited for my reply. Slowly I started. "I think, first of all, you're underestimating men in general, and me in particular. Secondly, you might likewise be underestimating God's healing power, not to mention the healing that comes from time." I chose my words carefully, trying to reassure Trish of my concern.

"Next, you need to know two things about me, my dear Trish. First, I certainly hope I've not added any pressure on you in any way. I don't believe I have verbally, but maybe unintentionally or through body language or something. I'm certain we have a future ordained by God. If that's marriage, which I might add even makes me nervous, God will reveal that at the appointed time. If not, well, He'll reveal that also.

"The other thing you should know is you are not alone in the situation you just described because I can't present myself a virgin to any woman I might marry. I regret that, but it's a fact I just can't alter. I deliberately and regrettably sustained a loss of virginity. No excuses because although I was not always a Christian, I was an adult. Until now I haven't really thought much about it, especially knowing it's under the blood of Jesus. If He's forgiven me—and He has; and if I've forgiven me—and I have; and if you forgive me, then I'm completely forgiven.

"Frank lost his chances for what I would consider to be a lifelong, romantic, exciting life with you by refusing your love. I pray to God I'll someday be the recipient of all the love I know you hold inside your heart. Maybe in cases like this, God gets two people together who can understand and relate to each other's past experiences. Remember this my dear, beautiful Trish, you went into your marriage with a commitment Frank apparently didn't have. That's not a blemish or spot. That's not even your fault.

"Trish, there's the one big difference between your case and mine, you don't need forgiveness. You need understanding. Understanding by you to not to feel guilty, or like you're damaged goods, which you're not. Understanding on my part, to accept you wholly and completely, just as you are. I promise you that understanding and acceptance, no matter what the future holds for us. Can I ask the same in return?"

Trish stopped again, faced me with tears streaming down her cheeks, looked up at me and nodded in agreement, then threw her arms around me and held me as tight as possible. We held the embrace for several minutes. All the while I could feel the heaving of her deep cry as she released all the hurt, anguish and fear.

"Oh God," I cried, just barely loud enough for Trish to hear. "Help me to be all the man she needs, and all that You want me to be." We wept, locked in each other's arms.

CHAPTER SIXTEEN

The computer work at the photo shop required little effort from me. As the printer was busy spitting out bills or receipts, I made phone calls to clients with appointments in October, offering them the opportunity to reschedule to September; keep the appointment but change the location to my house; or cancel altogether. Most opted for the latter when they learned I would soon be out of the business. I couldn't blame them. Many of the people I had previously corresponded with wanted to purchase their negatives. Complying with their request, I readied them for the mail.

I wanted two things that evening. I longed for Trish to be with me and I wanted WPFH to be on the air so I could tune in. I could have neither. Trish's overtime kept us apart, and the fire had our station off the air. I glanced in the direction of the silent radio. For some reason it didn't look right. Then I saw why; Trish's cassette tape was still in the player from last night. Quickly I flipped the tape over and listened to the remainder of Pastor Glen's message "Just Who Am I?" His style of delivery, verbal mannerisms, and unique way of dropping truths into our spiritual laps astounded me. I found myself nearly mesmerized by the sermon. I was determined to get more of his tapes in hopes of catching up with the rest of the congregation, especially Trish and Jerry.

When the printer stopped, I busied myself stuffing over fifty envelopes. After only a few minutes I heard a knock on the studio door. The shades were down so I couldn't see who had knocked, but because it was nearly 9:30, I was certain it wasn't a shopper. "Who is it?", I asked as I approached the door.

"Three guesses, and the first two don't count," came the reply.

"I'd know that voice anywhere. It's Mae West! Right?" I toyed.

"Come on David, open the door. It's starting to rain again, and it's getting cold out here."

"Oh, is that you, Trish?" I feigned, reaching slowly for the lock.

"You got ten seconds, buster, or I'm breakin' in!" she said, working her way into the fictitious drama scene I had created. I opened the door but much to my surprise she had a policeman with her.

"I'm...ahhh...sorry for the delay officer. Trish, what's the matter?" I asked, stepping back to let both of them in.

Trish displayed a mysterious concern on her face as she said "The officer was in the process of checking your license plates when I parked my car in front of yours. When I confronted him and inquired about his purpose, he said he was checking out the car. He was interested why it was parked on the street this late at night when most of downtown is a ghost town. I told him it was your car and he agreed to investigate why your studio lights were on this late at night." At that she couldn't keep her straight face any longer and succumbed to a smile while saying, "Gotcha! Didn't we?"

"Yes, you did," I replied. "Again, I'm sorry officer. You see I'm just taking care of some late night business, but I don't know this lady. You might want to book her on vagrancy charges or something," I said, not knowing when to shut up.

"I've got no evidence of a vagrancy violation at this point, but you might want to introduce yourself, Mister, because the lady here says she knows you," the officer responded.

"What he'd better do, officer, is quit the comedy routine and take me out for a bite to eat."

"Ma'am, I think you've got the situation under control. I'll leave you two now. Have a nice evening."

"We'll do that officer. You do the same," she replied.

I closed the door, turning to Trish and scolded, "Now that wasn't funny at all. You did that on purpose."

"And it worked far better than I envisioned. Can we go get something to eat now?"

"You're worse than a shark; at least it stops eating once in a while."

Trish frowned at me with sad eyes, and a slight pout. "But I'm hungry, and it's getting so I just can't eat a meal without you."

"You sure know how to lay it on, don't you?" I asked, not really expecting her to concede anything. "Okay, I'm about done here anyway, but I want you to know that wasn't funny. I didn't know what that officer wanted when I opened the door and saw him there. You both looked like you'd seen a murder take place."

"Well you might not have thought it was funny, but I did, but not quite as funny as the 'Twinkie' you talked about with Jerry." As Trish finished that snide remark she jumped back about two feet as if she expected me to grab her.

"Did he tell you about that?" I asked, faking anger.

"No, Jason the chief installer did."

"How did Jason know that happened?"

138

"I guess Jerry told him, I don't know."

"Well, somebody knew Jerry and I had a misunderstanding."

"Oh! Is that what it was, just a misunderstanding?" Trish asked.

"Yes!" came my teasing yet sharp reply. "And that's all there is to that!"

After I batched all the mail together, I handed it to her to hold while I put on my coat. "Next subject," I announced. "Where do we go to eat?" Trish looked at me differently than I had noticed before. It was as though she was studying my actions or trying to decide whether or not she should speak what was on her mind. With one sleeve on and the other dangling from my shoulder, I paused. "Did I say something wrong, Trish?"

"No, not at all. I was just deep in thought. I heard you but I didn't know if I should answer you the way I would like," came her slow, deliberate answer.

"Well..." I posed again, "...are you hungry for anything in particular?"

"Yes, as a matter of fact, hot chocolate with whipped cream on top and apple pie."

"Now just where in the world are we going to get that? We're not in Marquette. Ridgemont hasn't got all the BIG TOWN conveniences like late-night restaurants."

Trish looked down at the floor, blushing slightly, then raised her eyes until they met mine saying, "We can get them at my apartment. That is if you're ready."

I felt a shiver of fear slide through my gut. Why, I can't say. It was okay for her to be with me at my house, but something kept me from accepting an invitation to hers. Confident that Trish was a Christian, and certain she had only honorable intentions; knowing too, that my intentions with her were pure, I made a compromise with the fear I felt. "I'll try, Trish. But this apprehensiveness or fear I'm experiencing seems so strong. If I start feeling uncomfortable and change my mind, you won't mind will you?"

"Not at all, but as we drive over there, think about this; fear is not of God. Maybe Satan is trying to get you to think or dwell on something that just isn't going to be a factor. Maybe he's trying to get you to second-guess your self-confidence, self-control, or even your faith in God. Worse yet, he could be trying to get you to doubt the strength of your spiritual man. This might be a real good opportunity for you to teach Satan a thing or two."

I had to admit her logic seemed to make sense, especially that part about fear not being of God. "Okay I'll follow you over, but stop by the front of the post office so I can put those things in the drop box."

The rain had turned to a light mist, and a slight ground fog had developed.

I followed Trish from the post office to the front of her red brick duplex apartment. Cautiously and timidly I got out of the car and shut the door. Trish had already arrived at my side. "I think I know what it is, Trish. I know why this is making me feel uneasy. It's not you, or me, or even the devil. It's that I don't want people, here in your neighborhood, to think things about you. Your reputation means much too much to me to cause that to happen by my being here. What are they going to think, a man going into your apartment at night? I just don't want them to think that way about you."

I leaned back against the door to my car facing Trish, the misty cold rain falling lightly on our faces. A breeze came down the street rustling some of the wet autumn leaves on the ground and lifted the gentle scent of her perfume to my nose.

Trish didn't say a word; she just embraced me and then kissed me. Stepping back about a foot she looked at me and said, "We're not going to let what other people think get in the way of what God has given us. For right now that's a very beautiful and blossoming friendship that I believe will be much more than that before too long. The world distorts, defiles and wrecks everything good that God has made. Where it can't succeed at that, it creates an illusion, a counterfeit—an impostor of the real thing. People are going to think exactly what they want to think. You can't stop that, David. I know the people in this neighborhood. I've lived here for some time now. They know me too. They also know what happened to my marriage. Small towns are just that way. I can't stop them from thinking what they might, and they can't stop me from living. What I live and what they think may be two totally different things. I will not be held accountable to God for what they think, and I will not be held captive to fear of their thoughts either. I invited you to my apartment for hot chocolate and apple pie, not an illicit rendezvous. I'd like you to come in but I cannot make you. I will tell you this: don't let what people think stop you—if that's what's getting in the way. Okay, Honey?"

I didn't give Trish an immediate answer. I reflected upon what she said, and had to admit she was helping me look at things from a different perspective. While she waited for my answer, God seemed to confirm our relationship by telling me, "Look how you two take turns helping one another through the troubles and tribulations of day-to-day living." Maybe He hadn't spoken it from the clouds for the world to hear, and maybe Trish hadn't even heard it, but I did, and I thanked Him for it.

"What are you thinking about, Love?" Trish interrupted, though she didn't know she had.

"Oh, I wasn't thinking as much as praying. God just ministered to me, not in the area we were talking about, but minister He did. Let's go have some pie and hot chocolate."

We looped arms and walked up the stairs to her front door. She unlocked and opened the door, stepping inside to turn on a light. In an effort to calm myself and start a conversation, I said, "You really should leave a light on or have a timer that will turn one on for you while you're away. It's much safer that way."

Trish hung up her coat in the closet and extended her hand to me for mine.

"You've been in the military too long, over-cautious from all the big city adventures, no doubt. This is Ridgemont. You've been here long enough to know nothing happens here."

I didn't pursue the conversation but followed her into the kitchen. There, a pleasing aroma greeted me, that of the fresh apple pie. It smelled good and triggered my hunger mechanism. Trish filled the teapot and set it on the stove, turning to get plates out of the cupboard and cut the pie.

Although her apartment was small, she had it decorated meticulously with graceful touches of her artistic ability. It was spotless, right down to new-looking bamboo place mats on the small, highly polished, wooden kitchen table. The curtains were lacy and folded back, held in place with delicate silver rings that caused a draped affect. Everything I looked at reflected Trish's charm. "Would it help if I turned the stove on?" I asked.

"It probably would," she replied, gingerly lifting the first piece of pie from the pan. "And would you get the whipped cream from the fridge? Hot chocolate without whipped cream is useless, don't you agree?"

I did.

Soon the teapot was whistling and I placed it upon a large ceramic hot-pad in the center of the table. Trish set the pie and two packages of instant hot chocolate on the table with the napkins, forks and spoons. We were ready to ask God's blessing on our evening snack. I was amazed how all my fear had subsided. That might have been a miracle of God, or it could have been the company I was keeping. Maybe both.

"Trish, can I ask you two questions?" I inquired breaking the momentary silence.

"Sure, David. What's on your mind?"

"What we were talking about out front, there's one thing that still bothers me. At first it didn't cross my mind, but of late more Bible verses seem to be staying with me than in the past. Specifically, and I don't know where it is, but in one of Paul's epistles I believe, it says something about giving the appearance of evil. Now I know what you said out front and I agree that we can't live our lives captive to what other people might think. If the true intent of that Bible verse, however, is to be applied to our lives, then shouldn't we be vigilant about our actions so we don't cause people to think less of Christ or our Christian witness? Am I right?"

"You are, David, there's no doubt about that. We must never intentionally discredit our Savior. But what we have here is two totally different things. First the scripture verse that you are referring to is, let me get my Bible...First Thessalonians, Chapter 5, verse 22, and here's the application as I see it. We have no power to know, let alone change, what people are thinking. When we go out to eat, neither one of us would think of starting to consume the meal without saying grace. Isn't that right?"

I nodded in agreement as she continued.

"There are going to be people in the restaurant who will understand what we are doing and admire it. Others will be indifferent. Still others will be offended at our display of what they think is religion, and harbor unkind thoughts about us. We're not going to let that stop us from giving God thanks for the food and asking His blessing on it.

"The other situation that should concern us, enough to change our actions, is when our action causes people to think ill of our Lord. Casual Christians do this when they walk into a bar; go to a questionable movie; buy lottery tickets; or light up a cigarette. These are deliberate actions that display lack of concern for the name and calling of Jesus Christ and what others perceive that name and calling to be. Are you still with me?"

I nodded. "Very much so."

"Then let's look at your visit here tonight. Which case is it here tonight, David?" she asked.

"Well to be perfectly honest I see both. I entered your apartment deliberately. What people think about me doesn't concern me. What they think of you and Jesus does. Help me please, but it's just like going into a bar to me."

Trish turned the Bible to me so I could read it as she asked, "But do you see this word right here? What is it?"

I looked and answered, "Appearance."

"Who's appearance, ours or theirs?" she asked, directing my thoughts in a logical flow.

I paused a minute then answered, "Ours, I guess."

"You're right. We can't change how somebody perceives something because it's based upon their frame of mind, background, experience, upbringing and religious teaching. As a believer, I've gone to office Christmas parties where alcoholic drinks were served. While there I've undoubtedly had a glass of ginger ale in the very same kind of glass as the mixed drinks. But whenever I go to such an event, I go intending to enjoy the friends and food. Those who know me will know that I'm drinking a soft drink but others may think I'm having something alcoholic. I can't change what they think, and won't even try.

"You and I, here tonight, are enjoying a pleasant time together at my apartment. It could be at a restaurant, a friend's house, your house, your studio, or at the station working late and any of those situations could be misconstrued by someone; but we are not giving an appearance of evil, the evil is in the mind of the one thinking the evil.

"Look, we're sitting at my kitchen table, in front of a window with the curtains open and the lights on. We even have the Bible open discussing spiritual matters. Certainly neither one of us is giving an appearance of evil. Now if the house got dark, and tomorrow morning those same neighbors saw your car still parked out front with frost all over it, THAT would be an appearance of evil."

"Thank you, Trish. I hope someday I can know God and His word well enough to live my life with confidence and assuredness like you."

"Thank you for the compliment, David, but I'm working at it, too. We will never get to the point where we can say we've fully arrived. And too, the Holy Ghost is the one you need to depend on for that kind of growth, not me. Just ask Him for His help. He will answer you and give you wisdom, knowledge and revelation."

"What about the 'counterfeit' you mentioned?" I asked.

She was quick to reply. "I said the spirit of the world will try to destroy anything good that God has made, and that's true. The 'world' is of course the spirit of the world. When the spirit of the world encounters something good that cannot be damaged or destroyed, such as a strong marriage, then it offers a counterfeit. A counterfeit for a strong marriage would be living together. But the spirit of the world is smart. They won't call it a counterfeit marriage. They'll call it something pleasing to their conscience like 'a trial marriage', or 'an alternative life style'. I think you get the idea I'm trying to describe. The list of things Satan attacks goes on and on as he seeks to kill, steal and destroy everything God has made.

"It's a shame, but people just don't see it. All they see is the immediate gratification. Notice I was careful not to use the word satisfaction because it seldom does, and even when it appears to, it's only temporary."

I closed the Bible and reached across the table for Trish's hand. "Trish, I love you. I hope you won't say our relationship is moving too fast or that it's getting out of control. Such a short period of time has elapsed since I offered you the job at WPFH, but look how far we've come since then. Can I, or even dare I, say what I just said without running the risk of scaring you off?"

"There's not a chance of that, David. And I love you too. If we had met under different circumstances; if you were not a Christian; if you, WPFH, and my confidence in God were not the answers to countless prayers, then I would say it might be moving too fast, way too fast. But it's not. I feel comfortable with where we are and how we've gotten here. Do you?"

"Yes I do, Trish. However there are several areas that I'm disappointed in and one is my spiritual growth, and regretting the years I've wasted until now. Will you continue to help me grow spiritually by studying the Bible with me?"

"I would be glad to, but remember this, and then I think it's time we said goodnight. Paul said, 'I look not at the things which are behind me, but I press on to the mark of the high calling which is in Christ Jesus.' Don't languish over the past or worry about the future; just concentrate on the now."

"Trish, you seem to make those verses I've read take on useful day-to-day meaning—something I can use and apply. Well, I'd better leave now. It's too bad that this weekend couldn't be free for us to just go somewhere and make a memory instead of working tomorrow and Sunday. There is at least one ray of sunshine for the weekend in addition to the station going on the air."

"Oh, what's that, David?" Trish asked, handing me my coat.

"I have a portrait appointment with an angel tomorrow evening and I can't wait."

"Good night, David! " she insisted firmly, and then grinned.

I reached for the door. "I guess I've overstayed my welcome. Are there any special instructions for bedding down Nutsy tonight?" I asked, searching desperately for any excuse to linger in Trish's presence.

"No! Now good night again, David."

I drove home thanking God for the beautiful time He had given Trish and me.

CHAPTER SEVENTEEN

The busy schedule and shortened daylight hours made my normal autumn activity impossible. I usually enjoyed field excursions and scenic tours through the woodlands, and by this time would have already walked at least five nature trail hikes and ridden on the Algoma Train at Sault Ste. Marie, Ontario, to take fall foliage photos. Although I had missed them this year, and hadn't experienced the peace and tranquility they usually yielded, the events of this September were equally rewarding.

Saturday arrived with a chilling breeze from the north. The air coming in from Canada was cold, but fortunately, Lake Superior was still warm enough to temper it. This same warming affect would soon cause the southern shoreline to be buried in mountains of lake effect snow. For now though, all we could expect was a blustery day with gray rolling clouds and an occasional sprinkle.

We expected an active day at the station and the entire FM staff would be in, preparing for the dedication as well as next week's programming. The AM staff of announcers would still be on their fire-forced vacations. The team of installers and technicians would be putting the finishing touches on the equipment and turning the facility over to us later in the day, ready for broadcasting.

We had already received a number of phone calls from inquisitive people who had heard we would soon be on the air and were asking when we expected to start broadcasting. Jerry had planned to announce the start of the new FM station over the AM side, but the fire took care of those plans. Instead, he bought a full-page ad in the Ridgemont Inquirer. That ad was to run in this afternoon's edition. I had sent letters to nearly 100 known churches in the signal area for announcement from the pulpits or in the church bulletins. Because we were not going to be a commercial station, thus not seeking advertising dollars, we hadn't informed individual businesses. We had also told many of the area Chambers of Commerce of the new station in those cities that had chapters.

The programming for just about all of the upcoming week had been scripted, scheduled, and, for the most part, produced; a chore made more difficult by not having a studio B in which to rehearse and record production work. I hoped a private talk with Mr. Gramswald would alleviate that problem.

It appeared as though many of us had used the same alarm clock this morning as we approached the parking lot at the same time. Jerry was making a right hand turn and had the right-of-way as did Ted, Jim and Trish. I waited patiently to make my left turn. It was still dark but I recognized my Trish as she drove in and up to her parking spot. Jerry ran up the sidewalk to unlock the door, bracing himself against the wind while I greeted Trish. "Did you sleep well last night?" I asked.

"Yes," she replied pleasantly, "I sure did. How about you?"

"Very well, thank you," I answered while yawning. "You're working the morning training session, right?" I asked as we approached the front door to the station. Ted held it open as we went in.

"Thanks, Ted," we said in unrehearsed unison.

"Yes, and remember, Annette won't be in until just after nine. She doesn't have a Saturday morning sitter for the kids, so she won't be able to leave the house until her husband gets in from work."

Jerry started the coffee and we sat chatting in the break room, waiting for it to brew. "What time did Mr. G want me to go and get him, David?" he asked.

"He said around noon, but you may want to call him to see if he has a more specific time in mind."

Jerry looked at me like I was out of my mind for making such a suggestion. "No," he responded, "You call him and confirm the time. Maybe, if I'm lucky, he'll change his mind and have you pick him up."

"I'm surprised at you, Jerry," I chided. "A strong Christian like you still relying on luck."

Trish smiled widely and said to me, "Very good, David! Just what are you going to be like when you get even more mature in your faith? He got you, Jerry; you know that, don't you?"

Jerry hung his head, faking a childish pout, then said, "You're right David. That's a worldly statement and it has no place in a Christian's vocabulary. I repent, and I accept your chastening in the love that I hope it was intended."

"Well, actually, Jerry, I was only pointing out what's become obvious to me. I wasn't trying to correct you, although it may have appeared that way. I just don't believe in luck; never really did even as a non-believer. Your use of the word simply took me by surprise."

"Whether you meant to or not, I stand corrected!" he stated.

With our coffee poured, we headed to our workstations. Ted, Jim and Trish went into the studio, while Jerry joined me in my office. "It's just about ready, isn't it, David?" he remarked, looking about and turning a full 360 degrees, making obvious reference to WPFH-FM.

"Yes," I replied. "I sure hope the technicians give us the okay early today so we don't have to worry over any last-minute problems."

"Hey! Now it's my turn, Dave!" Jerry quickly retaliated.

I looked puzzled at him as he made the statement. "Your turn to what?" I asked.

"My turn to correct you! You used the word 'worry'. Christians shouldn't worry! We may show some concern or attention, but we don't worry. Both AM and FM stations are in the Lord's inventory of responsibilities. That means they are under His care and as such we needn't worry about anything. The same holds true in our personal lives as well. If we've turned our life over to Him, then it's no longer our life but His, and all we do is walk in the steps that He ordains. By all means we should pray, turning the situations of life over to Him. And we should, as the Word says, pray without ceasing. However, that doesn't mean we have to pray over every detail like 'Oh God what record should I play next?' It's part of living our faith to trust God in directing our steps. Our decisions should always be under His jurisdiction. Have you ever considered that, David?"

"Maybe something like that, but I just didn't realize that God enjoys and desires to be a part of our lives. I guess He's willing to get involved whenever we extend the invitation. It makes sense that He would want us to live life trusting Him to see us through all the circumstances we encounter each day. Going through life with that perspective would alleviate most of the harmful stress, and probably give the devil fits."

"What about you and Trish?" he asked, quickly changing the subject.

"Why do you ask?" I answered with a question.

"I tried to reach her last night after she left work because she seemed upset—no, not upset—more like subdued in her spirit. That's just not like her. She didn't seem to want to talk about it, no matter how much I tried. Apparently she didn't go straight home either. You two didn't have a disagreement, did you?"

I paused for a moment, recalling the events of our evening together. Trying to determine if I had missed some emotional signal from Trish; or if she had displayed anything that should have alerted me. I couldn't recall one. Then turning back to Jerry, I said, "She came over to the photo shop after she got done here. She seemed in a good mood then, in fact she and a policeman even played a trick on me."

Jerry perked up momentarily and then asked, "A tall, stocky, dark-haired policeman...badge number 723?"

"I didn't catch the badge number, Jerry, but I would say he matches the rest of your description, maybe 210 pounds and rather large feet, about 11's or 12's."

"That's him! What kind of a trick did they play on you?" he asked continuing his impromptu interrogation.

"Oh, just a thing about my being in the office so late at night, not very significant in retrospect. Do you know that officer?"

"Sure, that's Trish's Uncle Charlie Lawson. Didn't she introduce you to him?"

"No, but wait until I let her know I'm on to that little secret. Thanks Jerry, you may have just taken a weapon out of her arsenal."

"Well you're welcome, I think. She may very well cancel our previously arranged confidence agreement now, but can I return to my original question?"

"Sure Jerry. What was it?"

"How are you two getting along? As I said, I tried to reach her at home but couldn't until after eleven. By then she seemed okay, at least over the phone."

I once again returned my thoughts, momentarily, to the night before. "I can't for the life of me remember anything about last night, or yesterday that would have caused her to display that kind of emotion to you. We left the shop and stopped at the drop box at the post office. Then we went up to her apartment. I didn't want to go in at first. After a lengthy talk out front I finally went in. That's probably why you couldn't get her on the phone; we were outside, standing by my car. Once we went in we had some hot chocolate and apple pie. Very good apple pie, I might add. Then we talked for some time about the neighbors and other things too. Then I left to go home. That must have been around 10:45 because I was in bed by 11:30."

Jerry strolled across my office to the window, looked out at the dreary, gray sky, and then sat in the easy chair facing me. "Maybe I just picked up vibes that weren't true. But she just seemed uneasy about something. You're sure there's nothing wrong?"

I didn't even get a chance to start my answer.

"Why? Should there be?" came Trish's question from the doorway. We both recoiled, looking in her direction. I immediately turned beet red as she came closer. She looked right into my eyes and said, "That's cute, David! You look good in red. But this guy..." she continued while turning to point at

Jerry, "...this guy needs to get shot like a double agent spy. I'm paying him good money to spy on you David, and he's in here spilling his guts to you about me." I could tell by her smile she was teasing and attempting to start another game.

"I've got work to do," I said, reaching for a stack of papers from my in-basket. If you all don't mind I should get with it."

"Not until I get an explanation," she retorted, poking her finger tenderly into my chest while I stood there, desperately wanting to hold her in my arms.

"You'll get the same explanation I got about your Uncle Charlie!" I sternly informed her, removing her finger gently from my chest.

"Ooops! I just remembered Jim needs me for something back in the studio."

Trish turned, starting a hasty retreat from the office but not before I said, "We'll continue this later!"

"Jerry, as you can see, we're fine. Trish and I have some learning to do about each other but plenty of time to do it. We each may have our own areas of insecurity about the future of our relationship, but by the direction of God, we'll get through them. Hopefully, during this learning process, we'll know just what it is that God has in mind for us."

"Sounds good to me, David. God bless both of you." Jerry headed to his office and I picked up the phone to make the call to Mr. G.

The phone rang seven times, and I was about to hang up when I heard that not-so-familiar voice of Mr. Jerome Gramswald. "I didn't wake you up sir, did I? This is David Post in Ridgemont."

"Of course not, David. How are you this morning, and why are you calling? Let me guess. Does it have something to do with Jerry?"

"Well, sir, he did ask me to call you and get a firm time for him to pick you up, or to see if there was any change of plans."

"That rascal! Undoubtedly he's hoping for a change of plans. He doesn't really want to come and pick me up does he?"

I didn't answer.

"That's as good a confirmation as I need, David. Then you come and pick me up around two this afternoon, at the hotel. Wait till I see him!"

"Sure thing Mr. G. I'll see you then."

"Fine, son. I'll be in the lobby and ready to go when you get here."

After quickly punching Jerry's intercom number, I informed him that he was off the hook. He seemed relieved. "Some day you'll know him a little better than you do now. He really hasn't upset your apple cart yet, but mind my words, give him time; he will. Thanks for going in my place."

"Okay, Jerry. I'll talk to you later."

I spent the rest of the morning getting my "Manager Moments" scripts organized for the week, giving them one more editing for grammar and content. Annette came in at nine and we chatted for a while about her program and the training progress of Jim and Ted. During the talk I asked, "Annette, have you given any thought to those things we talked about during your interview? You know about Christ, salvation and eternal truths?"

She squirmed uneasily in her chair and then answered, "I really don't get a great deal of time to sit down and think, with the kids and all, especially now that I'm working again. I know a lot of things about Jesus. I'm not ignorant about spiritual things. I just haven't sorted through all of them yet. Maybe someday."

"Annette, I'm not trying to preach to you. I wouldn't, I'm not a preacher, but the Bible does say 'today is the day of salvation'. It also says 'tomorrow is promised to no man'. Yes, you're young, healthy and full of life, but whether you want to admit it or not, a turn in health is as near as the next cough, cold or flu. There is a being out there, referred to as the prince of the power of the air, or the prince of darkness, who is intent on keeping you away from God. A God you're going to face someday. We are here on this planet to make a choice. By not taking time to make an informed choice, or by putting the choice off, you are actually making the choice. There is no neutrality with God. We are either with Him or against Him."

I could tell that what I had said to Annette had gone into her spirit. Maybe while working at WPFH, one of the staff members might get the privilege of leading her to the Lord. She looked ready to me yet seemed unyielding to further prompting on my part.

"Are you still planning to be with us for dedication tomorrow, Annette?" I asked. She answered she was. "Bring the family if you want to; we will have juice, coffee, Danish and milk. Pastor Glen Hershey will be with us as will Mr. Gramswald, Jerry McFarland, and the rest of the FM staff. The dedication will last only about forty-five minutes at the most."

The remainder of the morning went fast. Soon it was time for me to leave for Marquette. On the way out I spotted Jerry and stopped to ask him a quick question. "Tell me, Jerry, why doesn't Mr. G. get a rental car and drive himself around?"

"He doesn't drive. In fact he hasn't for some time. I guess it has something to do with living in Chicago. If you've never been there, well, it's just like what you would imagine big-city traffic to be like. Besides, he's got money and can afford to have a chauffeur and take taxis. Not to mention the fact that as long as he's the primary financial backer of WPFH, and the one who pays the bills, he'll also call the shots. Are you on your way to get him now?"

"Yes. I'm just going to ask Trish to do me a favor and then I'm out of here," I replied pulling on my coat.

"Okay, I guess I better get ready for him. I'll see you when you get back. Don't hurry!" Jerry yelled over his shoulder, heading down the hall to his office.

Trish wasn't in the break room nor was she in my office, so I checked in studio B as I went by. If she's not in here she's got to be in the main studio, I thought to myself. Maybe they broke for lunch already and I missed her. She was busy working with Jim. Slowly and quietly I entered the studio. Acknowledging my entrance, she placed a finger against her lips. I responded accordingly by holding my ground and keeping my mouth shut. Soon Jim had finished his PSA practice. That's radio talk for Public Service Announcement. After she told Jim and Ted the training session was over and it was now time for lunch, I moved over behind her and placed my hand on her shoulder. "I'm sorry if I interrupted. Don't you think it's time we start using the 'On The Air' light above the door? You know, to keep dummies like me out of here when there's important stuff going on?"

"No way, David!" she sternly corrected. "We don't cry wolf around here. That sign is used only when we're actually on the air. Studio B will need one also, plus one that reads 'RECORDING IN SESSION' for when we're taping or doing interviews and things like that. I'll put that in with my plans and ideas for you to consider."

She finished getting the studio ready for Annette's afternoon session. "Trish, do me a favor, please. There's been a change in plans, and I'm running over to Marquette to get Mr. G. this afternoon. I couldn't reach Madame this morning to let her know about all the details of the dedication. Could you call her and fill her in on the times and all?"

"Sure, I'd be glad to," she answered with a smile. "Are you leaving now or do you have time for lunch?" she inquired.

"Actually, I'm on my way out the door right now. I was going to stop at a drive-thru for a burger. Man, I'm hungry. I didn't get to the break room all morning."

Trish pouted and then looked up at me. "You mean I have to eat lunch all by myself?"

I reached up and patted her head, saying, "Looks that way, Sweetheart." but the Bogart impersonation apparently wasn't good enough for her to recognize; she stood there looking at me as if she wanted me to explain. I didn't. "But listen, I'll be back probably by 3:30, and I plan to work until six or so. Maybe we can catch something to eat before we go to the photo shop for your portrait."

Trish's expression changed quickly as she remembered my request. She immediately started revealing a side of her I hadn't yet encountered. "Oh my. Oh my! Is that tonight? I didn't wash my hair. What should I wear? You didn't tell me what to wear! Do you still want to do that David? I mean REALLY want to do that?"

I put my arm around her as we walked to the door. "Now I don't see any reason for you to get so hyper about a portrait session. If your hair looks as great tonight as it does right now, well, that'll be perfect. Maybe just one of your casual dresses will be fine. Trish, what you wear to the shop doesn't really matter to me; it's you I want a portrait of, not your clothes. Oh brother, that didn't come out right at all. And yes! Yes! Yes! I really want to do this! After all I don't have even a billfold picture of you." I paused. "So is it still on then for tonight?"

"Okay, but...."

I stopped her, lightly pressing my index finger against her lips. "No 'buts' about it. I'll see you when I get back."

CHAPTER EIGHTEEN

"Excuse me, are you ready to go, sir?" I asked Mr. Gramswald, who was dozing off behind a magazine.

"Oh! Sure, David. You caught me taking a siesta. I'm sorry about that."

"No problem at all, Sir," I replied. "Actually it's I who should apologize. I'm running a few minutes behind. I made a personal stop at a store in town before picking you up. My watch needed a new battery and I wanted to pick up a little something for a friend." I grabbed Mr. G.'s suitcases and headed for the door. He stood, straightened himself as though he were stretching then followed behind.

"I hope you don't mind, but I used my car," I said as I opened the passenger door for him, and then turned to get his luggage in the back.

I slid behind the wheel and started the engine. Mr. Gramswald settled back into the seat, adjusting it to the reclining position, and said, "Okay, I'm ready. Shall we head for Ridgemont?"

Without answering, I put the car in gear and drove out of the Soumi Hotel's parking lot. There was one more thing on my mind that needed to be addressed, but Mr. G. looked like he was settling in for a nap so I postponed asking. About fifteen minutes went by in total silence.

"When's the AM side going back on the air?" Mr. G. abruptly broke the peace, nearly scaring me out of my seat belt, through the windshield, and halfway down the hood. "Oh! I didn't mean to scare you son," Mr. G. apologized.

"You may not have meant to, but you did a super job of it," I fired back, giving a laugh to let him know I was teasing. "I really haven't talked to Jerry about the AM side for a couple of days now. I do know he's getting shipments of replacement equipment, almost every day. Most of it was already on order, according to him, before the fire. Other than that, you'll have to talk to him."

Mr. G. returned the seat back to upright and continued, "How about your schedule? Is it still set to go tomorrow morning?"

"Yes, and that sure sounds good, 'tomorrow morning.' I mean I haven't been in the radio business two weeks, and tomorrow we go on the air. I'm excited, nervous, anxious, scared and humbled all rolled up in one." The smoothness of the conversation and the ease with which I answered his question left me feeling more comfortable with him now than when I first picked him up.

"Well I'm sure glad to hear everything's going well. I'm also glad you can talk to me in terms I can understand. Most of the time Jerry likes to blow radio jargon my way, but I know he's a good man to have on the job."

As abruptly as he started the conversation, he quit. This was my golden opportunity to do some personality investigating of my own. "Mr. G. can I ask you a most direct question and know that it will be held in the strictest of confidence?"

"Son, you disappoint me. You don't have to ask me for confidence. I didn't get to where I am in life, spiritually as well as financially, by kiss and blab tactics. If you have a question, even a discreet one, fire away. If I can answer it, I will. If not, I won't. Either way, it goes no further than the interior of this car."

"That's what I was hoping for, sir, and I meant no insult by that first question. It was just my way of getting the conversation started." I took a deep breath, and then began. "What's the real story between you and Jerry McFarland? I know last time we talked you said it was some kind of a game. Quite frankly, sir, if it is, it seems to have gotten out of hand. I personally feel very uneasy about being around the two of you together this weekend. Anything you can tell me, any light you can shed to dispel this uneasiness would be appreciated."

Mr. Gramswald sat stone quiet at first. Studying my face for what seemed like an eternity, I wondered if he understood the question or was upset at me for asking it. His countenance changed to a most pronounced somber look, and then answered my question. "This likewise goes no further than the inside of this car. I've never told anyone, and I don't believe Jerry has either. It's no deep, dark mystery, conspiracy or trickery. A long ways back we agreed; so we just don't talk about it.

"It was nearly thirty-five years ago now, I guess; seems like yesterday though. Needless to say, I hadn't met the Lord yet. I had just been discharged from the service. My dad was expecting me to come back to Chicago right away, to join him in the family business. I guess he was still somewhat disappointed in me for wasting those three years in the military. The fact that I had been an enlisted man, and had turned down a commission, nearly put him in his grave. At any rate, the army life kind of taught me how to live fast, reckless and carefree. I really didn't want to go back to Chicago and get locked in behind a desk, but I didn't want to kill my old man either. For about six months I kept putting him off, not making a decision, even though I had moved home. I kept telling him I had to burn off all the energy that the army

154

had put in me. He bought that for a while, but soon he started hounding me about getting back into the work force.

"To make an old, long story short, I went to work for him. After I had been there for a while, I met this young, attractive lady at the office where my dad assigned me. She was a single lady, quite cute with a very pleasing personality. I soon found myself falling in love with her from across the office. She was perfect. Well nearly perfect. She had one liability—an illegitimate son—not thought about much in today's society, but it was back then. I dated and eventually married her, rest her soul, against my father's wishes. He threatened to write me out of his will if I ever adopted the boy or gave him the name Gramswald. Remember, I still didn't know the Lord as my savior yet. At any rate, I agreed not to adopt him and we raised him with his mother's maiden name, Gerald Frederick McFarland. You know him as Jerry.

"Since coming to know the Lord I have confessed that sin of not giving Jerry my name through adoption many times. But, and this is the hardest part, I don't believe Jerry has ever forgiven me. If he has, he hasn't said so, and I'm afraid to ask. So now we play this game. He makes it look like I get under his feet or bother him. I, for my part, play along, letting him make me out to be the heavy. It's not too hard a part to play."

The silence in the car was deafening. All that resounded in my mind was that Jerry McFarland and Mr. Jerome Gramswald were family, maybe not in bloodlines, but family just the same. They were as close as father and son could be without blood or adoption decree. That revelation didn't simplify things, but it sure did clarify them.

We were about halfway back to Ridgemont when again the silence was broken by a question from Mr. Gramswald. "How are you and Trish getting along, if you know what I mean?" he asked with a wink.

"Well, sir, we've been taking our time to get to know each other; getting an idea of our likes and dislikes. But more importantly, she's helping me to grow spiritually. In fact, in just the short time I've known her, she's helped me understand how to get my own revelation out of the Bible by studying rather than by depending on a preacher to spoon-feed me. Now don't get me wrong. I know I need a good pastor —we all do—to 'perfect' each of us as part of the corporate body of Christ. However, in my own quiet times alone in prayer and Bible study, it's nice to read and learn about God in ways that I know are designed by Him and meant just for me.

"If you don't mind, I'm going to change the subject. I'd like to ask you a favor. If it's none of my business, you can tell me so. Since we first talked on the phone, back when I decided to join Jerry at the station, finances have never been discussed, at least not in detail."

He didn't give me an opportunity to finish, but said, "Do you want a raise already, son?"

I took my eyes from the road long enough to look at his expression to see if he was teasing. He wasn't. "Oh, dear me no, Mr. G.! What I was leading up to was to ask you to explain how things get done at the station. You know, from the money side of the business. Jerry seems to keep that to himself. He did say that you provide the vast majority of the station's financial backing and therefore pretty much call the shots. Assuming his ambiguous explanation is accurate, could you, or would you help me understand how that works?"

"It's really not too difficult or involved, David," he began. "I do supply the majority, nearly ninety percent, of the finances needed to operate the AM station. Obviously, until the FM side starts attracting its own supporters, I'll back one hundred percent of its operations. The same holds true for the television station, once it gets rolling. Yes, I probably do call most of the shots, at least the real important decisions. The day-to-day stuff I leave to Jerry. No offense intended, but it will probably stay that way for the FM. How much authority he delegates to you is strictly between the two of you. You see, I really didn't want to keep the AM side going. Maybe Jerry's told you about that. That's his idea to keep it going."

I nodded, indicating that Jerry had told me that.

"Maybe someday Jerry will see that there's really no need for both of the stations, but I'll yield to his enthusiasm and reasoning for the time being, provided the FM side rallies its own support base. Does that give you the facts you need to understand the financial side?"

"Yes and no," I answered. "But let's take a hypothetical situation, if we can."

"Oh-oh!" he responded. "That usually means 'here's the situation I've got,' but go ahead, David."

"Well, okay, seeing as how you've put it so succinctly, here's the situation I've got," I echoed. "Our main broadcast studio is now complete and the FM goes on the air tomorrow. We'll get the technical papers today from the electronics people giving us the okay for broadcasting. However, that still leaves the FM side without an auxiliary studio. If you're looking for dollar signs, this is where they should start appearing. How do we get the funding required to equip an FM studio B? What's the procedure for getting that

156

need to you and then the cash to start making expenditures?"

Mr. G. rubbed his hand across his mouth, thinking through his reply. "I guess the best way to put this is straight forward. You see David the pot is not bottomless. I advanced Jerry some large sums of money for the FM addition about two years ago. The next large sum he got was to get the attorney fees, filing fees, and FCC license fees. Then came the equipment purchases, and lastly came the AM upgrade and replacement expenses. Fortunately the fire didn't hurt us financially, but to be quite frank, with the purchase of the Marquette land for the television station, which I will be committing to on Monday, I'm about tapped out for this year. I hope that doesn't put too much of a damper on your spirits or plans for the other studio. Does it?"

"No sir, not totally, but I suppose it does for now. We'll just have to work that problem out some other way if we want to do anything real soon. Maybe we can arrange a shared schedule for the AM's facility. What you've said hasn't diminished my enthusiasm or desire to draw up plans though. I don't think it's bigger than our God. Maybe going slower might be a better course for the station and me right now."

Only a few minutes remained until we would arrive at the outskirts of Ridgemont, so I asked Mr. G. if he needed to make any stops before going to the station. He asked me to stop at The Northern Lights Motel southeast of town in order for him to get a room, unpack and freshen up. He refused my offer to stay with me. As soon as he finished we headed for to the radio station.

Susan greeted us at the door and handed Mr. G. a station coffee cup that displayed the call letters and dial locations for both the AM and FM frequencies. "Hey! Where did these come from," I whined. "I didn't get one. I've been drinking my coffee from a Styrofoam cup ever since I hired on."

Immediately, she turned to the table behind her, picked up another and handed it to me, saying, "They came in this morning, just in time for the dedication and open house. Jerry wanted the first one to go to Mr. Gramswald when he arrived."

"Well thank you, Susan," Mr. G. said leaning over the counter to kiss her cheek. "And where's that rascal anyway?"

"He's in his office, sir. He's expecting you."

"I'll just bet he is," he replied. He turned to me and said, "Thanks for driving over to get me. I know you're pretty busy, so I'll let you get back to your duties. I want a little time with Jerry, if you know what I mean, David."

"Oh, yes, sir!" I quickly replied, turning to go to my office. "Let me know if there's anything else you need me to do for you."

"Thanks again, David."

Someone had been extremely busy while I was out. The break room was all cleaned and rearranged. There were party decorations strung all over the break room, down the FM hallway, in my office and in the studio. Susan told me that Jimmy had done all the cleaning and straightening while she and Trish had decorated for tomorrow's celebration. Annette was in the studio with Ted and Jim.

Trish was working in studio B with Jimmy, trying to figure out the mock-up studio's layout. I stopped in to see if she had gotten in touch with Madame.

"Yes, I did." Trish answered. "She's feeling stronger by the minute. I told her about tomorrow's schedule. She said she was still planning on being with us. She did ask who was going to be here, so I told her. She seemed most inquisitive about Mr. Gramswald. By the way, is he here now?"

"Yes," I answered. "He's in with Jerry right now. I asked him about the funding for studio B and it looks like it might be out of the question until next year, but I still want your plans and ideas as soon as you can get them drawn up, Trish."

"Oh, that reminds me," Trish interjected, "Madame says she doesn't want anything to get in the way of her special gift to the station, so just in case she isn't able to attend tomorrow, she has sent it over by her chauffeur. It's in the pink monogrammed envelope on your desk. Did you see it when you came in?"

"No, I didn't. Did she say what was in it?" I asked as I retreated to my office at a speedy pace.

Trish tried to keep up with me but couldn't in her high heels, lagging behind me she said loudly, "No she didn't! But she did say you were to open it with Jerry. I think it says that on the front of the envelope!"

Trish finally made it to my office with her heels in her hands. "Did you hear me, David?" she asked.

"Yes, I did Love," I answered holding the envelope, then tapping it against the palm of my other hand, then studying the writing on the front:

To my dear friends at WPFH, David and Trish.
   Open in the presence of Jerry McFarland, President of
WPFH AM-FM. God bless you two and the station as it goes
on the air.

   Madame F. DeVille

"Shall we take it to Jerry's office now?" Trish asked.

"I would, Dear, if Mr. Gramswald weren't in there with him."

"That's okay! Let's just knock on the door and see if we can go in," she said excitedly.

"No. I don't think this is the right time for that."

Trish looked perplexed as she asked, "Now what's that supposed to mean. Is there some kind of trouble?"

I turned my gaze from the envelope in my hand to Trish, catching the sparkle and mystery of her beautiful eyes. "No, there's no trouble. I'm just under the impression that they need some time together to work out some details that just couldn't be handled over the phone—maybe the television station or the land purchase, or both. This just isn't the right time for this, no matter how important we might think it is."

Trish yielded to my judgment and went back to work, while I returned the stack of papers on my desk. Periodically I would pick up the envelope, hold it up to the light, and try to determine its contents to no avail. Repeating the futile activity once too often, I was caught red-handed by Jerry, who quipped, "You could read it better if you opened it".

"I suppose so, but I can't. Well I mean I couldn't, but now I can. No I can't, Trish isn't here!"

Mr. G., who had followed Jerry into my office, turned to face him and said, "You sure you haven't been working the boy too much? I'm sure he's got all his marbles but his shooter doesn't work."

We laughed. Then Jerry asked, "Just what does all that gibberish mean? I sure hope you can talk better than that on the air."

"Why doesn't everyone sit down for a moment, and I'll explain."

I refreshed Jerry's memory about Madame's promise to make a gift to the operation of the WPFH-FM that she made while she was in the hospital. I then went on to relate to Mr. Gramswald who Madame Francene DeVille was and the circumstances of her heart attack, salvation and subsequent healing.

"That brings us up to now, and this pink envelope," I said, holding it up to the light again. "Madame plans to be here for the dedication tomorrow, but just in case she has any difficulties, and I don't expect her to, she sent the gift over while I was picking up Mr. G. in Marquette." Jerry reached out for the envelope as I continued. "The instructions on the envelope, as you can see, Jerry, state the envelope is to be opened by Trish and me in your presence. That's why I couldn't open it before, because I didn't want to bother you and Mr. G. in your office. Now we can't open it because Trish is in studio B."

While I was walking toward Jerry, Mr. G. stood up and said, "Why don't you go get the young lady so we can clear this matter up and get rid of the suspense?"

Jerry handed the envelope to Mr. G. and said, "Good idea. David..."

I was already on my way before Jerry could finish. Trish followed me back into my office and the four of us stood there for a moment waiting for someone to make a move. Finally I took the envelope from Mr. G. and handed it to Trish. "You open it, Dear. I'm too nervous."

"Okay," she said, calmly.

There was a check and a short note. The check was for $10,000; the note said:

> *Although this check is to the radio station, and for the radio station, I really only know Trish Ivey and David Post who work there. They have befriended me and led me to the Lord. It is their prayers and faith that resulted in my miraculous healing. I would ask that they determine the needs most pressing for the FM radio station and apply these funds to that project or projects. I hope to be with you tomorrow as together with Jesus, we dedicate the station to its purpose of telling the people of the central Upper Peninsula of God's plan for their lives.*
>
> *Madame F. DeVille*

Jerry turned to Mr. G. and said, "I believe we can comply with those requests, can't we Mr. G.?"

"Why sure, Jerry, and I believe David and Trish have a very specific need in their minds. David, remember our conversation in the car?"

"I sure do, sir. Trish, this money might go a long way, if not all the way to setting up studio B. Would you agree with that?"

"That was my first thought when I saw the amount of the check."

The small celebration moved to the break room for coffee and sharing the news with the other employees.

Soon the spontaneous party was over and we were all back working. Jerry, Mr. G. and I returned to Jerry's office where we put the final plans together for the dedication. Jerry double-checked with Pastor Glen to make sure he had his alarm clock set and appointment schedule marked to include our first broadcast.

I returned to my office. It seemed like I had only worked a few minutes when Trish entered and said, "It's nearly 4:45 and I'm beat. I'm going home now unless there's anything you need me to do."

"Gee, is it that time already? I still have about an hour's work left, but you go on home. Take it easy and I'll give you a call when I leave my house for the studio. It'll probably be close to seven. Would you like me to pick you up?"

"Yes, please do. You'll call me then?" she asked in an effort to reconfirm my stated plans.

"Yes! I'll call you first."

"Bye, David."

"Bye, Love."

CHAPTER NINETEEN

"Hello, Trish. Have you had some time to rest?" I asked when she answered the phone.

"Yes, David, I really feel refreshed. After getting home, I fixed a light meal and relaxed in a bubble bath while listening to a new praise and worship tape. How about you? What time did you get out of there?"

"Oh, it must have been about six, maybe a little after. I did about the same thing as you, except for the bubbles, that is. This afternoon's drive to Marquette and back was more tiring than usual. But now that I've eaten and showered, I feel much better. If you're ready, is it okay for me to pick you up now?"

"Sure! Say in about twenty minutes?"

Checking my watch, which already showed ten after seven, I said, "Yes, I'll see you in twenty, Trish. I love you!"

The statement must have taken her by surprise because she was silent for a moment. "I love you too, David, very much. See you soon. Bye."

When I pulled up to her apartment, she was standing on the porch. I couldn't tell what she was wearing except for a long, tan, quilted stadium coat. As I turned into the parking space she started down the steps. It was dark. The only source of light was the streetlights. Though they were dim, they illuminated her face and hair; she was radiant. The thought of Frank relinquishing his hold on such a beautiful, talented and charming woman came to my mind and simply astounded me. "Thank you, Frank," I said softly under my breath as she approached the car. I knew I should get out and open the car door for her but I was captivated, no, make that hypnotized by her glow and couldn't seem to find my door handle. It was almost like a slow-motion film sequence as she opened the door, entered the car and then turned toward me looking happily into my eyes.

She didn't say a word. We looked at each other with a pure and holy attraction. When I could no longer stand the spell her radiance cast upon me, I slowly leaned in her direction. As if reading my mind, she reciprocated, leaned toward me, and we kissed. As our lips parted, the now dangerously familiar fragrance she wore bypassed my mind, intercepting my heartbeat. "You're going to have to stop wearing that perfume, Trish. I can barely contain my emotions. What is it, anyway?" I asked, never allowing my eyes to part from hers.

"It's my favorite. It's called 'Suddenly'. Does that mean you don't like it?"

"Are you serious? Haven't you been able to tell what happens to me when we're close while you're wearing it? Yes, I love it, almost as much as the person who's wearing it. It's just that I've never been affected by a woman's perfume so profoundly before."

"Well thank you! I hadn't really paid attention to what my perfume did to you. Should I stop wearing it?"

Trish was off and running with her game plan. I was certain of that. She knew not only what affect it had on me; she also knew I liked it. "No, don't stop wearing it. I was just teasing. Just make sure you know that it's a powerful fragrance. Shall we go?"

"I'm ready if you are, my love. But I guess the honeymoon, so to speak, is over, right?"

"I'm sorry, Trish, you've lost me. What do you mean?"

"What I mean is, don't you open car doors for me anymore?"

"Oh, if you only knew," I answered, trying to excite her curiosity while driving up the street.

She looked at me and asked, "Knew what? Are we starting another game?"

"Don't ask me that! I believe you're the one that started it. What I meant was, watching you as you came down the porch steps and as you walked to the car, all I could do is fumble to find my door handle. If I could have just gotten out...I could have...well...been a gentleman and opened your door. There, do you see what kind of affect you have on me?"

Trish turned her head to face out the side window. I couldn't tell but I believed she was blushing. Then she replied, "You're so kind, loving and fun to be with. I don't deserve you, David."

"Now what's that supposed to mean?" I asked, realizing she was not blushing but crying.

"I think you know what I mean. What we talked about in your back woods. I'm still dealing with that. I feel better about myself since then, but please don't expect me to be over that in an instant."

I could feel my own tears about to begin. My heart was aching as she spoke those words. "Trish, my lovely Trish, it's I who don't deserve someone as sweet, pleasant, charming and wonderful as you. At the risk of being too bold, let me tell you something very personal. I had determined many times over the years that I would probably not have a 'someone' for my life. Now I'm not so sure about that. It hasn't surprised me in the least that God has so quickly confirmed that YOU were the 'someone' for me. If that is indeed

God's plan, and I truly believe that it is, then I'll consider myself the most fortunate of men. I pray that is what God has in store for us. And I pray I can be to you what you've already been to me."

Trish didn't answer. I started second-guessing my boldness and started thinking I might have said way too much. After I parked the car in front of the shop I waited to see if she had composed herself.

"Thank you, David, for not pressuring me for an immediate answer. I'm not going to beat around the bush. You weren't too bold, but you might think me so after I say what I'm about to. I know we need more time to get to know each other better, but I don't have any doubt about what our future holds. God has given back to us '...the years the locusts had eaten.' My prayers have all been answered and YOU are my 'someone.' And do you know when I knew that? The day we met for lunch and you asked me to come back to WPFH. I felt a lot of the hurt inside me leave as you approached the table. God seemed to say 'All three answers in one package. A sign of My Trinity.'"

"I think I knew something about us in the back of church when Jerry introduced us," I said softly.

I got out of the car and opened the door for her. We walked up to the door of the studio where I wrestled with the lock. It finally yielded to my twisting and I reached into the darkness of the room to turn on the lights. Stepping back, I allowed Trish to enter the shop, studying her face as she did to see if her tears had left traces on her cheeks; they hadn't. "Let me turn the heat up just a tad before we get started," I said. "The spots and floods will soon have this place as warm as toast; then when you feel comfortable about posing, we'll start. Would you like me to make some coffee?" I asked, trying to get her to open up to more conversation.

She shook her head no and by the way she did it I could tell she felt uneasy.

"Would you rather not do this tonight? I'll understand if you don't feel up to it."

She still had her coat on with her arms crossed in front of her. She made no effort to remove it. She did answer me as she selected a chair and sat down. "No that's quite all right, David. I'm actually looking forward to this. I've often wondered what those cover girls go through in a photo session."

"Well, let's hope I'm not that demanding. They have sessions sometimes lasting hours on end. All I want to do is take a couple portrait shots, not make a portfolio spread for a cover to a women's magazine, although your face on the cover of 'Woman's World & Fashion' would be nice," I said, trying to help her to relax and show a smile.

"Get serious, David!" she retorted, signs of a smile tracing their way across her lips.

"That's much better, but I know you've got a bigger smile than that. Do you want me to get my squeaky rubber duck or bouncing ball like I do for the kiddy pictures? You ought to see me pull my hair out trying to shoot those little crumb-busters."

Then she displayed the smile I had come to love so dearly and remarked, "You're just not going to get serious about this at all, are you?" She stood up to take off her coat as the room warmed to a more comfortable temperature.

"Why should I? I'm with the woman I love. I'm about to take some glorious portrait shots of her, and then we're going out for a late supper. What is there in all of that to make a fellow get serious? If anything I should get goofy."

She laughed, announcing, "You've already arrived at goofy; I think you're moving beyond that now."

As she unfastened the buttons on her coat I reached toward her to help her slip it off her shoulders revealing the most beautiful, lacy white dress I'd ever seen. It wasn't like a wedding gown, but more like a party dress with half sleeves. She gracefully adorned herself with a single strand of pearls. They draped across her lower neck, just above the neckline of the dress. She had matching pearl earrings. Her hair was just as perfect as it had been the day I met her. The way she had accomplished her make-up accentuated her natural beauty. She allowed me to slowly remove the coat from her left arm, which exposed the totality of her charm.

"Oh, Trish!" I whispered. For several long moments I filled my heart with the beauty that my eyes beheld; then I forced my mind to make the necessary camera and lighting computations for the eventual photographing. "Step over here, dear, in the center of the light," I said, taking her hand. She followed my prompting when I motioned for her to sit on a small stool. The brightness of the light heightened her beauty even more. I wanted desperately to touch her face and gaze into her deep blue eyes, which followed my every move. Tenderly I placed her hands on her lap and adjusted the level and position of her head. She sat motionless except for her eyes. She studied my movements while I fought the urge to call the whole thing off just so I could embrace her.

"How long will this take?" she softly asked, again showing a pleasant tentative smile.

"Not long, Trish. Let me know if you get tired, you feel a sneeze coming on, or if your nose itches. I'm just going to take about five or six of this pose and three or four with a hazing lens; then we'll do one or two other quick settings. Okay?"

"I guess so, whatever you said. Am I doing okay?"

"You're doing beautifully. If I could I would kiss you."

"Why don't you, then?" she teased, knowing full well I wouldn't.

"Hold that thought!" I quickly replied heading to the back of the camera. "Ready? Nutsy!" She smiled and the flashes fired off in response to pressure on the shutter release.

When the flashing stopped she immediately scratched the end of her nose and said, "I wondered if you were going to say 'CHEESE', but I never figured you would say 'NUTSY'."

"I wondered if it would work," I grinned. "It did. I also wondered if you would touch the end of your nose."

She turned directly to me while I reset the camera and asked, "Why would you wonder that?"

"It's simple: power of suggestion. In nine out of every ten portrait settings that I've done, when I've suggested, as I did to you, about having an itch, the subjects inevitably do."

"I don't believe that," she responded, rubbing her nose again.

"See, I just did it again," I pointed out as I resettled her in a different pose. "This will be it for the big camera, so sit pretty. Now that was stupid," I sternly chided myself. "Just what other way can you sit but pretty?" Soon the camera shutter was clicking and the strobes flashing. "Now, don't move yet," I instructed, grabbing my 35 mm camera from the desk behind the background screen. With the aid of the motorized film advance I took about twenty pictures before she knew what hit her. "There, cover girl, these are just for fun. Smile...turn your head left...now right...look up...now over here...stand up...blow me a kiss...want to go for pizza? ...Perfect... food... food... food... food, all done."

"Now what, David?" she asked moving back to the armchair.

"Let me take care of the film, lights and what not; then I'll make out your bill," I joked.

"You just can't get serious tonight, can you?" she reprimanded me.

"I beg to differ with you, Trish. Will you marry me?"

I continued putting away the cameras and other equipment acting as if I had said nothing out of the ordinary. Trish sat frozen on the chair. I went around the room turning off the photography lights, and then paused, standing

166

directly in front of her. She still hadn't moved, sitting with a somewhat dazed expression on her face; then spoke.

"What did you say David?" she demanded.

"Well, I said it will just take a minute or two and I'll get your bill for you, but I was just joking."

She stood to her feet and looked me straight in the eyes and said, "No more joking. It's time for you to serious up. This has been fun and you've made me feel so beautiful and special, but what did you just say?"

"Well Trish, I believe the words were 'Will you marry me?' Is that what you heard?"

"That's what I thought I heard. Did you mean that? You've only known me for just a short time. How could you possibly know you're asking the right person at the right time?"

"Trish," I began. "I couldn't be more sure of my asking you, or asking you right now. What I'm not sure of is when, if you accept, that we get married, but I do know this: if you're not just as serious about me and your relationship to me, then now is the time for me to find that out. I don't want to play a game. I'm forty-four years old. If there's even the slightest chance of your becoming my wife, I want to know it now or else let's stop right here.

"Remember when you said how amazing it is what God has done in the short time we've known each other? I'm certain God has given us to each other and ordained us to be together, but if you're not that sure, I think we ought to face that. I'm not asking you to marry me out of impulse. Like I said, I have no idea of when—we'll wait on God for that. I'm asking out of love and a desire to spend the rest of my life doing for you what you have done for me. That is to make you the happiest person alive. I don't want to wait until I'm fifty, or even forty-five. Will you marry me, Trish?"

"David, I don't believe a simple answer would be adequate to describe the joy that's welling up inside my heart. I've told you how I feel about you and what I believe our future holds. I don't have any idea either, when marriage might become a reality, but I certainly accept your proposal, doing so with thanksgiving unto our God for His benevolent, unending love. In His gracious mercy He has heard my heart's cry and given me the desire of my heart. He is a great God and I am most grateful to Him. Yes, I'll marry you, and, as proof of my gratitude, I'll love you with all the strength that's within me."

Trish threw her arms around me and we held each other amid tears of joy. After kissing her I stepped back, beholding her beauty and said, "A simple 'yes' would have sufficed."

At that she teasingly hit me in the arm saying, "Let's go eat!"

This was not the time to hit a drive-in for a burger and fries. The situation called for a romantic dinner by candlelight. Nothing else would do except a secluded corner of a restaurant. Ridgemont is not exactly a booming metropolis. It's a small community of just over eight thousand. In terms of the Upper Peninsula, that's a fair sized town, but it only had one such nighttime dining spot, The Ravenwood Supper Club.

As we walked to the entrance to the restaurant Trish looped her arm around mine and softly whispered, "This is absolutely the most memorable night of my life. David, I feel so complete, full of joy and overtaken by such a warm peace. What more could any woman want. I know my destination is heaven; I have someone to go through life with, and I'm back working among friends and fellow Christians. I doubt there's any good thing I lack."

"I can only make one correction to that, Trish, but I hesitate to do it because it's just a matter of time until that is resolved," I said.

"What's that?" Trish asked.

The doorman held the door open and we entered. "Annette: she hasn't accepted the Lord yet; everyone else at the station has."

"You're right, but I'm glad you said 'yet' because she will be too if she stays with us for very long."

The hostess seated us in the most private location of the restaurant, secluded, dimly lit and quiet. We viewed the menu out of habit, but each of us had already determined what we wanted.

Trish spoke first. "I believe a New York strip would be nice; I hope they have a small one though."

"That's exactly what I wanted, Trish. You want a baked potato?" I asked.

She nodded, folding the menu and setting it on the table. She reached over and placed her right hand on top of mine saying, "I'm really at a loss for words, Love. Isn't that a terrible thing for a radio announcer?"

"Yes it is, but fortunately you're not on the air right now. If you were this would probably throw you into a panic like thirty seconds of dead air." I retrieved the small, square, velvet covered box from my suit coat pocket and opened it as I spoke. "I hope you don't find this being overly prepared or presumptuous on my part, but let's see if it fits."

Her soft, smooth hand began to tremble as she extended it toward me. Raising my gaze to her face I caught the warm glow of the candle reflecting in her eyes. Eyes, I could tell, that were just moments from filling with tears of joy. "Trish this is the only part of this evening I planned. The rest of what has happened tonight has been footsteps ordered by the Lord. Had you said 'no', we wouldn't be here. Had God not said 'ask her', I doubt if I would have wanted to see tomorrow's sunrise. I know you said you would marry me, but before I place this ring on your finger, I ask you again, Trish, will you marry me?"

"Yes David, and forever."

We placed our order and then nibbled on the salad and breadsticks as we waited. Trish, keeping her composure, asked, "You know, David, the church has a twenty-four hour prayer room that's always open. I think it would be a perfect way to solidify our engagement by stopping there before going home for a few minutes of prayer together. Do you think we could do that?"

"I'd love to. We have always tried to keep Him at the focal point in our thoughts and conversations. I know, for me, I couldn't have made any of the recent decisions in my life, including asking you to marry me, without His guidance. Certainly we would never want to enter into anything as important as marriage without committing it to Him and seeking His help, strength, wisdom and peace during this engagement time. Trish, I pledge to you my love. I pledge that that love will always remain pure and holy in your eyes and the Lord's. Should I ever get out of line in any way, tell me so, okay?"

"I will, David, and likewise, if I ever do anything that would or could lead to sin, I ask you to be strong, as you should be, and warn me."

Just as we finished exchanging our spontaneous engagement vows, our steaks arrived. The sight of the delicious meal set my neglected stomach to growling. Trish heard it and laughed, "Can't you do anything to stop that! You're embarrassing me! I think the people across the room can hear it."

Looking into her mischievous eyes, I replied, "If you'll allow me enough time to say grace, I'll do my absolute best to stop the racket and see if I can do a vanishing act with this New York strip."

We laughed softly, then held each other's hands, bowed our heads and asked God's blessing on the food.

After eating, we went to the church for a time of prayer. At this late hour I really didn't expect to see anyone in the prayer room, yet at least ten people were there. Several of them were on the phones taking prayer requests. I reasoned this must have been where Trish called, the night of Madame DeVille's heart attack. The room was rather small, about the size of a grade school classroom, maybe twenty feet square. The phone-bank, consisting of five semi-private stations, was positioned against the sidewall. There was a small altar at the front of the room. The remainder of the room was filled with short pews and kneelers. This was the first time I had seen kneelers since my Catholic days, and I immediately found myself out of habit looking for the holy water font at the door, but of course there wasn't any.

Trish led the way into the room and selected a pew. We both knelt and went into silent prayer. I can only speculate what Trish prayed. Although our eyes were closed, I could tell she was weeping. Her soft, gentle sighs were nearly more than I could bear and reminded me of our backwoods conversation. I hoped, though, that her tears were now tears of joy. Still, I sensed that there was a trace of hurt remaining that through the events of the evening and the grace of God, she was apparently releasing. Whatever the cause might be, I vowed that I would never be the cause of her crying.

Lord God, who gives life to us, abundant life, who gives to us mercy and forgiveness, and who has now given me this precious, loving and wonderful companion, empower me to live unselfishly for her and for You. It's just not enough, oh God, for me to want to; I must be empowered to do so. Listen to her sobbing, Lord. See her tears. Let there never be a day, in all the time you ordain for us to be together, that I ever cause her to shed a tear because of hurt, selfishness, bitterness, unkind words or actions. May my every breath be purposed first for You and then for her.

God, please forgive me, but would you mind terribly if I pinched myself to see if this is just a very pleasant dream. David, the psalmist, said it best when he asked, 'Who is man that Thou art mindful of him?' Sometimes I really wonder who am I that you concern yourself with me. I'm most grateful, Lord, for this dear person, my love. Thank you for her and the pleasant spirit you have placed within her. Bless us as we seek to learn and know each other, and as we follow the Holy Spirit's leading. Keep us in Your care Father; help us to meet our desire and pledge of remaining pure and holy before You and each other, in Jesus' name. Amen.

At first I hadn't noticed it, but tears were flowing down my cheeks too. As I looked up Trish had already finished her prayer. She offered me a tissue and quietly whispered, "We might want to add a prayer for the dedication tomorrow as well. Don't you agree?" I nodded in agreement, held her hand and began praying once more for tomorrow's events. She followed my lead. Then, having finished, we stood to leave.

On our way back to the car, I said, "This sure has been one special day, hasn't it, Trish?"

"It has indeed, David," she answered, looking at her ring glistening in the parking lot lights. "It's a beautiful ring, David. When did you get it?"

"Yesterday when I went to pick up Mr. Gramswald in Marquette. I had phoned a jeweler friend there and he had several ready for me to look at when I arrived."

"Did you know at that time that you were going to ask me?"

"I must have, dear, but for the life of me, I was still wondering how it would come about. It was like God was telling me to be ready, but nothing more. Because I was all by myself in the car, I prayed in tongues nearly all the way to Marquette. Every now and then I would stop praying and listen to see if either the interpretation would come or if God would have anything to say to my spirit. I knew I was to stop at the jewelry store to buy a ring for you, but what I didn't know was how or when I would get the opportunity to pop the question.

"I just kept asking God, 'Show me when. Make it plain to me. Don't let me guess or mess things up with my timing.' I've kept the ring right with me since yesterday afternoon, and I was just waiting on the Lord and trusting Him that you would say yes. Deep inside I knew you would; you've made it clear to me that we're not just good friends. You mean more to me than that, and I hoped I meant more than that to you. Apparently I do."

"Of course you do," she responded, placing a kiss on my cheek as I pulled up to the front of her apartment.

We kissed good night. "It keeps getting harder and harder to say good night or good-bye, Trish. I love you so much."

"I love you too, David. Thank you for asking me to marry you. Thank you for the beautiful ring, and thank you especially for your love," she breathed softly. We kissed for a brief moment longer then she got out of the car and walked up the sidewalk to her porch. I waited until she was safely in and then praised the Lord all the way home.

CHAPTER TWENTY

"'In the beginning was the Word, and the Word was with God, and the Word was God. The same was in the beginning with God. All things were made by him; and without him was not any thing made that was made.' This is WPFH-FM, 101.9 megahertz, broadcasting under license of the FCC. The words just spoken were those opening verses of the Gospel according to Saint John. The word gospel means 'good news'. The purpose of this radio station is to spread the Gospel, the 'good news', of Jesus Christ. Those first words from John's Gospel identify Jesus as the 'Word'. There's something very significant about the word 'Word' as used in the Bible. That significance is that Jesus not only was the Word, but He spoke the Word. Not just any word, but the Word of God. The Bible also states that '...hearing comes by the Word of God.' Thus the first part of the two-part purpose for WPFH-FM is to get the Word of God out to those who haven't heard it. The second part of our purpose is to edify, that is, to build up those who already believe.

"This is Jerry McFarland, president of WPFH-AM and FM. At this time I would like to introduce to you, Pastor Glen Hershey of Lord of the Harvest Church which is located on the south west side of Ridgemont, Michigan: Pastor Hershey."

"Thank you, Jerry. Friends, let us pray. Father God, unless you build the house, he that builds it labors in vain. We ask that you not only build but also bless and keep this house, which is purposed for the lifting up of Your Son's name. It started as a missionary vision of one man from Chicago, his gift to the beautiful people of Michigan's Upper Peninsula. It started as an AM station and has now grown, through your benevolence, to both an AM and an FM station. We know, Father God, that anything alive grows, anything dead does not. The world that you created proves that very point. The body of Christ, His church, is growing; that assures us that He is alive. A truth that keeps our hope alive, thus our hope grows.

"Keep the vision alive by Your power. Keep the facilities safe and functioning by Your care. Keep the staff protected and filled with Your Holy Spirit. Keep Your saving mercy seeking out the lost. And Father, keep Your hand upon the purpose, commitment and fulfillment of this station's goal – completing the great commission given to us by Your Son, in whose name we pray. Amen."

"Thank you, Pastor Hershey. Now for a few words from David Post, manager of WPFH-FM. David."

"WPFH-FM will be a Christian station with a format similar to WPFH-AM. We will have a mix of music, religious programs, news, weather and some sports news, but mostly music. We will also provide public service announcements, school closings and other information of general interest. This station will operate 16 hours per day initially, with expanded hours as resources allow. We are not a commercial station so we will not be airing advertisements of any nature. We will, however, rely upon the love gifts and offerings of the listening audience.

"I would like to identify those you will be hearing on this station. In addition to myself, you will hear the pleasant and experienced voices of Trish Ivey and Annette Chandler. You will also hear Jim Osborne and Ted Munson, who, although not as experienced as Trish and Annette, are joining the WPFH-FM staff ready and able to minister to you through this station. I am proud of this fine FM staff and I trust you will lift them up in your prayers as we embark on this adventure in Christian broadcasting. Our mailing address and phone number is identical to those of the AM station: Post Office Box 77, Ridgemont, Michigan 49926. We welcome your comments, suggestions and prayer requests. The only way we can be true to our calling, and likewise true to the God we all serve, is to be true in our service to you. May God bless you, the audience of WPFH-FM and this new radio voice in upper Michigan."

As I stepped back from the microphone, Jerry resumed his M.C. role. "I again ask Pastor Glen Hershey to come to the mike and lead us in a devotional. Pastor Glen."

"We are told in the Old Testament of a unified nation of people who labored to build a tower in a human attempt to get to God. Today, with our modern, advanced knowledge, we smugly laugh at such a thing. However, it is much more important that we understand the truth behind the recorded incident. The truth is that we can never get to God by our own efforts. In the opening prayer I mentioned that a man labors in vain who builds the house without God. That truth of God, dear friends, is true in every facet of life. The man who attempts to reach God within the limits of his own strength is wasting his time. It takes God to get us to God, first through the shed blood of Jesus on Calvary, and secondly, through growth in Him which must come about by the indwelling person of the Holy Spirit. Any other attempt at spiritual growth is a human attempt and guaranteed to fail.

"Too be sure, we may succeed in our meager attempts to gain knowledge, power, wealth, and happiness, but these things are temporal and will not stand the litmus test of eternity. God promises us in His Word that all these things will melt away with a fervent heat. He also promises us that the only thing that will not pass away is His Word. His Words are life. His Words are promise, and in His Words we place our faith. We must inevitably come to His Word, if not voluntarily, then certainly under compulsion when we meet Him, face to face. WPFH will send forth His Word and it will not return void. The acceptance of His Word is up to you.

"Jesus is the Word of God. Jesus is the way, the truth and the life. Let His way, His truth and His life go forth from this station to win every soul to the kingdom of God, until He triumphantly returns. Blessings from the almighty, eternal God be with this station and its staff. Be blessed! Proclaim the Word with power; proclaim it with urgency! Proclaim His Word with fervor and commitment, but proclaim it to the people!"

With that, Pastor Glen stepped back from the microphone, yielding to Trish. "Good morning, I'm Trish Ivey and I'll be your morning announcer Monday through Friday. I've selected a poem about the blood of Jesus. The Bible says that without the shedding of blood there is no remission of sins.

The Miracle of the Blood

I found myself once standing where I'd never been before.
Seeing strange surroundings, not knowing what's in store.
And then I raised my head a bit, looked upward at a cross.
Knew where I was that moment, and yet felt so at loss.
There was that man named Jesus, pierced and hanging weak.
Tears and blood had mingled as they trickled down His cheek.
My mind now coursed the pages that I'd read in times before,
About the blood of Jesus, His life and so much more.
But now the scene was real enough, I stood just feet away.
I now could see, first hand account, just how He passed away.
I'd read the reason why He died, I knew it was for me.
I looked again upon His face that hurt so much to see.
And as I looked, I saw one drop of blood as down it came.
I ran and caught it in my hand, then watched it write my name.

Jerry returned to the mike and introduced a musical interlude. Annette was at the control board and closed the microphones while starting the music.

We all stood there for several moments looking at each other somewhat dazed, not really comprehending the fact that we were now officially on the air. Jerry interrupted the moment by asking, "David, do you have your music ready for today?"

"I sure do, Jerry," I answered, lifting three large reels of prerecorded music for him to see.

"We'll wrap up the dedication and you can put on one of those reels; in fact why don't you set it up now, then we'll all go into the break room for breakfast."

Annette got up from the announcer's chair thereby allowing Trish to be seated. As the musical interlude ended, Trish cued up the station identification cartridge on which she had recorded my station promo. Upon its completion she introduced Mr. Gramswald.

"At this time we introduce to you the man with the missionary vision that has brought about WPFH-AM and now WPFH-FM, Mr. Jerome Gramswald."

Mr. G. slowly began his remarks. "Good morning, people of the central Upper Peninsula. God bless you on this Lord's Day. Let me start by apologizing for the delay in getting this station on the air. I also apologize for the temporary loss of WPFH-AM due to an electrical fire. It gives me great pleasure to announce that WPFH-AM will be back on the air by the end of this week, thanks to some diligent, tedious labors of love by Jerry McFarland and others. For right now, though, we are gathered this morning to praise the Lord our God for the blessing of WPFH-FM and to joyfully celebrate this first day of broadcasting.

"While not diminishing in any way the graciousness of our God, there have been the human labors of a very humble and caring man who has been responsible for the recent preparations—a peaceable man with a heart for doing the will of God. He single-handedly put the initial broadcast staff together and helped plan this dedication. He has overseen all the countless tasks necessary to get this station on the air. Tasks that included scheduling programs that will, we pray, edify and uplift you, our listeners, as well as draw the lost to Jesus. He has moved a mountain of paperwork and administered an avalanche of new files. That man is Mr. David Post, manager of WPFH-FM. In the short time I have known David, I can attest that you will enjoy his pleasant personality and come to love his dedication to the Lord, enthusiasm for the station and sincerity to service.

"I'm at a bit of a disadvantage in that I reside in Chicago where my family business keeps me. In spite of that, I have come to know and love you, the

175

people of the Upper Peninsula. After discovering your need, we asked God to provide a way to establish Christian radio here. The result was WPFH.

"When people in Chicago ask me what's up here that I get so excited about, I'm quick to tell them: First, an unblemished view of what the world looked like when God finished his six days of creating. Secondly, the joy of experiencing a peaceful and tranquil time without leaving planet Earth. And thirdly, the sight in the natural of the vision that God gave me.

"Maybe someday the Lord will allow me to have a long, enjoyable stay up here with you. Until then, know that I will be here, if not in person, certainly in spirit, as WPFH AM and FM gladly bring you the Gospel of peace and salvation."

Jerry returned to the microphone. "We now close this dedication service with an invitation to you to stop in next week to view the facilities that God has entrusted to us; to meet the team God has assembled, and share in our celebration unto the Lord. The remainder of our first broadcast day will follow a musical format. Thank you for joining us for this dedication service. I would like to close by thanking Mr. Jerome Gramswald, Pastor Glen Hershey and the staff members of this station for their hard work and sacrifices. And heavenly Father, above all else, we thank You. Without Your intervention, the evil one would have stopped us in our tracks. He certainly tried, but Your power sustained us and gave us ultimate victory. To You we give glory, honor, power, dominion, praise and adoration forever. Continue, Oh Lord, to be our strength and purpose. We pray in Jesus' name. Amen."

Trish started the first reel of music, and we went to the break room for breakfast. Madame seemed to be enjoying all her newly acquired friends but none more than Mr. Gramswald. She hung on his arm like a young schoolgirl. They must have had a natural tendency to gravitate to each other, being the oldest two in the group, and sharing a common bond of experiences. Though Madame was every bit Mr. G.'s senior by over fifteen years, they were an attractive couple with similarities that went far beyond their years.

Annette had invited her husband and family, and Ted escorted his girlfriend. Others present included Jim and Mary Osborne; Susan Jacobs and her husband Tony; Jerry and his wife, Carol. Trish and I served as host and hostess, seating those present while Jimmy Thomas started pouring coffee and orange juice. Pastor Glen gave the blessing but couldn't stay for the breakfast.

Eventually, as the festivities wound down, only a few of us remained. Jimmy started cleaning up the break room at Jerry's direction while Trish put the refrigerator items away. Jerry and I folded the large tables and returned them to the storage area along with the folding chairs, all the time listening to the break room speaker as sacred music played to us, and to the central Upper Peninsula, prompting joy in our hearts and smiles on our faces.

"Jimmy," Jerry said, "you can leave after you get done sweeping the break room and rearranging the furniture. I'll mark your time card for a half a day overtime. Trish, you're free to go too; I know you'll want to get home and polish that ring."

Trish looked sternly at him and then jokingly reprimanded, "David didn't give me a ring that needs polishing."

"You know I'm just kidding, Trish. I'm real happy for the two of you. With the dedication, none of us got a chance to talk much about the engagement. Have you set a date?"

"No, Jerry," I quickly responded. "We're waiting for the Lord to reveal that to us, but we're not going to sit around doing nothing, we're going to pray, talk and worship together until we get that release from God in our spirits. Isn't that right, Trish?"

Trish nodded in agreement as she wrapped up the left over Danish.

"Hey! Don't put those cheese Danish away!" I said. "I'll nibble on them as the day progresses. I believe I would have lasted longer than Adam in the garden as long as the temptation was only an apple. But if God had made the forbidden fruit cheese Danish, well, good-bye, paradise!"

Everyone laughed at my analogy as they went about their clean up chores. Soon everything was done and Jerry and Ted left for church. Trish and I were now by ourselves so we went into the studio. Several phone calls came in congratulating us on the start of our broadcasting, but for most of the morning it was just Trish, me, and the Lord. We prayed. We celebrated the Lord and our engagement. We sang praise and worship songs too—most of which she had to teach me. We had our own communion service of bread and juice and then sang along with the taped music.

"Trish, I want to know more about you, and that includes knowing about your childhood, family life, growing up, special events in your life, and everything else there is to know about you. Would you mind sharing that with me if I promise I'll do the same for you?"

She answered me as she sat down in the announcer's chair. "Okay, but I really don't enjoy talking about me. It's not that I have an inferiority complex or low self-esteem, but rather that that subject is boring to me. I know, however, that for us to get to know each other, we must share our backgrounds. And certainly we should relate our hopes as well, so here goes.

"My parents, who still live in their very first home in Grand Rapids, are Ed and Ruth Griffin. They have two children, Benjamin, now 35, who lives in Manistee and is a computer operator for a small plant there. Their other child, Patricia Marie...well you know about her. I already told you of my college days and coming to the Lord. You know I was married to Frank Ivey after a long period of dating and engagement. We didn't have any children. The reason for that, I later found out, was he had gotten a vasectomy without my knowing it—long before we were married. I guess he just didn't want children, but he knew I did. So he had that done, pretending all along, at each month's disappointment, that maybe we were trying too hard. It turned out to be one of his many continuing charades. You know my most recent history, so I guess that brings you up to date. Well not completely. I've recently met a handsome gentleman who has asked me to marry him, and of course I've accepted his offer."

"Now who's having trouble being serious?" I asked. "Last night it was me; and listen, you ain't told me nothin' I couldn't find in your 201 file," I teased, trying to be funny.

"David! Don't ever say 'ain't' in the studio. Jerry will have your hide!" she reprimanded.

I scrunched my shoulders and ducked as if I were about to receive a whipping. "I was just trying to be funny, but I guess I shouldn't be in here."

"That's right, and you also used a double negative. I would highly recommend you don't do that in here either. Now, what's a 201 file?"

"Never mind, my dear. It has to do with military personnel records in the army. I do know that you are 33 years old. In fact, your birthday is November 8th, just about two months from now. When I checked to see when it was, I knew there would be no way I could wait until November to ask you to marry me. I also found out that you're five feet, eight inches tall...."

"Make that five feet, eight and one half inches tall," she quickly corrected.

"Okay," I yielded, "if the extra half an inch is that important... You're a natural blonde—a beautiful blonde, I might add—and you weigh...."

"Now hold it right there, buddy! That's not in any '201 file', I know that, so don't you dare say anything that might jeopardize YOUR engagement."

"Well I was only going to make a guess, Trish," I said coyly, trying to squirm out of the predicament. "As an observer of your eating habits, I was only going to make an estimate. But on second thought, seeing how succinctly you issued that warning, I'll forego the guess-work and stick to the facts."

Trish smiled, edged back into the chair, and said, "Wise move."

"Tell me then, what was your childhood like?" I inquired.

"Pretty much normal, and by that I mean no traumatic events that I can remember other than the death of my grandparents. They were killed in a car crash on I-96 one late October evening on their way back from Detroit. I don't know for sure, but Gramps was driving and either fell asleep at the wheel or had a heart attack. The car plunged down the embankment to the Grand Rapids River, just outside of Lansing, striking a culvert and flipping over. The thing that makes it so vivid in my mind was that it was just before my tenth birthday, and the concept of death hadn't been fully explained to me. Before that I knew animals died, but I didn't know people did. The reality of it hit me when I went into the funeral home. Fortunately, the caskets were closed. Grandma and Grandpa meant a lot to me; if I had seen them laid out I might have been marred emotionally for life. I'm not certain there wasn't any damage as it is.

"It's your turn now, David, but before you start, why don't you set up that next tape player? I'll watch and help if you encounter any difficulty."

"Good idea, Trish, or is it Patricia?" I teased as I walked around the control table.

She threw a wadded-up sheet of paper at me told me in no uncertain terms not to call her that again.

"Why don't you get your name changed if you don't like it?" I asked.

"I did, over ten years ago; my name really is Trish."

I loaded the large second reel of music and set the appropriate switches that would cause one tape player to begin as soon as the other finished playing its two sides. Each tape held just over four hours of music, a little more than two in each direction. While they played, Trish and I were free to continue our conversation except for station identifications on the hour and half-hour.

Sitting back down, I began my story. "I'm forty-four years old. My birthday is August 24th, which by the way, means we're just over ten years apart—you don't think that's too much, do you Trish?"

Pausing before she began, she said, "I've wondered about that several times, David. Right now I don't believe it is, but it may be something we'll want to discuss and ask God for guidance on. After all, He knew that when He brought us together."

"Let's see if I can continue to bore you. My hometown is in the Detroit area; Trenton to be exact, so we're both down-staters and probably Tiger fans, at least I hope so. My parents are deceased. I have two sisters and one brother, all of them living in different states across the nation. There are a whole lot of aunts, uncles and cousins, but we've been out of touch so long, primarily due to my military career, that I wouldn't know them if I bumped into them on the street. At one time I did have a distant cousin teaching school over in Marquette, but I don't know if she's still there. I've even forgotten her married name.

"Well, to make a long story short, I didn't do too much as a kid; I somehow managed to be selected editor of the high school yearbook and student manager for the football team two years, but most of my adventures have been a result of my Air Force assignments. I was in the personnel career field so I learned quickly how to manage my career according to the regulations, planning my assignments to coincide with my personal wishes, for the most part. I even pulled a three-year tour of instructor duty at Keesler Air Force Base in Biloxi, Mississippi. Once retired, I got into photography, and now here I am, but we covered that territory the last time we had this kind of conversation.

"What really interests me now, more than ever, is for you to help me make up for all the lost ground in my spiritual life. I know that starts with a good solid understanding of the Bible, so let's start there."

Trish opened her Bible while I retrieved mine from my office. We had a marvelous time as she guided me through an overview of Old and New Testament books with a brief description of each. We decided to start with the Gospel of Matthew, getting through nearly all of the first four chapters by noon. Trish didn't let me forget lunch, though. We had pizza delivered about 11:30, after which she guided me through some training on the console.

Sunday morning was now gone and Jerry stopped by shortly after noon to take some readings and check the equipment, telling us about the morning's church service. "We had a special prayer time just for you two and the station this morning at church. Pastor Glen felt very honored to be here with us and talked for about five minutes about the dedication prior to the prayer time.

"Oh, yes! Guess what! Mr. G. took Madame out to lunch after church."

Trish looked up at me and then at Jerry, she had surprise written all over her face and asked, "You mean they went to church...Madame went to church with...Mr. G...together?"

"Yes, and then out to lunch," Jerry reiterated.

It was time for me to be extremely cautious as the topic changed to Mr. Gramswald. I didn't want Jerry to know that Mr. G. had entrusted me with the knowledge of his and Mr. G's relationship, so I kept quiet.

"Do you think they like each other?" Trish asked. "I mean they hung around each other here at the station during the dedication."

Jerry grimaced slightly and shrugged his shoulders. "I won't ever try to outguess that old coot, but I will say this, his getting romantically involved might just be the kind of deliverance from his meddling I need."

"Jerry, I'm surprised at you!" Trish scolded.

"You're right," Jerry replied. "That may not be such a good thing now that I think about it. If he does get romantically involved with Madame, he'll be up here every weekend until he retires. Then maybe...dare I even think it...he might retire up here. There goes the neighborhood," he quipped.

Once Jerry left, Trish and I resumed our conversation and Bible study. We soon found ourselves in the fifth chapter of Matthew, specifically the portion that deals with divorce and adultery.

"Trish," I asked, "Have you worked through the difficulty, hurt and emotions of your divorce?"

She turned her eyes toward me and answered, "I believe most of it's behind me now. I know that I've forgiven Frank, and that was the hardest thing to do. The emotional roller coaster I was on during the final months of our marriage and through the divorce has been smoothed out. The only thing that's not totally gone is the hurt, but God has blessed me with you, and you've done a lot to ease that. You've been right there when I've needed someone."

I said, "I hesitate to ask this then, Love, but feel I must. Are you sure that accepting my proposal is for the right reason or reasons and not because I happened to meet a need of yours for understanding or kindness?"

"David, my dear David, you are indeed kind, understanding and compassionate, but those are your natural attributes and you would have displayed them to me even if I had never been married, hurt or divorced. That's your character, and that's why I love you. I didn't accept your proposal because I'm on the rebound. I accepted your proposal because I know deep within me that I love you and that you love me. I know also our being together is what God wants for us. I hope that answers your question and that you have no doubt as to my intentions or reasons."

"It certainly does, Trish," I admitted. "It was something I needed to ask, and your reply was exactly what I wanted to hear."

Trish took my hand in hers and said, "Besides, buddy, you don't think you're going to get out of your marriage proposal, do you? You're not getting cold feet, are you?"

"No, not at all. In fact, I kind of like the idea of getting married, even though I wasn't as sure of myself when I asked you as I am now.

"Have you heard from Frank since he left or since the divorce?" I inquired, hoping I hadn't pursued the topic too far.

"Yes, a couple of times, primarily because we wanted to work out the property settlement before we went to court. That can get nasty if you don't have most of it worked out beforehand. We owned a house near L'Anse that we had to sell. I certainly wasn't going to live in it with its memories, and Frank was living with...with her...in Lincoln Park, so he didn't need it. We hadn't had it that long so we sold it for the payoff and real estate agent's fee. We each might have gotten a few hundred from it once everything was finalized.

"He also communicated with me a couple of times just to talk things out. He called me; I never called him. I guess he felt guilty and wanted to soothe his conscience. I listened and let him say what he needed to get off his chest. Maybe underneath he still cares about me. He sounded like he was sorry for having hurt me but never actually said so in words. Apparently he's been fighting a spiritual battle he just isn't strong enough to win. After all that's transpired, I can't even be sure he's a Christian, and if he's not, he'll never win.

"In all of it, the thing that hurt me the most was his deception; deception that spanned our dating, engagement and marriage. I might have understood, if after we had gotten married I hadn't met his needs or failed to be the wife he envisioned, but he was keeping secrets from me from the day we met."

"Speaking of meeting him, when did that happen?" I asked further, because of her openness to the topic. Too, I desired to know how deep the trauma and pain had gone so that I might be better able to adapt to her emotional needs.

Trish closed her eyes for a moment and bit her lip before answering. I could tell this was not an easy thing for her to relive, but I felt it would be better for it to come out at my prompting rather than for her to hold it in, waiting for another time.

"I've known Frank for a long, long time; much longer than most people would guess. We first met while at a college fair. I went to a couple of the small ones in the Grand Rapids area, but this was a much larger one and was in Lansing with most of the major schools represented. I was sitting in the Michigan State booth waiting for my turn with the counselor when Frank, who was also waiting, introduced himself and we started talking. We exchanged addresses out of sheer boredom and because, as he put it, 'If we end up selecting the same school, we can get in touch. That way we won't be all alone on the campus.' It sounded like a great idea, but I have a suspicion that he was exchanging names with a lot of girls. Sure enough though, we both ended up at Michigan Tech, in Houghton. Somehow he found me on campus even though I had long since lost his name and address. I remembered him as soon as he made contact with me and we started out just hanging around together. Soon that led to dating. Eventually we got engaged. It was during the time before we seriously dated that I came to a personal, saving knowledge of Jesus. Prior to that we went to church together, but when you're not saved, it doesn't have much impact on your life.

"Up to the time I accepted Christ, I was, thank God, still very much influenced by my parents' Christian morals and training. I hadn't made any life-damaging mistakes—if you can read through the lines, David. We dated just about all the way through college and got engaged shortly after graduation. We never really had any intentions of getting married right away; the engagement was, at first, our way of having a sense of security and freedom from young adult peer pressure or pressure from home. The engagement gave us an excuse not to follow the social dictates of having to date others, party, drink and; ahhh, you know... engage in premarital sex the way others were. All the while, Frank spoke like a Christian, acted like a Christian, and prayed like a Christian.

"Another reason why we had such a long engagement was he went on to get his master's degree while I continued a department store job I had started in my junior year. I was also busy preparing my resume and getting interested in radio. Mom and Dad wanted me to come back home after graduation, but I just wasn't ready to surrender my independence. They were afraid I would make some mistakes while out from under their guidance. I guess I did make one mistake, marrying Frank, but he had everyone so convinced of his Christianity that even my parents gave us their blessing."

I sat almost mesmerized by Trish's story, and I admired her ability to tell it while maintaining her composure. It was a strong composure that until now I hadn't seen in her. Certainly, as open as she had been with me in reliving the sequence of events, I would have expected her to break down in tears. She wasn't even fighting off her emotions. It was apparent that she had, with God's help, been restored from most of the trauma and hurt.

"Can I change the subject, Trish?" I asked softly as I cradled her hand in mine.

"Sure, Love. Change it to what?"

"Us and our future, our plans, our marriage. I would like to start somewhere else but I can't because of something you said earlier. I just have to ask what your desires are now, as far as children are concerned, especially in light of what has transpired, and the length of time that has passed?"

She sat motionless for a moment. Her only movement was that of her eyes as they darted around the studio; not looking for an answer as much as how to phrase her reply.

"The thoughts that just raced through my mind were based on facts that I've read recently. Facts that support current medical beliefs that people our age have a higher risk of having children with birth defects. I happen to believe I have a few more so-called safe childbearing years. I've also read that men over forty are more likely to have children that experience genetic difficulties. Here again, I don't believe God has brought us this far to leave us. This is one of those areas that we haven't talked about, so I'm at a loss as to what your feelings are. David, I know all of that sounds evasive. The bottom line in my heart is, if God would give us a child to care for, no matter what kind of child, I would like that. At least one, so that I might experience pregnancy, labor, delivery and motherhood. I hope I haven't disappointed you, David, or influenced you, but what are your feelings on children?"

"Oh my!" I started, then paused a moment. "It's been so long since thoughts of being a daddy have crossed my mind. When they first did, shortly after meeting you and wondering if we might be...right for each other, they took me by surprise. If I had met you ten years ago, I wouldn't have had any reservations about a family—even a large family. Now don't start pouting! I'm not about to tell you I don't want any children now, but there is one thing that causes me apprehension. That one hang-up is the future. A child born to us right now wouldn't cause me any problems. But ten years from now, when he's ready to throw a football with the old man, he really would be throwing a football with an old man.

Trish laughed exuberantly, standing to her feet and stretching. "David, I love you so very much. I can barely believe, except by the grace and love of God, that I have someone like you to say that to. You will never be too old to love children or me. Trust me, there's just too much love, care, understanding, and unselfish concern inside of you to do anything but love. Once God releases us to marry, promise me we can have a child right away. Will you?"

I sat there looking up at her for just a moment, lingering on her words, drinking in their charm and warmth. My mind raced over the past few weeks, and I wondered how so deep a love could be realized in such short a time. "My dear Trish, I can deny you nothing. Yes, we can have children right away. The same complete abandonment of self that Christ showed on Calvary, He has placed in me. I give to you myself, completely and as certainly as God has ordained the remainder of our lives to be spent together. And I pray He shall give us yet another gift from His vast storehouse—children. But of course, to keep things in proper order, sequence-wise, that is, how will we know when the time is right for our marriage?"

"We'll know, David. He won't leave us or forsake us, as the Bible says. That's a promise that has more than one application. If what I know about God is true, and I'm certain that it is, He knows our ages and won't make us wait too much longer. Be patient, Love, we'll both know when the timing is right."

"Speaking of timing," she said, looking at her watch, "it's time for a station I D. We don't want the FCC all over us for missing those things. You stop the music after the this song; I'll start the I D cartridge, and you can log the spot, okay?"

"Okay, Love."

CHAPTER TWENTY-ONE

I spent the better part of Monday morning interviewing for part-time help after having arrived earlier than normal to make sure the building was open for Trish. Her first "Good Morning, Lord!" show started at six o'clock on the dot and she worked as smoothly as I expected. While listening as she signed on and made her opening remarks, I breathed a silent prayer of thanksgiving, calling to mind how quickly God had arranged her availability. The first weekday broadcast had begun, and with it came the realization that I would likewise be on the air for my first "Manager Moments" program. I didn't get the exact count, but there were about 700 butterflies that took to the air in my stomach.

The rest of the staff arrived. Jerry and the AM staff were busy in their preparations for getting back on the air. Susan and Jimmy came in about nine to start their shift.

I hired George Sinclair and Holly Carlson on the spot to complete the weekend crew and work along with Jim Osborne. That action finalized the FM staff selection, with one exception. Those presently on staff were so specific on shifts and hours they could work, it left me with virtually no rescheduling flexibility. To remedy that situation, I called John Dwyer to see if he would be willing to fill in as the need arose. Although he was disappointed when I had told him last week that we had no more full-time positions available, he did agree to come in for a week of paid training and then to remain on-call. His desire to get into radio broadcasting was more important to him, as he put it, than holding out for a 40-hour workweek. I promised him he would be the next employee hired, but cautioned him that I didn't foresee any immediate vacancies.

Trish finished her show at noon and started the national satellite news service while I prepared for my first "Manager Moments" show. The hour-long script I had created called for small segments of devotions, music, prayer and information on the station, as well as updates on the status of the AM repairs and renovation. I thought everything went well, once I got over my nervousness. Trish stayed with me for a while, watching my awkwardness slowly smooth out. Eventually she left to have lunch in the break room, where she listened to the monitor in case I got into trouble. The uneasiness I felt at first, though, reminded me of my first day of instructor duty at Keesler Air Force Base, in Mississippi. I'll never forget it.

Normal mornings in those days never included breakfast. For some reason breakfast just wasn't something I could stomach, pun intended. However, on the morning of my first day of solo instructor duty, I fixed two fried eggs – over hard; two crispy strips of lean bacon; two golden slices of toast, with butter and jelly, if you please; one large glass of orange juice; and topped it all off with two medium cups of freshly brewed coffee with cream and sugar. It was a satisfying, great-tasting breakfast. Then I walked over to the counter, set my dishes down, sidestepped to the sink and lost the entire breakfast. I can't remember a time I've ever been that nervous since.

I stuck strictly to the script and felt comfortable after about twenty minutes. While a musical selection was airing I arranged the next several segments of dialogue, cued another record on turntable #2, and readied a cartridge in one of the tape players. With all that finished and the music still playing, I had a few moments to catch my breath. As I slowly looked around the studio my eyes caught sight of Trish peering in at me through the small, square window. She motioned for me to "stretch it out". Apparently I was talking too fast and if I didn't slow down, would end up with more time than script. I blew her a thank-you kiss and smiled with a confirming nod. She returned an airborne kiss, and then disappeared from view.

Soon my first hour on live radio was over, and I yielded the microphone to Annette who was ready to start her six-hour shift. My feelings were mixed as I returned to the less stressful atmosphere of my office. After closing the door, I sat and reflected on those feelings. First was the feeling of accomplishment. That was good. The first show was now history; half of the first weekday programming was now behind us with no trouble from either the equipment or my inexperience. That too was good. The staff selection was now complete and the training sessions were going well. All of that was good, but yet there was one more feeling inside of me that needed to be explored.

For some reason, in the midst of all the successes, I felt uneasy. Uneasy about the challenges I had taken on. As I let the thoughts flow freely I could soon tell my spirit, and not my mind, was processing them. My spirit studied each one to determine its origin. I prayed softly in my prayer language as the thoughts continued. Were Trish and I really engaged, and had I truly heard the voice of the Lord in that area?

That second-guessing came from Satan. So did the thought about having taken on too much of a challenge by changing jobs.

I paused in my prayer to allow the Lord to speak if He so desired. He did — not in an audible voice, mind you, but with that voice that speaks from Spirit to spirit, Deep calling to deep. Not content with listening internally, I began to say the words I heard. "Be at peace, David. My Son is the giver of peace, and His peace passes all understanding. He will keep your heart and mind. You have surrendered your life to me; now I will honor that by providing you with a life that will, if you obey, bear fruit and have success. Be submissive to those challenges you wonder about. Not submissive in the sense of surrendering to whatever will happen will happen, but submissive in accomplishing them. You will succeed: I have declared it. It shall surely be as I have said. This is your appointment in life, to bring in part of the harvest through the work I have assigned to you. To edify those who have accepted the cleansing power of My Son's blood; to reach those who are not otherwise reachable, to console, to strengthen, and to teach. You shall do these things because they are your work and you have accepted My commission to do them. Thus, I bless you in your effort. Likewise, I have given unto you, for your comfort and joy, the one who is to be your wife. Hold her dear and watch your growth by her guiding. I have spoken it so, and so it shall be, sayeth the Lord your God."

I resumed my prayer in tongues, not fully realizing what had just happened. Trish knocked on my closed door and quietly entered. She approached my desk and I stopped praying long enough to stand and offer her a chair. I was about to continue, knowing she would understand, when my eyes met hers. Her face radiated like Moses' did after his encounter with God on the mountain. "Did you just spend some time with the Lord, Trish?" I asked.

"Yes, and by the look upon your face, I'd say you did, too."

"Love, you know I'm spiritually too young to know all that you do, but I would stake my life on the fact that God just spoke to me more vividly and directly than He ever has. He said many things of a personal nature but He also...He confirmed...well, that you and I...."

Trish jumped in, "That we were for each other?"

"Yes, how did you know that?" I asked.

"Because He just said that to me while I was in studio B working with Jim. How did He say it to you, David?" she inquired, eyes glistening.

"It went something like this: I have given unto you, for your comfort and joy, the one who is to be your wife. Hold her...."

Trish continued, "...dear and watch your growth by his guidance."

For about fifteen seconds we stood looking at each other, waiting for the other to say something. Neither of us did, so we just embraced.

"Hey, you two, you're on the clock. Do I need to remind you of that?" Jerry said, entering the office through the door that had been left slightly ajar. "I'm just going to have to give you two some real time off so you can get out of this place and be by yourselves without work getting in the way. How about tomorrow afternoon?"

Trish and I quickly accepted Jerry's offer!"

"By the way," Jerry interjected, "I just took a call from Mr. G. As you know he's back in Marquette working a property deal for the television station. He called me five minutes ago; that's why I came in here, to let you know he just closed on the site he went to see the other day. I guess his next move is to apply for that license with the FCC. Keep that in your prayers, if you will, okay?"

"We'll do that, Jerry," I answered. "If it's okay with you, Trish and I are going to start spending that money Madame gave us."

"Go ahead; it's in the bank, and you may as well have a studio B that's the talk of the industry, or at least the talk of all the other U.P. radio stations." At that he turned to leave, adding, "Just make arrangements for tomorrow afternoon so that training will go on as planned, and then have some fun."

I turned to Trish and asked, "When will you have some time to go over this equipment catalog with me? We really should phone in our purchase order as quickly as we can."

"Let's do that tonight after work at your place, okay?" she answered.

"Sure, that'll be fine, say six thirty, or would you like to come over earlier and have one of my not so famous homemade, bachelor meals?"

She paused before answering to study my face, and then said, "It all depends on what you're fixing. Besides, there may not be all that many more bachelor meals for you."

I don't believe the full impact of what she said hit me because I only answered the first part of her question. "Probably something out of a jar like spaghetti. I could make it from scratch, or I could stop and get something else. What are your taste buds calling out for, Dear?"

"The spaghetti will be fine. What time should I be over?"

"Let's make it five thirty. Is that okay?"

"Sure is! Just make enough for an army," she said as she left. I laughed at her words, knowing so well she meant exactly what she said.

The afternoon airtime with Annette went well. The equipment hadn't shown any signs of malfunction or breakdown in the nearly two days of broadcasting. Jerry had previously warned me that radio equipment was similar to other electronic equipment in that if it was going to fail, it would probably do so in the first ten hours of use. We had managed problem-free broadcasting through twelve hours on Sunday, and now almost nine hours today.

Ted had arrived and was in studio B with Trish and Jim, working on the mock-up studio. Annette was airing her afternoon show, so I took advantage of the tranquility of the afternoon to catch up on a mountain of paperwork. As a personnel technician in the Air Force, I had learned to make quick work of administrative routines. Before long, the organizational skills the Air Force had somehow planted in an eighteen-year-old delinquent had developed into managerial skills, and were now most useful. Soon all the files in my office were organized, labeled, and placed in their appropriate file cabinet locations. The in-basket was now empty and the out-basket full. As the workday was nearing its end, I took all my outgoing mail down to Susan for metering. There was one very rewarding benefit of being employed by WPFH: no more licking stamps; this place generated enough business mail to warrant a postage-metering machine.

I stopped by the break room on my way back from the front office for a candy bar. Jimmy Thomas was there, and a conversation eventually ensued. Jimmy was one of the few employees I hadn't gotten to know too well. I suppose that was because of the separation of work from the AM folks. We talked for about twenty minutes and he gave me an in-depth instructional tour of his traffic department.

"You see, Mr. Post," he explained. "I receive and mail taped programs to and from the ministries we air on either the AM or now the FM stations. When they arrive, I check them against the schedule to see when they are to air, and then get them to the proper studio at the time they're needed. Then when the announcers are done with them, I prepare them for mailing back to the ministry headquarters. I also catalog all the music as it comes in, tapes, albums, or compact discs. It's part of my job to order new musical releases that are first okayed by the board of directors or authorized by Jerry. Another thing I'm responsible for is the wire service terminal. That includes making sure it's operating properly, has plenty of paper in the printer. I also get the news flashes to the newsroom for broadcasting."

"You have far more responsibilities than I presumed. How long have you been doing all these things?" I asked.

Jimmy beamed with pride as my questioning reflected my interest and brought out his importance to the station. "I was hired on at WCDP right after I graduated from high school, initially as summer help when other staff members took their vacations. It worked out so well for the station and me, that Steve Busadis, the station manager at the time, said he didn't want to lose me at the end of summer vacation. Steve told me that I was a good worker, and rewarded me with permanent employment. I've been here ever since."

I asked him how old he was and he told me he was about to turn 25. If my math didn't fail me, that meant he had about seven years with the station; more than enough time to see all the personnel come and go. He agreed with my assessment and related that if Trish hadn't left, she would be the only one who would have been there longer.

When our break ended I shook Jimmy's hand thanking him for the tour and the WPFH history lesson, asking him not to hesitate to visit with me in the future. I was certain he had access to a great deal of station history that would prove interesting.

I returned to my office but for the second time in the afternoon, I just couldn't get my attention on the few remaining tasks. Maybe it was because the workday was nearly finished; maybe it was something else. My thoughts drifted from one topic to another: first Trish, then the station, then church, then spiritual matters, and then back to Trish. I desperately wanted some time to just sift through things. Again I found myself listening with my spirit as Jesus came and gently answered the call of my uneasy mind. "Let not your heart be troubled. You believe in God, believe also in me."

I assumed the same thing held true for a troubled mind.

"The evil one has tried to infiltrate your mental reasoning," God began. "He has no power over your spirit. Actually he has no power over any part of you; unless that is, you surrender it to him. Trust in your God. He who is able to save you is also able to keep that which you've committed unto Him against that day."

Many of those words I had read before in my private Bible study or had heard during church services. Maybe at one time they were merely words, but now the Word of God was alive and apparently they hadn't just gone in one ear and out the other. It was now obvious to me, they had lodged somewhere in my spirit-man, and the need I was experiencing at the moment called them up from their inner sanctuary to help—the kind of help I needed right then. Peace entered my mind. No, not just my mind, the entire room seemed filled with peace, a gentle peace that relaxed me and soothed me. Quietly at first, I started praying in tongues, then stronger and more boldly I spoke forth that still slightly unfamiliar language that had been placed within me. Before long I was praying with all the assuredness and confidence I had previously witnessed in others, including Trish and Jerry.

With my work finished I joined a few other staff members in the front office. Trish was in the front office with Jerry, Susan and Carl Worth debating the Tigers' remaining pennant chances. After the topic had run its course Trish and I walked back to my office as I related the two experiences of the day. She listened intently, and then replied.

"No doubt you were under some kind of spiritual attack. Did you rebuke it?"

I stood looking at her.

"Your facial expression tells me I just went to fast for you."

"Did I what?" I managed to respond.

She grabbed my hand as we entered my office, shut the door and started explaining the power Jesus had given us to bind and loose. "You see, David, Jesus knew we would need to build ourselves up gradually, over a period of time, as our revelation in the knowledge of Him increased. He knew we couldn't possibly handle it all at once. That's why He gave us the Bible, so we could learn and apply truth as He revealed it to us. At any rate, we have within us the power of God. Satan does all in his power to keep us from learning that. If he can't keep us from learning it, then he wants to keep us from using it. And lastly, if he can't keep us from using it, he, in a very cunning way, will cause us to use it often, hoping we get weary in the flesh from using it. Not weary OF using it; weary FROM having to use it. He also knows human nature tends to devalue things once they become routine or familiar to us. Let me slow down a bit."

"Please do," I responded.

"Did you ever knowingly get in fights with the devil before you accepted Christ as Savior?"

"Of course not, Trish. Should I have?" I asked.

"No, at least not very big ones. You know right from wrong on the big-ticket items, murder, stealing, adultery, etceteras, but what we call the 'little things' wouldn't bother your conscience. If you cheated on your taxes by a few dollars; or drove five miles per hour over the speed limit; these things wouldn't even cause a second thought. So naturally, why would the devil ever bother you over those things, you were in his camp?" she asked rhetorically. "But once you accepted Jesus, remember how things like that started bothering you right away?"

"I sure do," I replied. "I couldn't listen to off-color jokes without feeling dirty for having done so. I couldn't take more break-time than what was authorized or come to work in the morning five minutes late or slip out early. Yes, I remember those things. You mean those were fights with the devil?"

"Yes, they sure were! And what's more, they wouldn't ease up when you surrendered to them. If I know anything at all about you, David, you were probably pretty miserable each time you sinned. Is that right?"

I nodded in agreement. "I still am."

Trish settled into the chair in front of my desk while I paced the floor, listening intently to her every word. "The reason for those fights was that Satan was trying to wear you down and get you to give it all up. He's fairly confident that after several real good failures, you'll think a perfect life was impossible. Isn't that smart of him? He knows that his constant attack, coupled with our failures, will slowly erode our joy and destroy our fellowship with God. Satan has several thousand years experience with the human race, and he knows all too well how to manipulate our flesh. The trail of human tragedy reflects that after Satan's covert influences, many people often do give up. When they do, they return to their pre-salvation lifestyle, and to the habits that used to entrap them. And when that happens, the power is gone.

The power I have been alluding to is the power that Christ has, the power to be victorious over Satan. Remember though, and this IS important, while we can be VICTORIOUS like Jesus, we won't be PERFECT like Jesus. Not in this life anyway. I dare say most of us missed the mark of perfect shortly after reaching the age of accountability—that point in our life when we first knew right from wrong. But remember what Jesus told the woman caught in adultery? He said 'Go and sin no more.' He wouldn't tell her to do something she wasn't capable of doing.

"The other day, when Madame asked me to pray for her healing, I wasn't so much praying that God MIGHT heal her as I was taking authority over the evil that had been placed on her by the devil. To put it another way, David, if it's not good, it doesn't come from God. I know you would agree that Madame's heart attack didn't come from God. He can, and did, use the event for good. Her salvation is proof of that, and the Word tells us that much, but the heart attack came from Satan. 'The thief', that's Satan, 'came to steal, kill and destroy'; that's his occupation. But with God living inside us, specifically in the person of the Holy Ghost, we have His power resident within us as well. All we have to do is to learn how to employ that power and the victories in life are ours.

"Do you understand what I've said so far?" she paused to ask.

"I believe so, Trish, please continue."

"Okay, hang on to your hat then. If you've got the power of the almighty, eternal, all-powerful God resident within you, and the devil must obey God's authority, then you must likewise have the ability to scare the living daylights out of him. And here's the kicker: he must obey you just as he must obey God. If your mind is being attacked, that's a pretty good indication that you've got something the devil wants to destroy. Based on what you've told me, you've had two attacks right here in this office. Let's rebuke Satan's presence in here right now. Let's take authority over him and flat kick him out of here.

"In the name of Jesus Christ, Satan, we take authority over you right now in this place. We rebuke you and bind you from any further attack on David in this place. You are not welcome here, you have no authority here, and you must go. Leave this office, and the entire building, for that matter, now! Be gone! In the name of Jesus, YOU MUST GO!"

Trish's voice softened as she continued. "Now precious Jesus, we thank You for the authority over the evil one that You give us in Your name and we praise and thank You that what we have spoken is accomplished. Great is our God, mighty and holy and greatly to be praised. Honor and glory forever unto you, oh Lord, forever and ever. Amen."

As she prayed, Trish stood and joined me at the front of my desk. What a release I felt in my mind and spirit! She had taught me well, and had followed up that teaching with some practical application. I could now see what God had meant earlier in the day when He told me that "...her guidance would cause my spiritual growth". In just the span of a few short minutes I felt like leaping tall buildings in a single bound. Praise God!

Trish returned to the final hour of training with Jim and Ted. Jerry allowed me to leave early in order to check on my business mail at the post office and to terminate the postal box I had with them. After filling in a change of address and mail forwarding card I stopped by the photo shop to retrieve another carload of equipment and supplies. After all that, I arrived home in time to start a spaghetti dinner for two.

Let's see, one half pound of spaghetti noodles per army! Trish made one army; I made another. One pound should do it nicely, I thought. No, I'll cook two.

CHAPTER TWENTY-TWO

It wasn't so much that I had lost the skills or sensitivity required for seeking a wife. It wasn't even that I lost the art of being romantic. It was probably that I was a bit uncertain, somewhat unsure of myself; coupled with the fact that I was trying to make sure I remembered everything needed to provide a perfect evening. To be sure, I could whip up a mean plate of spaghetti. Whether from a jar or made from scratch, the sauce posed no problem and the pasta was easy enough to prepare. Any guy who, as a child, had stood in the kitchen and watched his mother cook as I many times had should be able to prepare such a simple meal with little or no difficulty. So what was my problem? I was uneasy and I just couldn't put my finger on why.

I did a quick check. The table was set exquisitely, starting with the tablecloth, made of imported white Belgian linen with a delicate embroidered border. Hardy white fall mums from the back yard, hastily cut and arranged, formed the centerpiece. Two tall, slender, pink candles with wicks trimmed to provide just the faintest amount of light, were stationed like soldiers on either side of the flowers. My best china graced each place setting, accompanied by the proper placement of required silverware. The serene flames of a three log fire reflected on the smooth marble hearth, and I dimmed the house lights to establish the best atmosphere possible. Yet in all this preparation, something was missing. For the second time in under a minute, I sat on the edge of the sofa, scratched my head and surveyed the scene. "What is it, Father? What's lacking?" There was no reply.

The phone rang. It was Trish. She was about to leave her apartment and would be arriving in less than twenty minutes. I felt like an awkward schoolboy at a dance with the class beauty, a girl who had quite unexpectedly captured his heart and, just as unexpectedly, awakened an interest in the opposite sex. Nervous? No, it went beyond nervous, but for the life of me I couldn't figure out why. We had been together so much of late, and enjoyed so many rich moments, not the least of which was our engagement. Maybe that was it. We were now really engaged and it had taken this long for the reality of it to hit me. It also might have been that I was apprehensive about the commitment I had made to her. Or maybe it was the realization that I was soon to have a wife. Although I didn't know how soon 'soon' meant, I was sure it was closer, through the grace of God, than I had previously envisioned.

The haunting feeling that something was still not right lingered. I stirred the sauce and checked the noodles; both were nearly ready so I lowered the heat. A sample taste of the sauce revealed it to be just right. A freshly prepared salad was in the refrigerator. All was ready. Actually, I had no reason to be so tense. Everything was going well. There were no chaotic or traumatic disasters like scorching the sauce or spilling the pasta. Though we had no specific plans for the evening, I was content, for the time being, to let the meal preparations fall into place. In the meantime I continued to fight off the uneasiness that pestered me. No matter how the evening turned out, as long as we were together, nothing else would matter.

"Spirit of uneasiness, torment me no more! In the name of Jesus Christ of Nazareth, I rebuke you. Leave me, and this house right now."

Wow! That felt good. I thought silently. *I wish I had known about that long ago. Lord Jesus, keep Your Spirit actively guiding me as I learn and grow in the truth that you reveal to me.*

I stood to look out the front window at the darkness of the outside. As I stared, trance-like, I felt captive to the anticipation of Trish's expected arrival. Within moments the blinding glare of a pair of bright headlights turning into my long, winding driveway, roused me to my senses. My Trish had arrived.

I opened the door before she knocked. "Hi Love," was all I could muster as I took in the beauty of her presence.

"Can I come in?" she asked, waking me from my blissful state.

"Of course, excuse me. Here's a key to the place, okay?"

"Thank you, but what do I need that for?" she inquired.

"I don't know. You may need it sooner or later. As the saying goes, 'mi casa es Tu casa.'"

As she stepped past me into the living room I noticed she carried a large brown cloth book bag that she placed on the sofa. I didn't pay much more attention to it other than I thought it made for a rather cumbersome purse.

"The spaghetti sauce smells great," she remarked, strolling back to the kitchen. "It smells even better the closer I get to the stove."

"Well, I'm nowhere near being a gourmet but I do like to cook. Tell me, will I have to step aside once we get married and relinquish control of the kitchen?" I teased.

"Heavens no. We'll share and share alike. My share will be the cooking. Your share will be the dishes and clean up," she teased back.

"Oh, it's starting already, is it?"

"What's starting?"

"You seem to be establishing your ground rules for marital bliss or an evening of wit. Take your pick," I replied.

Trish looked at me as she smiled. She too could tell we were off and running for an enjoyable evening together. "For right now the answer is wit but we do have something else to do tonight. Have you forgotten something?" she asked as she lifted the lid on the sauce.

"No! I thought so too at first, but now I believe everything is just right. The food is ready. The table is set. The candles are lit. What else could be missing?"

"How about some soft background music."

"That's it! I knew there was something I forgot. I stood in the living room and looked; I stood in the kitchen and looked; I stood in the dining room, and looked, but just couldn't determine what it was. You're right, we need a serenade of some soft gentle music." Quickly I readied a seven-inch tape reel of Montovani on the stereo, set the volume level low, and adjusted the tone for proper acoustics. "How's that?" I inquired.

"That's fine, David, I like Montovani. But there's something else you forgot." She slowly retraced her steps to the living room, purposely allowing me time to jog my memory. Soon she was in front of the sofa retrieving the bag she had placed there. "Think real hard, David. Did you forget what we were supposed to do here tonight, or did you have ulterior motives?"

I would have expected anything from her except those words. They jarred me deeply. "Trish! You've cut me to the quick. I have no ulterior motives. My love is pure before you and God. I promised you that. Why would you ask that?"

She could see her question was not received in the teasing manner she anticipated so she carried the bag over to me and set it on the easy chair, then wrapped her arms around me and said, "I'm sorry, David. Please forgive me. I didn't mean anything by my question. I shouldn't have tried to tease you about your forgetfulness. It's just that after you left the station this afternoon I needed to put some plans on your desk. When I went into your office I saw something that didn't look right. You see, if you remember, we're supposed to have a nice meal and then go over the studio equipment catalogs."

"You're right again," I admitted. "I left the equipment books on my desk, and I bet that's what's in the large bag you brought. Am I right?"

"Yes. Now without any more discussion...let's eat."

"There she goes again, folks," I playfully announced to an imaginary living room audience.

To say the least, the meal was as romantic and enjoyable as I had hoped. I caught myself looking at Trish's hand and the ring had I placed there just 48 hours earlier. "Has it settled in yet?" I asked.

"Has what settled in yet?"

"Being engaged."

She didn't answer right away. That caused me to get into a defensive mental posture, certain she was about to employ either extreme caution or levity. I was fairly certain it was the latter; after all I felt proud of the fact that I was getting to know how she operated.

"Naaaa! It's kind of old hat now."

I had anticipated her well. "I'm so glad the sparkle of the diamond lasted longer than the sparkle in your eye," I teased, throwing a crumpled napkin at her.

She smiled, caught the napkin in mid air, and rapidly fired it back. "I used to play softball rather well in college. I played shortstop on the statewide second-place girl's team a few years back. Don't think throwing things at me will be a useful tool in our married life."

I stood from the table and pushed my chair in, smiling just long enough to let her know I acknowledged her remark, then said, "Trish, all kidding aside, I'll never THROW anything at you. What I will do is GIVE you my love, care and understanding, forever."

Together we did the dishes and straightened the kitchen. I used the opportunity to show Trish where I kept the cooking utensils and how the cupboards were arranged. Then we went into the living room to sit before the fire and review the equipment catalogs. By eleven o'clock we had selected those items we felt would be necessary to build a functional Studio B. I got my electronic calculator from the junk drawer in the kitchen and started adding up the cost, totaling in the shipping and insurance fees as well. "Not to bad for an evening's work," I sounded.

"How much did it come to?" Trish asked, having moved to the fireplace and sat looking into the diminishing flames.

"Take a guess."

"Oh, maybe sixty-five hundred, give or take a hundred," she answered.

"Hey, not bad. Actually it's slightly less than sixty-four. That leaves us about thirty-six hundred for carpeting, furniture, track lighting and any other room modifications needed. I'll need your advice on that, Love, and I'll call in this order tomorrow morning as soon as they open up. I wonder how long it takes for delivery?"

"WJOH has dealt with that firm. They're in California. I suspect shipping time would be under two weeks," she offered.

"Well I don't know about you, but I'm getting tired, and you better get yourself home, too. Shall I get your coat?"

"Please do. David, it's been a very pleasant evening. The only thing we didn't do was make plans for tomorrow. Remember, we have the afternoon off."

"Let's do something really crazy for mid-September in the U.P.," I stated.

"I'm almost afraid to ask, but what might that be?"

"Listen, the weatherman said tomorrow would be mostly sunny, with highs in the upper fifties to near sixty. Let's have a picnic at the park, you know, where the acrobatic squirrels are. Okay?"

"That sounds great, David. Bring your Bible, and we can get a submarine sandwich at Papa ToJo's; they're the World's best. We can stop by my apartment and get the extras like Cokes, chips, blanket and whatever else we may need. Oh David, I can hardly wait! Thank you, Jesus. Thank you, Jesus! I'm saved! I'm happy, and I'm deeply in love!"

"Amen!" I added.

Sleep came quickly but so did the alarm. I could barely believe morning had arrived. I double-checked the clock to make sure it hadn't malfunctioned, or that it might be responding to restored power after an electrical outage. Like it or not, it was time to get up; the alarm hadn't lied. I believe it was a tie as to which thought crossed my slowly responding mind first—awareness of God or thoughts of Trish. "Father God, I love waking to thoughts of You. I ask You to be my first conscious thought each morning. I praise You and I greet You with thanksgiving and adoration. Spirit of the Most High God, empower this spirit-man within me to take charge of the day. I yield all my thoughts, words, deeds and emotions to You, Father, in expectation of how You will display yourself to me. I seek You now of my own free will and choosing. Your word instructs us to seek the Lord early in the morning. Lord, I believe this is early enough to qualify, and I do indeed seek You and Your guidance as I travel through the events of this day. In Jesus' name I pray. Amen."

Tuesday's work seemed to flow even better than the day before. Getting into a routine was undoubtedly the reason for that. Trish was on the air and I was already working some scripts for my remaining shows for the week. I kept looking at my watch, computing and waiting for the time in California

199

so I could phone in the equipment order. The catalog stipulated phone orders taken 7 a.m. to 7 p.m. California time. At ten I made the call and spent $6,384.79.

Just before noon I got ready for my time on the air. Trish prepared the studio while the news was on and then placed a note in my shirt pocket. As she turned to leave the studio I asked her to remain until I was into my program a few minutes. My confidence level had been elevated by successfully completing one show but certainly not to a point where I wanted to start without her right nearby. It appeared I didn't need her, but it was nice knowing she could bail me out if I got in over my head.

Once I got through my opening remarks and into the first musical selection she left the studio. After cueing up the next piece of music on the turntable I opened the mike and proceeded with my text. I was now well into the program. The script called for several back-to-back musical selections. While they were playing I opened Trish's note. That was a mistake. The first thing I read was, "I love you." I wanted to read on but yet a part of me kept going over that first line. It was like Christmas morning to an eight-year-old.

"The song is over David! You've got dead air! What's next?"

Trish's words jolted me back to reality. How much dead air had gone out, I wondered. She quickly ran the station ID cartridge, giving me time to regain my wits, and then stationed herself at my side as I continued with the next record.

"I think I made a boo-boo, didn't I Trish?"

She nodded in agreement, administering a stern look at me long enough to know I had just been reprimanded.

Checking the script, I got myself back on track while cueing up the next record. She stood by a few moments longer, knowing I needed her there until my nerves relaxed and I stopped hyperventilating. Tenderly, she wiped the perspiration from my forehead.

As the music played she leaned over my shoulder, picked up the note from the console and whispered in my ear, "It looks as though that was my fault. Is this what distracted you?"

I nodded.

"I didn't really expect you to open it up while you were on the air. All I wanted to do was let you know that I ordered our submarine sandwich and I'd be picking it up shortly. I'll be back here just about the time you're ready to go."

"That sounds great, Love. I'll be okay now. Go ahead."

Thank God, the rest of the show went without incident. Annette came into the studio a few minutes early and offered to finish the show but I declined her offer. I still needed every minute I could get in order to get more proficient. Soon my time-slot was over and I threw the switch to air the hourly satellite news service, picked up my materials and relinquished the chair to Annette.

Trish insisted on driving to the park for our autumn picnic. The weather had cooperated. The sky was blue with bunches of those fluffy white clouds drifting by on the breeze. The day reminded us of mid-May when spring fever strikes with incurable accuracy.

Trish turned onto her street and spotted something that made her flinch. As she maneuvered into her parking place she said, "Oh no! God, why today?"

"What's the matter, Love?" I asked, looking first at her, and then all around us, certain we were about to get hit.

"Frank's parked out front. He's waiting in his car for me. I wonder how he knew I'd be here now."

I could see the concern displayed on her face. She had gone from peaceful and happy to distressed. "What do you want to do? Whatever it is, I'm with you."

She started praying in tongues and didn't answer. She set the brake and turned off the ignition. "I'll take care of this!" she stated boldly while getting out of the car.

"Do you want me to go with you? Do you think he's got trouble in mind?" I asked, feeling helpless, yet knowing I needed to get involved somehow.

"Only if you want to meet him. Otherwise stay here. He's perfectly harmless."

I wasn't going to just sit in the car like a cowardly old man, but by the time we reached the front of Frank's car I had nearly changed my mind. I watched him carefully as he got out of his car and approached us. He extended his hand toward me and introduced himself. "Hi, I'm Frank Ivey, but you probably know that by now."

"Yes, and I'm David Post," I answered responding to his handshake.

He seemed to be sizing me up. I hoped it wasn't for a fight. Then he broke the momentary silence, saying, "I need to talk to Trish for just a few minutes in private, if you don't mind."

I turned my eyes to Trish who said, "It's okay, David. Here's my key. Can you get the stuff out of the apartment while I talk to Frank?"

"Are you sure?"

"Yes. Go ahead. It'll be okay," she tried to reassure me. It didn't.

Frank and Trish began their conversation while I slowly walked up the sidewalk to her apartment, praying softly as I did.

When I arrived in the kitchen I discovered she had enough stuff packed for a family reunion, not an intimate picnic for two. Wasn't that just like her? By the time I got it all packed into the trunk of her car, they were smiling cordially. Even with the smiles I still felt uneasy, like something was going to snap the tension in the air at any moment. I stayed alert. I kept praying, changing from English to tongues and back to English, glancing in their direction every so often.

With the picnic supplies neatly arranged to fit, I shut the trunk lid. As I did, their conversation appeared to be ending. They both approached me and my insides recoiled like an M-16 rifle. I sensed my defensive mechanisms taking charge. The space between us diminished, and it seemed like the north poles of two magnets being forced together. There was my fiancée and her ex-husband, smiling, both walking toward me. I wanted to run for my life but my legs wouldn't move.

"David," Trish spoke, "Frank and I have just had a very healthy chat about a few things. He's asked me to forgive him. I told him I already had. I've told him of our engagement and shown him the ring you gave me. He's genuinely happy for us. I just want you two to be friendly toward each other."

I looked intently at Frank's face. He was a handsome man. I could see why Trish fell in love with him, which likewise caused me to wonder momentarily why she would be attracted to me, much older and considerably less attractive. My words finally found order and filed out. "I can agree to that," was my first comment. "I have to be honest though, it is most uncomfortable for me right now. Frank, I extend my hand to you again in friendship but I will be relying on Jesus to sustain that friendship."

Frank took my hand, smiled, saying, "But David, you've got the easy part. You've got Trish. I had her and lost her. Living without her isn't easy."

"Frank," I said, not even knowing what would come out next. "Would you like to share a picnic lunch with us at Ridgemont Park?" The question surprised everyone, especially me. Even more surprising was Frank's answer.

"I'd like that, but I don't know if I should. Obviously you two have planned for a time together and a third wheel wasn't in those plans, I'm sure."

His words seemed sincere enough to me. I quickly glanced at Trish who seemed in agreement. "I would like you to join us, and I don't believe Trish would mind. We've got more than enough food. Please join us."

"Okay. Let me lock my car, or would you rather I follow you to the park?"

Trish quickly answered, "Why don't you follow us, Frank. I think that will work out the best."

In just under five minutes we were at the picnic area of the park, practically by ourselves. After we ate, a conversation started. Frank filled us in on what he was doing back up north. He related that things hadn't work out with the girl he had run away with, and he had caught her using drugs and stashing them in his car. The long and short of it all was that they had parted ways. He decided to come back up to the U.P. to get things straightened out with Trish but with our engagement he knew the best he could hope for was to ask for forgiveness and wish us the best of luck.

That's about where I joined the conversation. "Frank, I think you know luck really doesn't have much to do with anything. Luck might suit non-Christians, but you know where Trish is in that regard and I'm a born again Christian too."

"Yeah. I know. Some things never change. I've played Christian just about all my life. Up until the truth came out, that is."

Trish lowered her head.

Frank continued. "I knew all along Trish was a Christian. I knew she wouldn't do anything...maybe I shouldn't say any more...but...because I knew she was...well...a virgin, she was what I wanted for a wife. I played the game pretty well. I had her as my girlfriend and cheated. I had her as my fiancée and cheated. I even had her as my wife and cheated. Now that she's forgiven me I feel a lot better, but not very good about myself."

Trish and I sat, just listening, letting Frank get it out, but I could tell she was near tears. Trish, sitting next to me at the picnic table started rummaging through her purse for a package of tissues. I didn't know where the conversation would lead, nor how far or long Frank would continue his confession. All I did know was it seemed to be doing him good.

"My fooling everyone with my Christian act was like an academy award performance to me. I got so good at it that it just became easier and easier. Soon I was fooling myself. I was starting to believe I was a Christian. I couldn't help but believe it when I fooled Trish's parents enough to give us their blessing."

Trish had managed to regain her composure and was now holding my hand on top of the table. She turned her attention to Frank after looking at me for a moment. "Frank, have you ever really accepted Christ as savior, and I know you know what I'm talking about?"

The question took him by surprise. He looked up at the clouds drifting by and then back down at his folded hands on the table saying, "I don't even know. It's hard for me to tell the difference between what I've convinced myself of and what the real truth is. Maybe that's my punishment for trying to live such a deceitful life. What goes around comes around. You know, I deceived others; now I'm being deceived."

I wanted desperately to join the conversation but yet felt so detached from it that I thought it better to let it stay between Frank and Trish.

Frank continued, "I think maybe I need some psychiatric help. I know I need something."

"How about Jesus," Trish asked. "Are you ready to try him? I mean, really try Him?"

He looked at Trish and then me, distress and mental anguish etched on his face. He shrugged his shoulders. "I would like to say yes, but something won't let me. Maybe I'm just not ready to give it all up. Something inside of me won't let go of the lifestyle I've lived for so long. Maybe someday I'll get honest with God, but I don't think right now is the time for that."

For several moments no one spoke. Trish wiped another tear from her eye; Frank sniffled; and I just sat there, all of us waiting for someone to make the next move. No one made a sound. All that could be heard was the rustling yellow leaves of the birch trees as a gentle breeze nudged them. Several seagulls fluttered into a nearby clearing searching for scraps from previous picnics. The passing clouds caused the brilliant sunlight to dance on and off the table, intermittently warming us as we sat locked in silence.

Finally Trish spoke. "What do you want to do with the rest of your life, Frank?"

"I wish I knew," he replied, sighing. "I only know this: if I've lost you to David, then life's best gift to me is gone. Anything else will be second best. I really don't know if that's worth hanging around for."

That was about all my spirit could stand. "Frank, God has more than one plan for each of our lives. If He didn't as soon as we made our very first mistake it would be over for us. I believe God always has a plan 'B', or a way to fix what we, in our ineptness or rebellion, seem to mess up. I could share with you, as I have Trish, the mistakes I've made in my life, both before and after accepting Jesus as Savior. He isn't locked into just one plan for us because He knows the future and He knows what choices we're going to make each time we encounter a fork in the road.

"He knew all along what you were doing. It didn't surprise Him that you blew it with your marriage any more than it surprised Him that I went thirty years deliberately walking away from Christ and His light, and in the darkness of my own shadow. He wasn't even surprised when Adam and Eve messed up in the garden. He just had to activate plan 'B', and we know what that was—sending the promised Redeemer.

"But let's get back to you. If you're truly sorry for what you've done, as I believe you are, then you need to turn it and all the sins of your life over to Him. Ask him to forgive you, just as simply and earnestly as you asked Trish. He'll hear your prayer. Then ask Him to take control of your life, and give it direction and purpose. Then wait upon His healing and guidance."

I was startled by my own words. Did all of that come out of me? No, I silently replied in my spirit. It came from God Himself.

Frank just sat there, not responding verbally, but the look on his face revealed that the words had penetrated his spirit. I started praying softly as Trish took her turn being led by the Holy Spirit.

"God loves you, Frank. I'm concerned about your mental state right now. Let God have it. Give it all to Him. Promise me you'll do that. What David has just shared with you is true. There's just no purpose in life that satisfies or gives peace more than the purpose God gives. But first you have to accept it. And then by His power, live it."

"I'll promise you only that I'll think it over. I know what you're saying is true. I've heard just about all the same sermons you have, Trish. It just takes a commitment I don't feel ready to make yet. But I will think it over. Can I get back with the two of you later?"

"Sure," said Trish, "but here; here's the prayer line number at Lord of the Harvest Church – A PRAYER – 277-2937. There are people there who will pray with you and for you and help you get through the confusion and turmoil. Call them if you need someone and can't reach us."

He took the piece of paper with the phone number, saying nothing, smiled as he turned to leave the park. Trish and I started talking almost simultaneously, saying, "He's still having trouble making commitments."

I stopped while Trish continued, "There goes one very unhappy man. I'm really concerned about him. He sounded for a moment like he was contemplating suicide. Did you sense that, David?"

"Yes I did. When he said something to the effect that he didn't know if second-bests were worth hanging around for. Is that what you think he meant?"

"Uh-huh. David, let's war in the spirit for his soul, right now."

We did, praying as if Frank's life depended on us.

After Frank left and our prayer had finished we still had several hours together. We studied the Bible, discussed our future and prayed. It was rapidly becoming more than obvious to each of us that we were growing into an oneness. Our spirits were in union and we were helping each other grow and mature. The love we surmised and hoped existed only days before, was being confirmed and reconfirmed by the Lord with each event we encountered and during each moment we shared.

CHAPTER TWENTY-THREE

One of the many pleasant things about the northern part of Michigan is that crime, for the most part, is non-existent. Crime, like the criminal, is apparently affected by the substantially cooler temperatures this far north. The big-city homicides, rapes, burglaries and other vices are generally nothing more than distant newspaper headlines. And so it was with little thought of losing them that Trish and I left our picnic items on the table while we took a relaxing walk. We strolled along the nature and exercise trail, through the park and along the banks of the Big Trout River. The gravel path wound its way through a wooded area, over several grassy hills and then under Lighthouse Point Road to the jagged granite cliffs overlooking Lake Superior. The Park Service had built several wooden platforms that jutted out from the rocky edge nearly fifty feet above the crystal clear water. They provided an unobstructed view southeastward to L'Anse, and directly north as far as the eye could see along the eastern shore of the beautiful Keweenaw Peninsula.

We stood on the platform for nearly an hour, saying little, but loving much. I can't say for certain what thoughts crossed Trish's mind but I can relate what went through mine. First, there was the vastness of Lake Superior, stretching from Duluth, Minnesota, to Sault Ste. Marie, Ontario. Its great expanse of miles and countless gallons of water exemplified the greatness of its Creator, a Creator who had scooped out its bed with His hand and had filled it by His spoken word. The clarity of the water caused me to ponder the purity and righteousness of Jesus. Righteousness applied to me and to all who believe on Him. The blue of the water merged with the blue of the horizon, which typified an endlessness that hinted of the eternal existence of God. The repetitive onslaught of crashing white-capped waves had, over the expanse of time, worn the once-jagged rocks beneath us into smooth boulders, bringing to mind the limitless power of God. The beauty of the wooded shoreline nearly equaled the beauty of my Love standing beside me. And lastly, the sparkle of the sun, dancing and jumping from wave to wave, duplicated the glistening diamond engagement ring she wore, symbolizing our promised love. In all of this, the gratitude of my heart, mind and spirit refused to be limited to words. I held her tightly, expressing my affection with a kiss.

The evening's setting sun, slowly changing from orange to red, to muted violet, reminded us of our mortality, and that we were restricted to the earthly confines of time and space. Time—the daylight was coming to an end.

Space—we needed to return to the park and gather our things. The relentless gnawing of time upon our special afternoon had to be reckoned with, but not without making some very important headway in our personal plans.

Before leaving the platform I announced, "Trish, I'm ready to marry you."

She turned her gaze from some deep, infinite place on the horizon to look just as deeply into my eyes. She seemed to silently acknowledge that there was a love flowing between us that simply couldn't be denied or restricted much longer. "I agree, David. Let's set a date."

We began a slow walk back to the picnic area, which gave us time to discuss the many things that needed to be addressed. There was her apartment and moving her things to my house. There was the blood test and the ceremony. We needed to let her parents know. That, we decided, should be done soon, seeing as how they didn't know much about me and our plans. We discussed again our age difference and the desire for children. All of these things would hinge upon the timing of our marriage. We knew we might run into a certain amount of concern from Trish's parents and others too, who would consider my age and the lack of a long engagement as obstacles to a successful, life long marriage. We would just have to convince them of our firm belief that this love was ordained of God. We had already vowed to each other a promise of obedience to the Spirit of God; that part was now firmly established. As long as we stood sure and unwavering with Him, He would stand with us.

When we arrived back at the picnic area we started packing to go. As we stood by the trunk of Trish's car, the conversation continued.

"I think it would be nice," Trish spoke, "if Pastor Glen married us at the station, seeing that's where we came to know each other."

"That's a wonderful idea!" I responded excitedly. "But how about doing one better than that? What do you say to having the wedding performed live over the air?"

The suggestion must have triggered a myriad of thoughts. The reflective look on her face, coupled with the delay in her answer were proof of that. "I'm not too sure about that," she eventually reasoned. "Give me some time to work that through. Okay?" she asked.

"Sure, love. It was just a thought, but wouldn't be nice to share our marriage ceremony with all the people listening, rather than a few at the station? Think of the couples, young couples, those who are anticipating their own marriages, who might be leaning toward a civil ceremony instead of standing before GOD and man to make that important commitment. We have an opportunity to encourage or sway others to make their wedding more than a ritual with a legal document to establish joint housekeeping."

"That may be true, but most of our listening audience are already Christian; they're probably not even contemplating a secular marriage. No doubt what they are planning are traditional church weddings," Trish reasoned.

I had to admit all she said rang of truth. Yet I couldn't help thinking there just might be one couple, influenced by the airing of our marriage vows, and thus persuaded to involve God in their plans. "Trish, I could be wrong, but give it some serious thought. Our Christian example, like we spoke about the other night, might be just the thing some couple might need. And too, think of it this way, our wedding would certainly be unique when compared to the, quote, standard practices. What could be more exciting than having our own...special...meeting in the air?"

I could tell Trish was allowing all of that to soak in since she said nothing. We were in her car and on our way back to town before she said a word, changing the topic slightly as she did so. "What about a honeymoon? Where would you like to go? Or are things at the station too demanding for us to break away for awhile, assuming we were to get married in the very near future?"

Pondering all the intricacies her question raised, I delicately answered. "I hadn't really thought about a honeymoon. Forgive me for that. You would have never asked that question without something specific in mind. Am I right, do you have something in mind? Or should we pick a date first to see how that fits the schedule first, before we make any specific itinerary?"

She answered right as we reached her apartment. "My desires aren't that important. It's what's best for us together and for the station too."

"That's where you're wrong, Dear," I continued as we unpacked the car and went up the sidewalk. "We should have a marriage, and that includes the ceremony and honeymoon, that will not only solidify our love and commitment to each other, but be all that you ever dreamed of, yet maybe never realized with Frank. Maybe that's too blunt; I don't know. I'm just speaking what's in my heart. Your desires are my desires. You're just too important to me; how can your dreams not be important to me as well? Tell me, what in your wildest and grandiose dreams would be your idea of a perfect honeymoon?"

Her answer was very simple yet specific: "A trip around Lake Superior."

"You mean...all of Lake Superior?" I asked, astounded not by the simplicity of her desire, but by the vastness of the Lake.

"Uh-huh," she shyly responded, "All of it."

"Well, I've got only one thing to say to that—no make that two. One, your wish is my command, Love. And secondly, we'd better pick a date before the snow starts flying or we'll have to wait until next summer. Even if we left today we'd run the risk of getting snowed in somewhere."

Trish smiled coyly and said, "Now wouldn't that be nice and cozy. I kind of like the thought of just you and me, snowed in for...oh, say...six or seven months."

"I think you're beginning to sound like a romance novel. Let's get back to reality—we do have a radio station to operate. Unless we're otherwise able, we should plan a honeymoon of no longer than a week; less if possible. Wouldn't you agree, given the circumstances?"

"I would, David, but let me amuse myself with the 'grandiose', as you put it. Okay?"

"You got it! Now let's get the rest of this stuff unpacked; then you can get me back to the station so I can get my car and drive home. I think an early-to-bed situation tonight would be most beneficial to this old body."

Time seemed to shift into high gear as we raced through the end of September and into October. The days were filled with a flurry of activity and planning. The daily work at the station became more like routine; not with spiritual insensitivity, but rather in the repetitiveness of certain tasks. Daily Trish and I sought the Lord's guidance in our wedding plans, specifically in determining the date. We called her parents to let them know of our plans. Their voices over the phone revealed the surprise we expected, but what we didn't anticipate was their desire to visit with us on the weekend of October 17th.

In the meantime, the studio B equipment started arriving, piece by piece. Each unit was unpacked, tested and set in its place in the developing studio. Trish and Annette were working hard in their off-the-air times with carpet installers, lighting consultants, and furniture store sales people getting those things accomplished. I took the responsibility for getting a contractor to satisfy our electrical needs.

The many accomplishments of the FM crew during the first two weeks of October were astounding. First, the training program had almost magically made air personalities of all of us novices. Even I had gotten proficient enough that I didn't need Trish or Annette with me at the beginning of my show. Our combined efforts had nearly finished studio B, with the exception of returning for replacement one defective microphone. Jerry had gotten the AM side back on the air. Mr. G. had completed the purchase of the television land. Trish and I had diligently sought the Lord and arrived at an October 25th wedding date. And lastly, we awaited a phone call from her parents who were arriving sometime during the day for their visit and for us to meet.

Trish had assured me time and time again that there was nothing to worry about. She tried desperately to set me at ease about their visit. Although I knew there was no reason to worry, I just figured I would anyway.

One thing that hadn't happened during this time was that we hadn't heard again from Frank, although we continued to pray for him and his salvation whenever his name came up. We didn't even know if he was still in the U.P. or if he had returned down state. All we did know, based on our picnic encounter, was that he desperately needed our prayers.

Our wedding plans got progressively more intense as we neared our special day. One morning we met for prayer at the church and agreed to continue this new tradition of early-morning prayer through the remainder of our engagement. It meant a sacrifice of about an hour's sleep, but Proverbs 8:17 says, "...and those that seek me early shall find me" prompted us to dedicate that time of the day to prayer, to seek Him and His will.

In the past several weeks, Pastor Glen had taught us that God shows up where there is sacrifice to Him. Too, we had been taught that God desires obedience more than sacrifice. We believed if we could make a morning sacrifice of prayer and praise unto Him, in obedience to the prompting of the Holy Spirit, He would be pleased and honor our diligent search for Him.

I received nearly immediate confirmation to one of my morning prayers as peace about meeting Trish's parents replaced nearly two weeks of apprehension. The Lord knew I had no intentions of putting on a pretense or doing some kind of soft shoe shuffle, as Frank had, in an attempt to get them to like me, or put them at ease about our plans. My desire was to be able to address any questions or concern they might have about our recent dating and engagement. I could understand if they had concern; they and their daughter had been deceived before and had suffered tremendous grief and heartache. This time, though, it would be different. I knew that. Trish knew that. God knew that. It was now my wish to make sure her parents knew that.

Because it was Friday, Trish and I were fasting through breakfast and lunch. Instead of rushing off to a restaurant at the completion of my noon show, we went for a walk instead. The air had turned significantly colder. Although the calendar said mid-October, the temperatures insisted it was November. So did the sky and wind, flinging a flurry of tiny snowflakes all around us. Although they melted as they hit the ground, their pristine presence promised winter's eventual onslaught. Our winter coats proved inadequate in guarding us against the wind off the lake, broad-siding us as we walked. Trish prayed aloud in tongues while I prayed silently, listening as I did to her beautiful prayer language, hoping God would give me the interpretation. He didn't. I could only guess that whatever she had prayed, it was between her and God.

After walking for about twenty minutes we turned around, starting our return trek to the station. As we did she paused in her prayer to ask, "Are you still apprehensive about meeting my parents?"

"I was earlier in the week, but not now. There was a time when I was concerned that they might be close-minded about us and our age difference, and our lack of knowing each other for very long. All of that has subsided now. What they say or how they react has little to do with us in the long run. It's not going to change my feelings or love for you and I know you well enough to say it won't change you either. All I'm going to do is show them the real me. I'll relate what's transpired in our lives to get us to the point of marriage, and let God in His wisdom do the rest. If they like me, though that's not my objective, so much the better. If they are hesitant, and that's a real possibility, I'll just consider that an expression of their love and concern for their daughter—their once deeply-hurt daughter. There is, however, one area that still concerns me just a little. Trish, do you think I should ask them for permission to marry you, after all, I am in my forties."

"I believe that would be an appropriate thing to do. I know Daddy, and he would be most proud if you did, and may even expect it. He will more than likely use the opportunity to express himself more than he might if you didn't ask."

Then Trish smiled at me, adjusted her collar to block the wind, and added, "Don't worry, David, they'll just love you. I know they will. I'm not hurting any more; they'll be able to see that."

"Did you have anything special planned for their visit, or are we going to let them tell us what they want to do?"

"Oh, don't worry about that either. They've been up here a number of times and they'll tell us where they want to go or what they want to do. We don't need to make any special plans."

When we arrived back at the station, the snowflakes changed back into rain. The afternoon went fast and the work in Studio B included making some promotional tapes for the upcoming Thanksgiving and Christmas specials. With that finished, I went to my office to read some of yesterday's still unanswered listener letters.

Trish was still working in Studio B when Susan came across the intercom, "David, is Trish there? Her father is on line seven—oh."

I quickly tensed up, then took control of my emotions, and answered Susan's inquiry. "I'll take the call, Susan; she's in Studio B. I'll get her in a moment."

Picking up the receiver, I punched the 70-button. I didn't really know what I was going to say. "Hello, Mr. Griffin? This is David Post. Trish is in the studio making a tape. She'll be done in a moment and I'll get her for you. Are you in town now?"

"Hi, David. Yes, we're at Trish's apartment. We let ourselves in with a key we had. Mom...I mean Ruth...Trish's mother, that is – ahhh, is soaking in the tub trying to unwind from the trip so I thought I would let Trish know we arrived safe and sound."

I studied the character and quality of his voice, knowing it belonged to a loving father, kind man, and true Christian Brother. What I couldn't tell was whether he was evaluating me, and if so, how I was doing. "If you can hold the phone for just a moment I'll see if she can take your call. Okay Mr. Griffin?"

"Sure David. But please, call me Ed. Too bad about the Tigers this year, huh?"

"Well, to be honest with you, I know Trish followed them through the end of the season when they lost to Boston, but I've been just too busy to follow them the way I usually do. I'll be right back Ed."

I made a "cut" sign across my throat to Trish through the window then held my hand up to the side of my head indicating a phone call was waiting for her. She acknowledged and I returned to my office to continue my opening conversation with her father.

"Trish will be here any moment. How was the trip up, sir?" I asked, attempting to get the dialogue resumed.

"It was kind of tiring this time. We encountered some dense fog at the Mackinac Bridge. It was closed for just short of two hours. Then there was rain and fog again at Newberry, but we were through that in about fifteen minutes. Other than that, the trip wasn't too bad. Tell me, in Trish's last email she said you two were going to get married on the 25th; is that still the plan?"

"Yes, sir. Trish said she would like a honeymoon around Lake Superior and the only way we can get that in this year is to get married soon, before winter gets a hold on this area. We both agreed that waiting until next spring was not what God had spoken to each of us in our spirits."

"Now don't get me wrong, David. I just have a feeling that things are right this time for our daughter. But please forgive me if I'm a little gun-shy. Seeing as how you broached the subject of God, are you sure of your Christianity? Tell me what Christ means to you."

Trish had entered the office and was making a joking gesture about taking the phone out of my hand so I needed to end the conversation, even though I desired it to continue.

"Well, sir, Trish is here now and she is chomping at the bit to talk to you so why don't I answer that question when we meet?"

There was a pause before he replied, "Okay, but I'll bet you have the right answers. Call it a spiritual hunch. Go ahead, put Trish on."

The two of them talked for about ten minutes. Actually it appeared that Ed did all the talking, apparently mostly questions, because Trish responded with little more than "Yes Daddy" and "No Daddy" answers. When the one-sided conversation was over and the receiver back in its place, I asked, "That was certainly an interesting conversation from what I could determine. Was he giving you the fatherly third degree?"

"As a matter of fact he was. He couldn't seem to wait to find out about you first hand. He wanted all the answers before the two of you meet. He's just trying to make sure I know what I'm doing. He's always been that way, looking out for all the family members, concerned about their welfare more than his own. He also wanted to know if we were financially okay. There again, he's just always looked out for the two of us kids."

"Well, Love, we have a few more hours to work, then we can talk to them face to face. How are your shows for next week coming along?" I asked.

Trish thumbed through her schedule to give me a recap of the plans. "Monday's and Tuesday's shows are done—scripted and music pulled. Wednesday I'm having the pastor of Houghton's Church of God's Salvation in for an interview and call-in talk show. That'll start at about nine o'clock and run at least two hours. The main topic of discussion will be, let's see, yes, here it is, 'Are We Guilty of Taking God's Forgiveness for Granted'. I'll also air some of the more traditional hymns during that time. His congregation isn't Pentecostal so Pastor Thomms and I agreed to use the better-known hymns of the past during the time he's going to be on the show.

"The Thursday and Friday shows are still up in the air. Trust me, no pun intended. I've kind of been concentrating most of my attention on producing the promos for the upcoming seasonal events. That brings you up to date, David."

"Fine. I might need your help with ideas for a few other things that Jerry's suggested, specifically for the weekend staff to do. Let me know if you have some free time this afternoon or Monday, okay?"

Trish acknowledged my question and returned to Studio B. I took a stroll down the hall to check the mail and was on my way to the break room for a snack when I remembered our fasting. My first thought was that the afternoon's work would go much quicker with a Snicker's bar inside me but it really seemed trivial after my spirit took charge and rebuked my flesh.

Jerry stepped in for some small talk and then was soon on his way to Marquette to pick up some legal paperwork for Mr. G. Susan had a dental appointment so she switched the incoming calls to my office. Jimmy stopped in with an armful of requested albums and CDs, and there were still over twenty letters that needed my reply. That's how the remainder of the afternoon went.

Trish walked into my office about five minutes to four. "I thought you would be on your way home by now," I stated, looking at my watch. "It seems like you've been working ten or more hours a day since returning to WPFH. With your folks in town I thought you might want to leave early."

She wrapped her arms around me, kissed me gently, and said, "I was just on my way out. What time will you be over tonight so I can plan accordingly? I'm thinking Mom and Dad will just want to eat something at my apartment. They usually do after the trip up."

"I'm going home in about fifteen minutes. Give me at least an hour to get myself fed and shaved; maybe between 5:30 and 6:00. Is that okay, Dear?"

"Sure. See you then."

I watched her leave my office. October 25th seemed an eternity away.

CHAPTER TWENTY-FOUR

Arriving at Trish's apartment just before six o'clock, I found the three of them finishing their supper. Trish let me in and I entered the kitchen confidently. Ed greeted me with a firm handshake followed by a sincere hug.

"We've been discussing you as you might have guessed," he announced as he introduced himself. "Care to join us for coffee and dessert?"

"That sounds good to me, sir. Thank you. If you were discussing me you sure picked a boring subject. Maybe a recap of what's been discussed is in order so I might correct any errors or exaggerations Trish may have told you."

After Trish did the formal introductions, she served each of us a slice of peach pie. Ed and Ruth seemed as at ease with meeting me as I did with meeting them. They seemed to use the small talk of our conversation as a gleaning process, searching for information in a tactful yet cordial manner. Their inquisitiveness didn't bother me and I used the opportunity to learn about them as well. Soon Ed broke through the small talk by broaching the marriage subject.

"So the 25th is the day you two have picked, huh?"

I waited for Trish to answer even though Ed was looking at me. "Yes, Daddy. We're confident that's what God wants for us. I hope you don't have any problems with that. If you do we want to work through them so you will be as confident about it as we are."

"Good Lord!" I thought nearly out loud. "I hope he doesn't think her answer too confrontational. Then I put my tense nerves at ease by reassuring myself that Trish should know how to reply to her Dad's line of questioning.

Ed glanced back at me as he responded, "I don't have any problems with the date; it's just that Ruth and I looking for the assurance that you two are positive about this big step. We're confident both of you know about this commitment you're about to make as well as your love for each other. We also know that no couple, including you two, can predict the future. As Christians we are aware that a life-long marriage, free from trouble, is not the desire of Satan. As in our case, it takes a strong reliance on God to see you through those demonic attacks as well as keeping your promise to stick by each other with love and respect. Ruth wouldn't come out with it as boldly as I will, David, but we've been lied to before. We just want to know something about you and your commitment—considering the hurt Trish went through the first time. Do you understand that?"

"Yes, I can understand that, and I would be disappointed if you weren't concerned enough for your daughter's happiness to check me out. I know you probably did with Frank too; the fact that he was living a lie and deceived everyone so well is no reflection on anyone's ability or inability to discern a spirit of deception. Knowing all the right things to say and then saying them at the right time with an artificial sincerity can't be all that difficult to do. But you see, I don't guess, surmise, or even think I love your daughter; I know it. I know it not only in my heart and mind but I know it in my spirit. I'm not looking for a wife to get me through my youth; as you can see I'm well past that stage in my life. Trish and I are one in spirit already. That oneness came from and was confirmed by God in so many ways that it just can't be denied. Maybe she's already told you some of them.

"Ed, I think you asked me a couple of questions over the phone that didn't get answered. I'd like to answer them for you now so that Ruth can hear my answers. Without trying to be presumptuous about what words you might want to hear, I will answer as the Spirit of God leads me, trusting Him not only to give me the appropriate words to convey my thoughts, but to allow your spirit to hear the truth that I try to relate.

"I believe your first question was '...are you sure of your Christianity?' If you had asked me that question just a couple of months ago the answer would have been the same but with much weaker conviction. And if you had asked for proof, I would have been hard pressed to come up with any. You see, although I accepted God's plan of salvation nearly nine years ago, I remained a spiritual infant for most of the time since. My Christian walk was little more than trying to live as well disciplined a life as I could, reading the Bible frequently but many times fruitlessly, and of course regular church attendance. To be sure, my faith was real and so was the conversion that brought it about, but the fruit was scarce, if you can understand what I'm saying. But now that I'm working with all the fine Christians at the station and attending Lord of the Harvest Church— and of course being under the nourishing guidance of Trish—I've experienced spiritual growth that not only astounds me but prompts me, no, drives me to seek a deeper relationship with Christ. It was shortly after joining the staff at the station and coming to know Trish, Jerry and some of the others that I received the baptism in the Holy Ghost. Needless to say that baptism resulted in an awareness of spiritual truth that only the Holy Spirit can provide.

"I know that's a rather long answer. But unless I shared all of that with you, I might not have completely answered your question. And too, I might not have explained where I am in my Christianity. While I hope my answer is adequate to you, its much more important that you see your daughter's trust in my Christian walk, for it's been primarily through her help that I'm even able to evaluate where I stand with Christ."

Ruth responded nearly as soon as I finished. "David, I don't believe there are any right or wrong answers that Ed and I are looking for. It's not so much a verbal evaluation but rather a spiritual evaluation that's taking place here. We certainly don't want you to think we've come up here to give you some kind of litmus test. For that matter, we don't want you to think our questions and your answers as being some kind of standard by which we measure whether we will or won't be happy with you as a son-in-law.

"We know Trish has not only grown spiritually through her past experiences but we also know she's not an impulse kind of person. She hasn't just been divorced and she isn't just grabbing the first man that comes along. What she is doing is making a very important decision for the second time. Yes, we were all fooled by Frank; we may have been too involved in Trish's life at the time, and Frank may have felt it necessary to lie to get past us to get what he wanted. We won't make that mistake with you. You two are not required to give us some high and lofty reason for why you should get married. All Ed and I want to know is that you are sure."

Ed was about ready to start speaking as Trish jumped in the conversation. "Mom, Daddy, Frank is a part of my past but he's not a part of my present nor my future. The only space he occupies, beside two legal documents, is a part of my prayer life. This man, has pledged to me his love, care, understanding and support. He has asked me to marry him and I've agreed. He's the one I want to spend the rest of my life with. If you've ever experienced a miracle, and I know you have; if you've ever experienced and known the moving of God in your life, and I know you have; then allow me to tell you that David has been my miracle from God."

For a moment there was silence, as though everyone was digesting Trish's last words. Ruth cut each of us another piece of pie while Trish poured more coffee. Ed broke the silence and continued the conversation, asking, "The other question I had for you this afternoon was 'What Christ means to you?' I think you've answered that pretty well. I don't see you two getting married and then dropping out of your spiritual life. I'm convinced Christ means too much to the two of you, both personally and corporately in church membership. We've been to Lord of the Harvest with Trish before; we know as long as you continue there you'll grow under Pastor Hershey's shepherding. That's a great pastor and a great body of believers."

It was Ruth's turn again. "David," she began, "we had a long conversation during dinner about you two and of course your age difference. That, in and of itself, doesn't bother Ed or me a great deal, but your ages do cause us concern from the perspective of children. Trish said you both agreed to have children if God so blessed. I think that's wonderful. We can't have enough grandchildren; we already have three from Trish's brother's marriage. She also related that you are going to ask God to grant you children right away. That too, I think is great. But what I'm concerned about is the far-distant future. If Jesus doesn't return for the Church for another twenty years or more, are you prepared, that is, have you discussed how that age difference will be dealt with at that point in your lives?"

I glanced quickly at Trish, smiled, and proceeded to share with Ruth things our past discussions had revealed. "I have just recently turned 44, Ruth, and of course Trish will soon be 34. That ten-year difference right now is kind of a blessing because Trish knows she can trust and lean on my maturity more securely than she could trust someone nearer her own age. Of course the benefit for me, and I'm not trying to be funny, is that having a young bride makes me feel much younger. But at the heart of your question, which is a valid question, is the fact that I will always be ten years older. Trish will never catch up with me in age, and of course I will not slow down for her, but we are equally yoked in spirit. That's why when this discussion first started I said that she and I are already one spirit. By saying that I don't want you to get any wrong ideas. First we are pure before God. We've pledged that and have held to that. Secondly, I don't want you to think I'm on some spiritual ego trip. I have a lot, and I do mean a lot of growing and maturing to do as Trish says, in 'my spirit-man'. She has a tremendous jump on me in that area but I fully intend to catch up and assume my biblical position as head of the family. Trish and I will know when I get to that point; until then she and I will continue, as God has directed us, to help each other grow. Ruth, that growth is the ultimate answer to your question. Growth comes about by actions taken during the course of time. As Trish and I grow, we cannot encounter age difference difficulties that cannot be overcome by the One who confirmed in the first place that we should be together." Pausing just long enough to draw a good deep breath, I added gently, "I hope what I've said will put that issue to rest for you. It has for us."

Ruth reached across the table, lightly placing her hand on mine, and with a soft, reassuring voice, replied, "This time I think Trish has found every bit as good a man as I have. I'm not concerned about anything anymore. It's really kind of ironic. We knew Frank for a long, long time but still we didn't know him. He and Trish had a long engagement, but yet it didn't work. We've just met you and it seems we know you very well. Your engagement will be quite short, in comparison to Trish's first, yet I know your marriage will last. I don't have any doubt but that by your perseverance and by the grace of God, any obstacle including age will be successfully overcome. What do you say, Dad?"

Ed finished his bite of pie, wiped his mouth, nodded in agreement and said, "I couldn't agree more. David, I like you a lot already. Trish, Honey, I think you've got a winner. Now, can I be a pig and have that last piece of pie?"

Later, we went into the living room to catch the final few innings of the World Series game but found it was being rain delayed so we just relaxed and chatted about the wedding plans. Trish and I filled her parents in on a few preliminary plans. They advised us they would return down state on Sunday and be back up in time for the wedding, maybe a day before, if possible. Before I left for the night, I invited everyone to my house for lunch and a stroll through the woods tomorrow. They agreed, and I said my goodnight.

Trish walked with me out to the car. The air had gotten cold but the sky was clear and the stars brilliant. I embraced her for several minutes and then told her that my love for her was deepening beyond any of my pre-conceived expectations. She remained silent. Except for her breathing she made no movement, apparently content to remain in my arms till the sun came up, if that were possible. Of course it wasn't.

"My lovely Trish, if it gets any better than this I don't know if I can stand it. Is it possible, really possible, for God to bless us so much that humanly speaking, we can hardly restrain the joy?"

"He does love us, David. Everything we know about the extent of God's love was evidenced by His Son's sacrifice on the cross. Every other blessing, including these that we now share and cherish so dearly, pale into insignificance when compared to that exhibition of God's love. To answer your question, yes, God blesses, and I don't think He blesses half way or with mediocrity. It's my belief, He goes all out."

"Do you think your parents are fully convinced of our Love?" I asked her.

"I really have no reason to doubt what they said this evening. I've never seen my parents be anything but straight shooters. They've never said one thing and meant another. There have been times when they've told me they were not in agreement with me but I have no reason to think anything other than what they said tonight is true. They genuinely like you, but then I told you they would. Didn't I?"

"Yes you did. I didn't feel uneasy or nervous with them. I certainly hope they didn't get offended, but it just felt natural to call them by their first names."

"I think that was a plus. If you had come off too stuffed shirt, they may have had some apprehension about your sincerity. But they saw the real you, the guy I'm going to marry and spend the rest of my life with. You're being at ease with them was probably just what they were looking for."

"Well I'm going to get home now Love. You bring them over about eleven o'clock. I'll have my laundry and house work done by then. We'll have a salad and sandwich lunch then enjoy a slow walk in the woods. Too bad all the leaves are gone. Oh well, they've probably seen the autumn foliage up here before."

"Yes they have, Love. You get going now before I fall asleep in your arms."

"Soon you'll be able to; now isn't that a pleasant thought to end the day on? Be blessed with a restful, peaceful night's sleep, in Jesus' name. Amen."

I was up before the sun getting the laundry started, taking the time between loads for prayer and Bible study. After consuming both the entire book of Ephesians and a pot of coffee, I started the house chores. It was amazing how I had gotten so busy of late to clutter up a house the size of mine by myself, but I had. I put away the vacuum cleaner and made my list for a quick trip to the grocery store. It was nearly ten thirty by the time I got back, making the lunch preparations as hurriedly as I could.

The table was all arranged as Trish and her parents arrived. Letting them in I excused myself to shower and change. When I returned I saw Ed standing in the living room looking at my large grouping of framed enlargements.

Catching sight of me out of the corner of his eye he said, "David, I like all these photos but this little bronze plaque really captivates me. Where did you get it, and what does it say?"

"I'm glad you like it, it's one of my favorite memorabilia from my Air Force travels. I got that from a very dear friend while stationed in Mississippi. He was a much older gentleman, I would guess about his late seventies and had been a merchant marine during World War II. At any rate, my Biloxi

Grandpa, as I affectionately called him, picked that up on one of his many trips to India. So to answer the first part of your question; it originally came from India. To answer the second part of your question, I do not know how to speak, read or write the Indian language, but based upon what my Biloxi Grandpa told me, it reads, 'Each victory makes us that much stronger. Each defeat makes us that much more determined.'"

Ed smiled as he turned to the plaque again saying, "That's a very impressive truth, isn't it?"

Soon lunch was over and we strolled the woods of my back yard. We came upon a deer that could see us but couldn't get our scent because of the wind direction. Finally, as we slowly approached to within about thirty feet of the deer, it barked and skittishly ran deeper into the woods. Startled by the unusual sound of a deer's bark she apparently had never heard before, Ruth jumped backwards landing off the path and into some mud. Ed and I helped her back on the path with only the loss of one shoe, held tightly by the sucking mud. Trish laughed so hard she could barely walk which caused the rest of us to join in. Using a stick I got the shoe out but it was beyond usefulness for the time being, so we retraced our steps to the house. Once she regained her composure, Ruth laughed nearly all the way back, using Ed's shoulder as a temporary crutch. I promised her I would never make her walk through my woods again.

"Nonsense!" she said loudly, still laughing intermittently. "Next time I'll bark back!"

Trish kept laughing, trying to respond. Finally she managed to get what she wanted to say out so we could understand her. "Yeah Mom! You might what to make her give you a BUCK for the shoe!"

"Trish," I reprimanded. "You're folks will think you get that sorry excuse for wit from me. They'll let me marry you but might make me give them some DOE first."

Ed looked back at me, nearly dropping Ruth, and said, "Now that's enough, you two. Straighten up or I'll TAN your HIDES."

"Isn't this a beautiful and enjoyable family time?" Ruth asked.

Everyone agreed.

CHAPTER TWENTY-FIVE

The four of us spent the remainder of the afternoon and into the early evening sorting through and making wedding plans. For my part, I spent most of the time taking candid pictures while nonchalantly nodding in agreement to all that Trish and her mother decided. Ed fell asleep in the living room easy chair which, I had been assured, was his normal Saturday after-lunch activity. I felt good inside about how our first two meetings had gone, and felt even better knowing that Ed could feel so at ease in my home to take an after lunch snooze.

Soon the constant clicking, flashing and winder motor noises of my camera started annoying Trish. I found myself the recipient of her chastening as she gave me specific instructions to put the camera away. That was a side of her I hadn't previously seen and I was unsure how to deal with it.

"Please David!" she insisted. "Put the camera away and help us with some of these details..." She had nearly finished the sentence when she looked up at me from the table. Seeing my perplexed expression she changed her mind, imploring, "I'm sorry Love. That wasn't very fair of me was it?" She quickly stood up from the dining room table, wrapped her arms around me and placed her head against my chest. "Forgive me," she entreated. "I just got too wrapped up in all these silly plans and forgot who is the reason for those plans."

"That's okay Dear. I've taken far too many pictures anyway. This has just been a super time for me, with meeting your folks and all; I just wanted a record of it. You don't need to ask me to forgive you. I was the one that was being inconsiderate."

Ruth had gone to the kitchen, taking our three empty coffee cups with her. Upon returning she said, "That's the kind of response to conflict, or tension, that Ed and I have employed over the years. You ask Trish; I'm sure she can remember. Although Ed and I have had some differing opinions on things, we've always worked them out with kindness, compassion and understanding. What you two just did is the only viable way to work things out so that a marriage remains strong and void of turmoil and hurt.

"I realize that that might have been just a minor thing but rest assured, there's rougher ones on the way. The method you agree to employ at the outset, as to how you maneuver through troubles, is the method you'll employ automatically once you've discovered how well it works. Now, I guess it's my turn to apologize. Listen to me talking like I'm instructing two teenagers. I'm sorry, I didn't mean to preach, or for that matter David, sound like a meddling Mother-in-law."

"No offense taken Ruth. We may not be children, but good advice is good advice and always worth listening to no matter what one's age is. I remember something I once heard a preacher say, 'don't get marital advice from someone who's been divorced; get it from someone who's had a successful marriage.' That just makes a whole lot of sense to me. You and Ed certainly meet the requirements."

"You and Trish will have a successful marriage too David. I just know that. Now, Trish Honey, maybe you ought to wake up Dad so we can get back to your apartment. Will we see you at church tomorrow David?"

"Yes. I'll meet you in the back of church near the tape sales. I certainly hope you've enjoyed yourself today, except for the ruined shoe, that is."

"Ed looks like he's just about awake so he can speak for himself, but I've really enjoyed meeting you last night and being with you and Trish today, not to mention seeing your beautiful home and the woods. Oh yes, the deer was pretty too."

"Yeah David, the same for me," Ed echoed, struggling to put on his shoes without untying them. "I've really enjoyed meeting you. I know our Trish will be loved and cared for. We know she's not a little girl anymore, but we like knowing she's made a good, solid decision. By the way, that's a real comfortable chair you have there. Excuse me for taking a nap in it."

Ruth handed him his coat, saying, "What do you mean a little nap? You've been asleep for nearly two hours."

"I think it's time for me to warm up the car. Trish, give me your keys before your Mother starts in on me. See you tomorrow David?"

"Yes Sir. And don't mind falling asleep, that chair does the same thing to me."

I walked Trish and her mother out to the car. Ruth got in while Trish and I embraced momentarily. "Have you ran out of 'Suddenly', or don't you wear it now that you've captured me?" I asked.

"No Love I haven't run out, and let me remind you you're not captured yet. Besides, I have an ample supply. It's just that I wanted you to behave yourself around my folks and be in your right mind. That's why I didn't wear it."

"Oh sure! You'll let me go on the air with the studio filled with that fragrance, but you can't trust me in front of your Mom and Dad. You've been trying to sabotage my show right from the beginning. Haven't You?"

"Shhhhhh! Mom and Daddy will think we're fighting. Let's continue this at some other more convenient time."

"Yeah sure, that's what you said about Uncle Charlie," I responded, tactfully reminding her of my keen memory.

Flippantly and without saying a word in retaliation she opened the back door of the car and got in while I knocked on the window to her mother's door. Ruth rolled the window down.

"We weren't fighting just then. We were teasing; something we've done almost from the first moment we met. If you run out of things to talk about, ask her about how I met Uncle Charlie, and about the perfume, and about Nutsy...."

"That's enough David," Trish tersely warned from the back seat. Let's go Daddy."

"Good night folks," I said, waving as they left.

The house needed some minor straightening and my self-imposed domestication required its accomplishment before going to bed. It also provided me an opportunity to thank the Lord for two very enjoyable meetings thus far with Trish's parents. I was certain they were good people. People who didn't practice putting on facades, and whose advice was certain to be beneficial in the future.

God showed up in all of His glory during the Sunday morning service. The praise and worship portion of the service seemed especially holy and reverent; as if God not only sensed our desire and need to be in His presence, but that He too wanted very much to be with us. Above the strong, relevant, and anointed teaching messages of Pastor Glen; right up there with the supernatural healings and delivering acts of God; and to me, equal to or even surpassing prophesies straight from His throne, was the thrill of being in the nearly raptured spiritual state of God's presence. At no other church I had ever attended, at no other time in my life, had I ever come into, with such certainty, the presence of God as I had since attending Lord of the Harvest, but even more so during this service. This body of believers had gained the knowledge and ability to launch out from the confines of this earthly habitation and into the spiritual ecstasy of face-to-face dwelling with the Almighty. That, no doubt, came from the sacrificial and faithful nurturing and guidance of Pastor Glen as well as the ability of the song-leader to identify and follow the prompting of the Holy Spirit in spontaneous song selection.

This was one of those uninhibited, Spirit-led, worship services where words fail to adequately describe the movement of God on each person present. To me, even the term 'High Praise' seemed totally inadequate. It was High-Praise as I had never experienced it, building both individually and corporately, to a point where the manifested, tangible power of God was moving with healings and delivering graces throughout the congregation.

There are terms, usually bantered about in strictly Pentecostal circles that describe such services. To use them merely indicates man's inability to comprehend, interpret and explain the experiences of being in God's presence. After nearly an hour and a half of continuous praise Pastor Glen instructed us, through prophecy, of what we had just accomplished in the spirit by our praise.

"You have entered! Yea, through your heart-felt, deep praises unto Me, you have entered! You could have done that long ago. Why did you opt for living in that despair? Why did you not come unto Me with your praise long ago? It was always there within you, desiring to be released through your spirit, yet you opted not to become involved in that which My Spirit placed within you. Do not hesitate in the future to come unto Me with that praise. My word says I inhabit the praises of My people. You are my people. I have people all over the Earth and you are some of them. I desire your true praise and I will honor it with My presence. Look closely at why you have not used that which I have given unto you. You were not hindered by shame for there is no shame in you. You were not hindered by inability because I have made you able. You were not hindered by even your sin for My Son overcame your sin. You were hindered by the thoughts that the evil one delivered unto you. Recognize his deeds. They are not parallel with My word. In fact, his deeds try to interdict and contradict My word. My word states over and over that praise is the way into My presence. Praise stills the avenger. Now that you have experienced this thing called praise, you will desire it more. Don't worry about what others who are not of this flock might say; just be obedient to the Spirit. Praise Me and see the power of your God descend from on high. I will teach you more and show you more but only as I find you faithful in your praise. Now as I said at the beginning, do not let despair rule in your heart. Replace it with praise and await your God to deliver."

Everyone in attendance, including the four of us, came out of that service changed for life. Ed and Ruth said their good-byes in the Church parking lot and started their eight-hour journey back to Grand Rapids. Trish and I went to her apartment for lunch.

With the wedding only a week away all our time would be spent in two areas; first by doing our jobs at the station, and secondly, by accomplishing all the remaining details of the wedding. We had already scheduled the ceremony, with Jerry's concurrence, at the station. Trish had been considering but hadn't yet agreed to the airing of the vows, but I could tell she was on the verge of going along with it. Pastor Hershey had already confirmed his delight to marry us. Invitations to those friends and family who we knew could attend had been mailed. I had taped five noonday shows in advance for airing in my absence. And John Dwyer was already scheduled to fill in for Trish on the week of our honeymoon.

All the preparations were going along well. Even a small wedding, as this was to be, had what seemed like hundreds, if not thousands, of tiny last minute details to decide upon and then accomplish. Trish's parents had made it back home safely and had already phoned us, confirming their plans to return on the Friday the 24th for the rehearsal and dinner. Trish left the honeymoon plans to me while she finalized everything else, including her wedding-day wardrobe, which I was not privy to. We were at her apartment Monday evening wrapping up a lot of the loose ends. Both of us were busy taking care of our areas of responsibility, exchanging ideas as we did, when she took me by surprise with a question that hadn't crossed my mind. Do you have any suggestions for a photographer?

"How novel an idea," I remarked. After all these years, both as a amateur and then as a professional, and all the weddings I had photographed in the past, I now found myself in need of one for my own wedding. "Call Cal Simmons. He'll do it for me, probably at cost. He really owes me a favor anyway."

"Why does he owe you a favor?" she asked.

"Because if it weren't for me, he wouldn't have his present job. But that's another story. Just give him a call and tell him where to be and when to be there. He'll be there."

A look of doubt etched its way across her face and I could almost read the words forming at her lips. "What if he's got a previous engagement?" came her question.

"Nonsense!" I replied. He's on the city payroll now. He's strictly a nine-to-fiver. I'll bet by now he's chomping at the bit to do a little exciting work for a change. Just tell him after he shoots our wedding, he's no longer indentured. He'll know what you mean."

I folded the large travel map upon which I had planned and marked our honeymoon route, including tourist and rest stops as well as overnight stays. For a few short moments I just sat there on the couch looking at Trish across the room as she made notes to herself. I prayed silently a prayer of thanksgiving and tried to envision our married life together that was to start in only five short days. Soon she sensed I was watching her as she raised her head and returned my smile with one of equal joy.

"What are you doing David?" she softly asked.

"Just trying to picture us married," I answered.

"What did you see?"

"Just a lovely, peaceful, fulfilling time with you in my arms."

"Anything else?"

"I don't know that I want anything else. Are you comfortable with that, Love? Are you still sure we're not moving too fast?"

She rose from her chair, strolled across the living room and sat next to me saying, "I'm more sure than ever. I've needed someone to love me for a long time. I've told you that. You know how I've prayed for that need to be met. I can't think of one emotional need in my life that has been resident within me as long. There's nothing, short of my salvation, I've wanted more than you and your love. Even if all the world's warning signs were shouting, and some of them are, that we're moving too fast, I wouldn't pay them any mind. I'm looking at our marriage with spirit eyes. God has shown us His will and confirmed it, time and time again. I'm not calling things that are as though they are not, but rather those things that are not as though they are. But maybe your question isn't so much for me as it is for you. Are you concerned David?"

"Not at all! Believe me when I say I have never been more sure about anything in my life. Well, let me qualify my statement as you did; I'm equally as sure about my salvation, and that's as certain as I can get.

"I'm also fairly certain that it's getting near my bed time. Let's have an early mid-night snack and call it quits for the day. Okay Love?"

"Okay, but all I've got in the house is some tin roof ice cream. Will that hold you till breakfast?"

"Provided I have a big enough bowl. Tin roof is one of my top ten favorites. Let's go to the kitchen and see how much of it we can eat, then I'll get myself home."

CHAPTER TWENTY-SIX

When compared to recent days, filled with the harried preparations for the wedding, Tuesday could have easily been called calm. Jerry and I were in my office, having an unscheduled late morning discussion of holiday schedules and program planning when Jimmy knocked on the door.

"Come in," I responded.

"Excuse me Sirs, I just took some albums in studio A for Trish and she asked me to bring you this note Mr. Post."

As he handed me the note I thanked him.

"Any problem?" Jerry asked while I started reading it.

"No, not at all. In fact, this just about completes the wedding plans."

Jerry looked at me with an inquisitive look, so I answered his unspoken question. "Trish just agreed to exchange vows over the air. If you remember, I asked you about that possibility a couple of weeks ago. Well the only thing holding it up was her hesitancy, but now that seems to have been overcome. I suspected she was leery of having a live broadcast due to the many people who know she's been divorced. She may have felt a quiet, low-keyed wedding would be more apropos, considering it's her second marriage. That's just my guess. She just hasn't said, at least not till now. At any rate, now she's agreed to do the ceremony on the air. That is, of course, if it's still okay with you."

"Sure it is! Did you want to make some spots to announce it; after all, it's just a few days away?"

"I'll discuss that with Trish at lunch and let you know. My guess is she won't want any publicity. You know, just do it unannounced. As for what you said about 'just a few days away', you're sure right there; Wednesday, Thursday, Friday, then a 9 AM Saturday wedding.

"Jerry, you've been married a few years. Can you remember if I'm supposed to be nervous or apprehensive? If I am I've got news for you, I'm not. What I am is excited. Maybe I'm anxious too, but not about the aspect of getting married, but rather that I might lose this precious, dear woman before she becomes my wife. I can't begin to tell you how often I think about Frank and how stupid he was to let her get away. No, correct that to how stupid he was to have driven her away. But truthfully Jerry, what should I be feeling?"

Jerry didn't answer immediately. It was never his style to give real quick replies to any question, and with the seriousness of this question he wasn't going to make this time an exception. Cautiously he addressed my concern.

"David, marriage affects men a lot differently than women. I don't put a lot of stock in psychology or things along that line. I even hesitate to make statements like the one I'm about to make, but no doubt you've already seen how getting married has affected Trish. Women, from my perspective and experience, seem to get all wrapped up in the romance of it. They seem to thrive on all the attention of friends and relatives, starting with the engagement, right through the waning moments of the wedding and reception. Women just seem enraptured by all the planning and preparations.

"Guys though, well that seems to be another story. We're more likely to get visibly apprehensive about the reality of locking in to a commitment such as marriage, even when we know it's what we want, what we need, and what we should do. Some men, just before the wedding, get what's called 'cold feet'. The reality of being responsible for the rest of their lives for someone's care, and any family that might eventually come along, makes a preemptive strike against our confidence levels. Couple that with knowing that most men our age have been raised to believe it's ultimately the man's career that's going to put the bread on the table, make the house and car payments, pay the bills and provide the nice things in life we just naturally want for our families. Those facts, bombarding me at rapid-fire speed, hit me right between the eyes exactly three days before I married Carol. I came so close to backing out it scared even me, and caused a frightfully emotional time for her. Is that anything close to what you're feeling?"

"I hate to disappoint you Jerry, but that's not it at all. In fact, you haven't even come close to describing Trish or I in any aspect. Maybe that's because it's going to be her second marriage, plus she's older now. Maybe it's because of my age. Yes to be sure, she's been enjoying herself in the preparations, but not at the level you described. As for me, I know of absolutely no apprehension about confirming my commitment to her in marriage. No fear of my upcoming role in her life. No indecision about whether she's the right woman or if we're right for each other. I'm just scared to death, and that's not a negative confession, just an expression, that I might wake up and realize this was all just a very long, pleasant dream. A dream where Trish was just a creation of my sub-conscience in response to some deeply felt yet unsatisfied need. Jerry, I love her so much it hurts. I'd just as soon go in Studio A right now, sweep her up in my arms, drive over to see Pastor Glen and have him marry us on the spot. If it's not a dream, then I want her now! If it is a dream, I implore you, please don't wake me up!"

Jerry stood up, walked across my office toward the door, causing me to believe he was going to leave without saying anything. Then, just as abruptly, he closed the door, turned back toward me and with one small tear rolling down his cheek, he said, "David you're very fortunate and blessed. Trish has told me many times in the past several weeks virtually the same thing as you've said to me just now. You've never opened up to me that deeply before. I wondered, to be perfectly honest with you, how sincere you were in regard to Trish. Nothing personal but, she's one attractive woman. I can understand how most men would react to her beauty.

"Remember our first encounter back in September? My God, it seems like months ago but it's not. After you accepted the job and while you were starting to line up a staff, we talked about Trish. I told you at that time I used to date her. Do you remember that?"

I nodded yes.

Jerry continued. "Do you likewise remember how I told you of her breakup and eventual divorce from Frank?"

"Yes Jerry, I do remember. Where's all this leading?"

"I'll tell you but you must promise never to tell Trish. Do I have your promise, your Christian promise?"

"Yes Jerry, I promise."

"Please don't get me wrong, and please don't read anything into this but what I tell you; this is straight from the heart. I grew to love Trish very much during the time we dated. It was only a couple of dates during a time when Frank and her were trying to confirm their future by dating other people. They had agreed to see if they were truly meant for each other by allowing each other the freedom to date someone else. Eventually they got engaged, as you know, and married. I was the only other person Trish dated, so far as I know anyway, and she was completely honest about it. Right up front she told me she was pretty sure about her and Frank.

"I know this sounds like a digression point, so I will. You see I have never really experienced the love of a father—at least not my real father. Can you imagine what it's like to look at the man who you call dad and know he's not really your father? I was blessed with a good man as my stepfather, yet each time I looked at him as I was growing up, I knew my physical makeup and appearance were different than his because I had none of his genes. As a boy and to a lesser degree when I had matured, I kept harboring ill feelings about not having my real dad. These feelings weren't directed at anyone in particular; they were just there, somewhere inside of me.

"I've said all that to get to this point. While growing up I wanted the love of my real father yet never experienced it. In other words, I felt the abandonment of being left behind and unloved by a man whom I'll never know, even if we were to pass on the street. Every time I saw my stepfather, the fact of my real father's absence would come to mind and cause me pain.

"Secondly, when I told Trish how much I had grown to love her during those few short weeks of dating, she didn't respond as I had hoped. Instead of the blossoming relationship and eventual marital bliss I had envisioned and dreamed of, I only felt the sting of another rejection, as kind as she was when it eventually happened. She said all the right words to ease me down gently, but it still hurt more deeply than I ever let her know. The result was all those suppressed feelings from childhood got stirred up again. There I was, a grown man feeling unloved and rejected again.

"David, we don't have all the answers. If we did, faith would be a most useless word. But I wanted Trish. As deeply as you just expressed that you did. Yet you've succeeded where I failed. That has stirred a lot of those inner feelings one more time. Can you possibly understand what it is I'm trying so desperately to express?"

"Maybe, Jerry; maybe not. Several questions hound me now as I try to understand all that you've shared with me. One of those questions is, what about you and Carol? Is everything okay with you two?"

"Yes David. I can assure you there's no problem there. I love Carol very much. She has been such a rich blessing to me, and there's no 'buts' in my statement. I love her and I know she loves me. What I'm saying is this conversation has stirred things up inside me that I've not felt in these past several years. I simply remember loving Trish just as certainly, just as deeply, and just as sincerely as you do. That's all."

"Well I'm glad to know there's nothing amiss with you and Carol, but why do you carry all that around inside you allowing situations like this to stir it all up again?"

"I really don't know, David. Maybe there's something else I still need to deal with. Maybe there's something God is trying to show me that will need His and my attention."

I walked over to the window where Jerry had finally stopped his pacing. Placing my hands on his shoulders I turned him so that we stood face to face. I embraced him with a brotherly embrace and said, "Jerry, I think I know what it is that's down there inside you. I could almost say I'm positive I know what it is, but I will not say it because by doing so I would violate a promise of confidence. If only I had release from the promise, then I believe you could be free from all those feelings that have piled up inside you over the years. Just one word of release from the right person and...."

"Call on 30 for Jerry. Is he in there with you David?" came Susan's abrupt announcement.

"Yes Susan. He'll take it in here."

I pushed the 30-line button and handed the receiver to Jerry.

"Hello...Well, Mr. G. How are things in Chicago? Oh, you're not? When did you get in? I suppose that's because of the television site? Yes, this Saturday at nine in the morning. I'm in David's office now. I'll be sure to tell him. Madame? We haven't heard from her since the dedication, except for seeing her at church. Yes every service and looking stronger by the day. I can come and get you. Well okay then, if you'd rather get a ride from her, after all a Cadillac probably rides better than a...sure, we'll talk then. Bye"

Jerry handed me the receiver and I placed it back on the phone. "Can I safely assume that was Mr. G. and that he's back in the U.P.?"

"Yes and yes. He wanted to come up for your wedding while taking care of some other business in Marquette. He'll be over there until Friday and Madame's chauffeur will bring him to Ridgemont for the weekend."

"I feel bad," I remarked. "Trish and I have been so involved in our plans we haven't checked in on Madame to see how she's getting along. We say our cordial hello's at church but we've not been the concerned, caring Christians we should be."

"Hey, don't get too guilty about that. She and Mr. G. have been busy on the phone with a friendship that's been developing into a closed party of two, if you can catch my drift. I dare say she hasn't noticed any lack of concern on your part," Jerry replied in an attempt to soothe my conscience.

"I'm certainly relieved about that but let's get back to you though, Jerry. It seems you're troubled by something that needs to be committed to God, prayed for and released. You know I don't want to feel awkward around you with my marriage to Trish. And I certainly don't want you feeling uncomfortable in our relationship, both as brothers in the Lord and as working partners here at the station. And besides, even though we've been together in a working environment for about seven weeks, we've never really had an opportunity to get together to develop or enjoy a friendship. I confess that also and ask for God's forgiveness."

"I rebuke that spirit of guilt you're trying so desperately to put on yourself today. Carol and I have been so involved in our hobbies in the evenings that we scarcely see the world going by. It's I who should apologize for not having had you and Trish over for a social evening."

"Well at the risk of sounding disinterested in further discussion, I feel I should get some of this paperwork done before I have to go on the air. I do want to continue this conversation and make some tangible plans for an evening for the four of us soon."

Jerry turned for the door, smiling and nodding in agreement to my statement. "We'll be sure to do that David. The important thing for right now, though, is to keep you busy enough to make it to Saturday morning before you decide to elope."

I laughed aloud while thinking, "My Bible doesn't mention anything about eloping. I wished it did."

As I signed off the air at one, Annette took control of the board and I raced out of the studio. "I'm starving, famished and also very hungry! Let's go eat!" I called out to Trish who was sitting in the break room reading her Bible.

I stood in the door to the break room and watched her return the marker ribbon to the page she was reading, close the Bible, and set it down beside her. This was no kids' kind of love that I felt. This was no infatuation or mere physical attraction. It wasn't even an emotional kind of drawing, although emotions were certainly involved. What it was; was a spiritual love and oneness that doesn't make one giddy and foolish but that reaches out to the other person with a desire to be a servant; to be protective and encouraging to the other. Yes, I couldn't deny the physical attraction, there was that, yet a holiness, and a pure kind of attraction in that area, but Trish just radiated the peace of her spirit and the love of her heart with even the simplest of moves and gestures. So it was, as she gently and respectfully set her Bible down beside her on the couch and turned her eyes toward me. I sensed within me, with confirming power, that I had already started looking upon her as my wife.

Helping her with her coat, I said, "I am most blessed and the happiest of all men because of you. If I haven't told you lately, thank you for loving me."

"What was that all about?" she asked. "I thought you were famished and had nothing on your mind but food. What triggered that display of gratitude?"

"You did. Jimmy gave me your note. When did you decide to have the wedding live on the air?"

"I can't say for sure when. All I know is I have a release in my spirit now that I didn't have a couple of days ago. Maybe I was just too concerned about who might tune in and hear us getting married, you know, Frank, John Fairbanks, others who know about my divorce. I guess I just didn't want to draw the attention of those people to our marriage, trying to keep it low-keyed, just family and close friends."

She continued as we walked out to the car. "After several sessions of prayer and meditation, I've come to the conclusion that what you said is probably true and it would provide a memorable facet to our wedding. Plus think of all the unknown listeners who will share our joy and be a witness to our promises. Speaking of promises, have you completed yours yet?

"Not yet Love. I've been working on them every spare minute I get, but I want the words to adequately express exactly what I know they need to. So far I haven't succeeded, even though I've written and rewritten parts of them five times. But don't worry; I'll get them finished in time. Now, where do you want to go eat?"

"I'm in the mood for a salad, a big chef's salad. Let's go to the Villa Cantine. That way you can have something else if you're not in the mood for a salad."

"The Villa Cantine it is."

CHAPTER TWENTY-SEVEN

We sat waiting for our lunch to arrive when I asked Trish if she wanted me to make any promotional spots for our wedding.

"What do you think about that idea?" she responded.

"I always assumed you knew better than to answer a question with a question, but since you've asked, I think we should air the wedding unannounced and those who are tuned in will get a surprise. Now, what are your thoughts?"

"Actually I'm in complete agreement with you. I don't want it to be a media event or have it appear commercialized. Love, this is our special day, first before God, secondly before each other, and thirdly before those actually present on Saturday morning. The radio audience is welcome to listen in, but to run spots seems too hyped up or contrived. Let's just keep it as it is, unannounced. Okay?"

"Sure. I'm glad we're in agreement on that. That's basically what I told Jerry earlier today, so now I'll confirm that to him this afternoon."

With our lunch finished we returned to the afternoon's work. Trish had a civic affairs interview scheduled for taping in Studio B with the Chief of Police and her Uncle Charlie on drug abuse in Upper Peninsula communities. I spent most of my afternoon answering mail. Jerry and I had a 3 p.m. meeting with the phone company representative to contract for new equipment. Because that decision would involve none of us at the station more than Susan, we included her in the meeting and decision process.

Soon the workday was over for most of us. Jerry left early after receiving a very exciting call from Carol. It seems the rabbit died. I was sorry to hear about that at first, thinking it may have been a family pet, until I realized what it was he was talking about. Trish and Susan left together. Trish told me she had an appointment at the Gown Town Dress Shop for a final fitting in what she called her "marital apparel." I just assumed that meant her wedding dress. Jimmy was reloading the wire service machine with paper and after he completed that he left. I followed right behind him, locking the AM and FM evening crews inside.

Once home, a hot bath helped me to relax. I fixed a light supper and sat to write a couple letters to family members neglected through the past several weeks of demanding changes and adjustments. As I did so, many of the evidences of God's handiwork were more clearly visible. I wouldn't call it hindsight; it was more like a chronological recap or reflection on the more significant events.

The time-old adage of "...can't see the forest for the trees" appears to have some spiritual truth as well as it's proverbial face value. Many times it seems, as we travel through life encountering the trials and tribulations that come our way, or even during the smooth times, we fail to see things with the spiritual acuity that a look back can produce. So it was as I wrote first to my sister and then to a dear aunt. Somehow capsulizing the recent events in the slower pace of longhand resulted in my emphasizing the more meaningful realities, while eliminating the superfluous and redundant. That exercise made the Divine intervention of God show through with unobstructed clarity. As I finished and sealed the second letter I breathed a prayer of thanksgiving and praise unto God. When I used up all my English vocabulary, I charged ahead with my heavenly language, confident in knowing as I did so, my prayer pleased Him.

I felt the day was through. I was physically tired yet not released to go to sleep. I wanted sleep yet it wouldn't come. I had been laying there several minutes, seemingly aware of nothing more than the ten o'clock chiming of my grandfather clock downstairs, the rhythmic beating of my heart and the motion of my breathing with its slight effect on the waterbed.

Suddenly I perceived something stirring and coming alive within in me. Not all at once; more like a slow, progressive, cumulative thought, building in intensity somewhere deep within, but definitely not in my mind. I knew it was my spirit man. It was a hungry spirit man. It was a spirit man neglected by relegation to a lower status on my recently established self-imposed list of priorities. After waiting a few moments for the words to form and then be processed in my mind, I focused on them. "What about My Word? You haven't spent time in My Word. I have many things in it just for you. Things you need right now. Make time to be obedient. Prepare yourself for your wife."

Immediately Ephesians Chapter 5, verses 22 through 33 came to mind. Not word for word mind you, but adequately enough to cause me to turn on the light, get my bedside New Testament, and read those scriptures. Initially I thought I had the wrong reference because the first verse I read was "Wives, submit yourselves unto your own husbands, as unto the Lord." I caught myself being smugly certain Trish should be reading this, not me. Apparently the Holy Ghost had the wrong address. But in the silent meditation that followed the reading of that verse came the revelation.

"Don't expect her to be submissive the way the world expects. Don't expect her to quit being who she is in order to become what you think she ought to be. Rather, expect her to acknowledge and accept your mandated role as head of the wife, as you acknowledge and accept Christ as your head and head of the Church. Submissive in this does not mean subservient. She is not now, nor shall she ever be subservient to you. Do not dominate. Do not dictate, and do not demand. Now read the rest of those verses and see how God has designed marriage, family, and the church."

My spirit devoured each verse in a way it never had before, pausing to receive the instruction of the Lord. There was a time when I thought I knew all this, yet by His Spirit, God had revealed something new to me. No longer did I feel responsible for running a household, orchestrating a family, or dictating directions to be followed to the letter because Christ died and had left me in charge. Now I felt a freedom to listen, evaluate and to employ empathy. I felt the explosive revelation inside me of knowing what the term 'helpmeet' was all about. It now seemed possible to not only understand what Trish might tell me, but to experience it as well.

The revelation nearly scared me knowing that without being obedient to the prompting of the Holy Spirit tonight, I might have entered into marriage without this indispensable instruction. That could have been disastrous. In ignorance I could have hurt the very one to whom I swore my compassion and understanding. As I came to grips with that awareness I felt the peaceful release to sleep. Soon it overtook me.

Wednesday was nearly uneventful. I say nearly because even though the routines of the workday were exactly that, routine, the mid-week service was not. Pastor Glen was out of town but he had taught us well not to look to him or any man, but rather to look to Jesus, the author and finisher of our faith. Jesus acknowledged our assembling together and came to consume the sacrifice of our praise. The congregation had long ago learned that when Jesus shows up, so does His healing power. As the song leader guided us through our praise and worship, he called the elders of the church forward to pray for and lay hands on the sick and afflicted.

Trish and I stood praying during this portion of service, as did many of the members. The nice thing about praying in tongues is that you can still use your mind to dwell on what is transpiring about you. So it was as I prayed. My mind recalled Jerry's prayer for my hip; Trish's prayer for Madame, and other reports from Pastor Glen of prayers for healing being answered by our mighty God. I thanked God for blessing Trish and I with good health. Over eighty people went forward for prayer and healing, many delivered immediately, giving their testimonies in praise and thanksgiving.

Trish and I said our goodnights in the church parking lot. Although we hadn't had much time by ourselves during the day, we knew we soon would have the remainder of our lives together. We confirmed lunch plans for Thursday and Trish read a list of events for Friday, including her parent's arrival, the rehearsal and dinner afterwards, and the final tasks for Saturday morning. The one thing she didn't call off was the one thing she didn't know I still needed to do. I had yet to drive to Marquette and pick up her ring. I had that scheduled for Thursday, after work.

"Oh yes," Trish added. "What are you doing tomorrow night?"

"Why?" I quickly asked.

"Don't ask questions! Just answer me!"

"Yes Ma'am!" I quickly snapped, popping a salute as I did so. "I'm going to be busy with something. Now can I ask why?"

"Yes, but before you do, I want you to know I'm going to be picking up my wedding dress and your ring, so don't be too upset if I tell you we won't be able to see each other tomorrow night."

I hung my head and put a sincere looking frown on my face as I feigned my response. "You mean lunch is the only time we have to be together tomorrow?"

"Uh-huh. And what's more, you know you can't stop by the apartment because Susan and I will be doing a lot of last minute things."

"Like what?" I quickly asked.

"Like none of your business, at least for right now."

Continuing my play for her emotions, which wasn't working I might add, I sadly replied, "You mean you're keeping secrets from me already? What are you and Susan going to do ALL evening long?"

"Just never you mind. Now kiss me and get yourself on home."

I figured it best to drop the play-acting and in this case, comply with her request. I kissed her then we got in our cars to drive home.

I wasn't ready to go to bed so I scanned the daily paper. It proved boring. Next I checked every channel on the television four times in hopes of finding something worthwhile. I didn't. About ready to scan the radio dial on the stereo, the Spirit of God chastened me.

"Why do you always come to me last?"

The voice was nearly so audible I caught myself looking around the house for where it came from before realizing it was God. The still small voice was becoming louder to me. I liked that. That was proof I was growing spiritually. I had to admit that my spiritual growth was not nearly as rapid as when I first encountered Jerry. Maybe that was due to the pathetic and anemic shape I was in spiritually. The best way to describe it would be a dried up, compressed and hardened sponge. Now, though, it is as though the sponge was nearly back to its full size and taking in water at a slower rate than at first. The warnings to man contained in the seven letters to the Churches in the Book of Revelation now had to be diligently applied to me; specifically, the warnings to the Churches of Ephesus and Laodicea. To the Church at Ephesus (and likewise to us) came the warning not to leave our first love, that being Christ. To the Church at Laodicea came the warning to not become lukewarm (complacent in our standing with God). These warnings were to be taken personally both by the Church and individually. I saw my need to take them seriously. If I was going to fill some time with the newspaper, television or radio, certainly that time could be spent in God's Word.

Immediately the flesh rose up against the spiritual truth God was employing in His chastening. First I grew tired. Then my mind started wandering while my eyes meaninglessly traced each line of print in the Bible. I stood from the couch and walked staunchly into the kitchen. I set the opened Bible on the table, prepared a strong, hot cup of instant coffee while resoundingly and loudly rebuking both my flesh and the devil.

"I will not be distracted from that which God has called me to do. He has a particular revelation for me this evening and I will not be denied. Spirit of sleepiness and drowsiness, be gone in the name of Jesus! Spirit of inattentiveness, be gone by the power of the name of Jesus Christ! Spirit of the Most High God, I welcome You here with me as I follow Your prompting. Show me Your truths and display Your power in revelation. I ask in the precious name of Jesus. Amen."

It might have been the coffee; it might have been getting off the soft couch. It might have been the combination of the two. Better yet it was probably the authority I took in the spirit, but whatever, I found myself nearly halfway through the book of Proverbs when the twelve o'clock chimes distracted me from my study. God had previously shown me a lot of things in those many chapters of instructions and comparisons. Things that I knew had value and relevance to living life not only to its fullest but in agreement with God's order and purpose. But this time there was more vivid value, and none more than the wisdom of Chapter 18, verse 22 as it leaped off the page and right into my spirit. Here was the missing part, the way I was looking for to begin my vows to Trish. "Whoso findeth a wife findeth a good thing and obtaineth favour of the Lord."

My mind lingered there for a while. Although I had not purposely gone about looking for a wife, I had certainly found one. And just as certainly in that find was the handiwork of the Lord. That logic led me to confirm to myself that I had obtained the favor of the Lord. With that spiritual encouragement, I finalized the draft copy of my vows to Trish.

CHAPTER TWENTY-EIGHT

Trish was very quiet during lunch. In fact, she had even been unusually serene during her "Good Morning, Lord Show". While there was nothing about her that showed a subdued or depressed appearance, she displayed a calmness I did not consider normal. She was obviously preoccupied with something distant that kept her deep in thought.

"A penny for your thoughts." I spoke softly, being careful not to jolt her too harshly back to reality. Holding her hand in mine as had become my custom, we waited for our lunch.

"You won't get rich that way," came her eventual and deliberate reply, amid a radiant smile.

"I know better than that. If they could be counted, and I doubt they could, I would easily be a multi-millionaire from all the thoughts you hold inside that precious head of yours."

My reply only triggered another smile but no reply while she appeared to be looking right through me. I pressed on. "Please tell me. What's on your mind Love?"

"I really don't know if there's anything on my mind or if it's just so complex a thought that words aren't capable of expressing it."

"Does it have anything to do with me? Can you tell me that much?" I asked cautiously.

"David, my Love, everything I am has something to do with you. I'm sure you're in my thoughts as much as you're in my heart. It's just that I'm so very happy and looking forward to our life together that I can't find words adequate to the up-coming occasion. That coupled with the fact that nearly everything is done and ready. With just a few exceptions all that's left is for us to get married."

I squeezed her hand slightly and said, "I was telling Jerry the other day that I didn't know how I was supposed to feel, you know, getting this close to being married after so long a wait. He went through a lot of explanations about what we guys can expect from our emotions, but none of it made sense to me. He didn't come close to describing what's going on inside of me. At any rate, I told him that I was terribly afraid I would wake up to find that you and all that's happened to us has been a dream—a very pleasant dream. I made it clear to him that if it were a dream, I didn't want to wake up!"

"David", Trish started and then stopped.

"What? What were you going to say?" I asked.

"Oh it's nothing. Have you finished writing your wedding vows?"

"It sounded like you were going to say something else but then changed your mind. What ever it was, I hope you feel comfortable enough with me by now to confide in anything. And yes, to answer your question, I finished the final draft last night. I'm going to go over it again this evening just to make sure it's right. How about yours?"

"All done. I'm going to have my mother go over mine tomorrow afternoon before the rehearsal."

"Hey that's not fair!" I quickly argued. "No one should know them before the wedding. And besides, I didn't get any..."

"Why did you stop so abruptly?" she inquired.

"Why? Because I was about to tell you a lie."

"Huh?"

"Yes, I almost unintentionally lied to you. You see, I was going to say I didn't get any help preparing my vows, but in actuality the Holy Spirit helped me. Is that okay?"

"Of course it is David. Let's not talk any more. Let's just enjoy each other's company."

"Okay, but one last thing, if you're experiencing something that's troubling you, please share it with me."

"I will David, but not right now."

I could only wonder at what she meant. For one very small instant, she looked worried. If I hadn't been watching her every facial expression at the time I would have easily missed it. What ever it was that troubled her, it would have to be overcome before the wedding or else.... I stopped my thought process right there. I prayed silently that whatever needed our immediate attention God would enable us to successfully resolve it.

At just after three Trish stopped in my office to see when I would get home. I told her sometime after eight o'clock. She kissed me and then went home. It took another hour of work for me to complete my unfinished tasks, and then I slipped behind the wheel of my car for the drive to Marquette.

Trish's ring was ready as promised complete with the minute engraving on the inside which read: W T G H J T L N M P A. Each letter representing the words in the scripture verse Matthew 19:6, "What then God has joined together, let no man put asunder".

It was nearly 8:15 p.m. when I got home and I could tell something wasn't right. There were cars parked on all sides of my driveway. As I drove past them I counted eleven of them. Some I recognized, others I didn't. The house was lit up like a Christmas tree and I could see people milling about, both inside and on the front porch.

"It's about time you got home brother!" came Jerry's voice from among those on the porch.

"Yeah! Nothing like being late for your own bachelor's party!" Trish's father chimed in.

"Hey gang, bachelor boy is here! On with the party!" someone shouted into the house.

"We're already partying!" came an anonymous reply.

Quickly I surveyed the faces of those on the porch as I approached the house. In addition to Jerry and Ed there were Uncle Charlie Lawson, Cal Simmons and Carl Worth. Inside I found Jim Osborne, Jimmy Thomas, Mr. G. and some other friends and associates. The biggest surprise was whom I found in the kitchen. Trish and her mom finished putting a deli tray on the table complete with various cheeses, meats and vegetables. With an astonished look I surveyed a wide variety of other snack foods and beverages that were available. Trish lightly placed a kiss on my cheek and whispered, Mom and I are going to be leaving now; we want you to enjoy this little surprise. I love you."

"Trish, I'm really overwhelmed and that rarely happens. How did you ever get all this planned without my finding out and on top of all the other arrangements you've been taking care of?"

Ruth heard my question and answered for Trish who was retrieving their coats. "Just never you mind. It's something that we wanted to do. We're just fortunate you had already given Trish a key. Now enjoy yourself and your friends David. Just don't stay up too late."

"Yes Mom. I'll be sure to do as you said. Thank you for this wonderful surprise."

"Come on Trish, Honey. Let's get back to your apartment."

"I'll be with you in a moment Mom. I need a final word with David."

As the others dove into the food, Trish pulled me onto the dimly lit back porch and said "I don't know if I'll get any more private moments with you prior to the wedding so let me just quickly say something about what was on my mind today. First I was concerned about my folks making it up here okay. You thought they were coming in tomorrow but they gave me the idea of doing this bachelor party for you and they wanted to be up here a day early for it. Dad's just thrilled about you being his new son-in-law. Mom's said he hasn't stopped talking about last weekend.

"Well, another thing that was on my mind was how we could surprise you but you helped us by not getting home until you did. By the way, where did you say you were?"

"I didn't say."

"Lastly, Satan stirred up two things I hadn't planned on. First he tried to get me thinking about being afraid to be with you on our first night. I know we've talked and prayed that one through but as that time gets closer, those fears want to make themselves evident again."

"Are you okay now?" I quickly asked.

"Oh yes. Love casteth out fear. I claim that promise of God's word," she stated matter-of-factly. "But," she continued, "there's one other thing that was on my mind and it shouldn't have been."

With deep concern in response to her changing expression I asked, "What ever could that be?"

"David, I think I've sinned. I tried to fight those fears about being with you with...with thoughts about us...alone...you know."

"I think I do and I'm not certain you're correct in calling that sin. Unless you tell me, I have no way of knowing what your thoughts were, but I've thought about us in that way a time or two also. Look at all the other preparations for the wedding and married life we've made; if preparations in those areas are important, why not that one? I don't know exactly how to describe my thoughts other than what it is—a part of our becoming one. There's a difference between lust and love. You know that. I've never lusted for you. I can't because I love you. Just a few minutes ago you quoted that scripture verse that says 'love casteth out fear'. I think love casts out lust too. Yes my love, I want to be with you too, in that special way God will give us, but that desire just can't be called sinful. As long as your thoughts, whatever they might have been, were under the umbrella of our promises of purity and love, and as such holy, then don't call God's gift to us sin. The world might call theirs sin, but not when God gives it and blesses it. Never. Does that somehow help you?"

A slight blush found its way across her cheek as a tear trickled down from her eye. Then she slowly lifted her head and agreed. "Uh-huh. Thank you David. I pray you will always be there to help me through times like this as they come."

"As long as I'm alive, I will be."

"Mom's waiting in the car. I better get out there. Have a good time tonight. I love you. Good night."

"I love you too. Thank you for the wonderful surprise."

CHAPTER TWENTY-NINE

The party ended at 12:30 a.m. Jerry and Ed stayed to help me clean up though I insisted they should leave. I wanted to be by myself but knew it would be selfish not to allow them to help if that's what they wanted to do. Ed straightened up in the living room while Jerry and I did the dining room. Then the three of us attacked the kitchen mess making quick work of the dishes, countertops and table, including wrapping the leftovers for the refrigerator. Soon afterwards they were on their way as Jerry drove Ed back to Trish's apartment.

I spent about a half hour reviewing my wedding vows and putting them in final form. It was nearly two o'clock and I was getting sleepy. Just before shutting off all the downstairs lights, I spied the calendar hanging on the wooden paneled wall by the front door. Stopping my assault against the remaining light switches, I studied the rest of the week. There were just two remaining numbers representing Friday and Saturday. It was now the early hours of the 24th of October. In just thirty hours Trish and I would be married. While sleep gnawed at my flesh, my spirit sang and shouted praises and thanksgivings unto God.

I must have been on autopilot Friday morning because I can't, for the life of me, remember anything that happened during the morning hours at work. The shortage of sleep the previous two nights had apparently taken its toll. Trish closed out her show as I stood by to start mine. I believe all went well, as best I can remember. At the end of the Manager Moments I switched to the one o'clock news, surrendering, as usual, the control board to Annette, and returned to my office. Trish left a note that she and her parents were having lunch together. They would see me in the evening for the rehearsal.

Jerry stuck his head in the door and told me to take the rest of the afternoon off. I did so gladly, hoping to catch up on some sleep. That wasn't supposed to happen. As I walked out to the parking lot I spotted Mr. G. getting out of a taxi and walking up the sidewalk. Instantly God instructed me to take him to the park and talk to him about he and Jerry.

"Okay Son," Mr. G. started his inquisition. "You've got me here but I don't believe its like you said, 'to see the squirrels'. What's really on your mind?"

Slowly I started, not actually knowing where to begin or what to say; just totally relying on the Holy Spirit to lead me. "Mr. G. I think it's time for you and Jerry to stop hurting each other, be it intentionally or not. I also think it's time you two stopped hurting yourselves, intentionally or not."

"David. You're going to have to be more specific. What are you trying to say?"

"Simply this, I believe you're carrying a load of guilt for not having adopted Jerry. Jerry's carrying a load of guilt for not having accepted you as his father, though I believe he loves you to no end. The two of you keep playing some kind of emotional cat and mouse game that may keep others amused but convinces no one."

"You haven't said anything to Jerry about what I told you, have you?"

"No sir. I could have. I mean there was an opportunity when Jerry was visibly upset. The Lord knows I wanted to, but without a release from you I kept my mouth shut. Actually, my knowing doesn't have any bearing on the situation at all. And the situation is, in my estimation, out of control. It has gotten out of hand and neither one of you seems to want to get it back under control."

"Excuse me for being so blunt David, but isn't this really between Jerry and I? If I had known you were going to butt in I probably wouldn't have confided in you."

I waited for my next words. I felt like I was into something way over my head and was mentally kicking myself for even getting into it this far. Then I spoke, startling myself as I did. "I think you confided in me, Sir, because you needed to get it out in the open where you could look at it. At the time it didn't really matter who it was that you told. Until you confided in someone, me or anyone else, you just couldn't get a good look at it.

"Jerry is more your son than if you were his biological father. I'd stake my life on the fact that you'd love to hear him call you 'Dad', just once, rather than Mr. G. In my mind I know absolutely nothing of this long term display of theatrics, but in my spirit I can't help feeling the two of you need to get this thing out in the open so you don't have to keep living in a charade. My guess is that Jerry needs to hear you call him Son rather than Jerry the Station Manager or WPFH Communications President.

"Nothing can change your decision not to adopt him. Time's taken care of that. But maybe it wasn't a mistake. What if you had? What if you had lost the inheritance? What if there was no WPFH-AM? Or FM? And what about the future of Christian television in the Upper Peninsula? What if without these ministries you hadn't reached one hundred souls for Christ? Or is it one thousand, Mr. G.? Or is it ten thousand. Or what will it be as the Gospel of Jesus continues to go out to this area of the country?

"Mr. G. do you see it all fades into insignificance when compared to how God has used your finances. You've yielded your heart to God in salvation. You've yielded your wealth and time to His purpose. But you've not yielded that one area that makes no sense to hold on to—a prideful, meaningless illusion. Jerry told me he always wanted his real father during his childhood. That seems to have been only half true. You know what I think, Mr. G.? I think he needs his real father more now than ever—that's you, the only real father in his life. He's an adult trying desperately to deal with an unresolved childhood problem. That's probably just as difficult for him as it is for a child trying to cope with an adult situation. Besides that, and Holy Spirit check me now if you're going to—Jerry needs a grandfather for his child."

"You know you're convicting the living daylights out of me, David. You make a lot of sense for such a young Christian who.... What did you say?"

"I said Jerry and Carol are going to need a grandfather for their child. My guess is you'd make a great one. I was hoping he'd already told you, but apparently he hasn't. I don't have any idea how he planned to do that, but since he hasn't yet, please, what ever you do, act surprised when he does."

A big smile formed on Mr. G.'s face, nearly obliterating all the age lines that had become markedly tightened as I spoke.

"Forget that," he cracked. "The shock value was what you needed to finalize your point and drive it home to the heart. Somehow, in all these years Carol and Jerry have been married, the thought of a grandchild hasn't entered my mind. Now you say it's a reality? When?"

"You'll need to get all those facts from Jerry. All I know is the test came back this week and Carol's pregnant. What do you think about that, Grandpa G.?"

Without turning his gaze from straight ahead he said, "You've given me a lot of things to think about. I'm not sure I'm even ready to make any comment other than you possess a whole lotta insight and it may even boarder on a word or two of knowledge. I'd certainly seek God in that gifting if I were you. I guess I'd also like to thank you for what I perceive you're trying to do. It probably is time for Jerry and I to start living as father and son, after all, that's what we really are. As for the thought of being a grandpa, my oh my, that really excites me!"

Once I was sure he was finished, I responded with a question totally unrelated to the conversation. "What, may I ask, are you staring at?"

"Did you see that darn crazy squirrel? He tried to catch that other one by the tail and fell right out of the tree. That screwball animal liked to knock himself plumb out."

"That's just normal stuff for these U.P. squirrels. It's almost like they know when someone is watching; they go out of their way to put on a show. What do you say? Are you ready to go to the station now?" I asked.

"Yeah David! I think it's time I had a long talk with my son. Let's go!"

As we pulled up to the front of the station I asked Mr. G. if he wanted me to go in with him. He thought it best for him to approach Jerry and the problem on his own, to which I agreed and returned to my original plan of a few hours of rest. This time I succeeded.

The rehearsal went well, starting at six and finishing right at seven thirty. We used Studio B, simulating what would be done in the main studio in the morning. The catered rehearsal dinner was set up in the break room. Trish was nearly beside herself. She radiated love, joy, peace, long-suffering, gentleness, goodness, faith, meekness, temperance; all those good things listed in Galatians Chapter 5, verses 22 and 23. That's why I couldn't help loving her. I see so much of the fruit of the Spirit in her life. The instructions I read in the Bible just seem to naturally flow in her life. I guess you could say she doesn't just go about witnessing, she is a witness.

While the guests were visiting with each other and milling about, I found it refreshing to sit on the couch and watch. I had been introduced to so many new faces I almost felt overwhelmed. Although the gathering of people didn't total more than twenty, most of them were out of towners on Trish's side. I enjoyed watching them spend time getting reacquainted and filled in on all the latest events of their lives.

After about a half an hour, Trish sat down beside me. Taking my hand in hers she asked, "Do you feel uncomfortable around all my relatives?"

"Not at all. I've been sitting her just relaxing and watching them make up for lost time. You know, Love, part of being in the military is the separation from family. During those 22 years I can count on my two hands the number of times I got together with my family. Selfishly, we servicemen and women think civilians can't possibly experience intense and lengthy separation the way we were required to. Nor could civilians be able to understand, let alone commiserate what we encountered during such times. I can see that's just not the case. You're way up here in the U.P. and all your family is down state. That may be closer than some but certainly not right next door. I'm glad to see you getting all caught up on your family happenings."

She squeezed my hand slightly and placed a kiss on my cheek while the others noticed her public display of affection and ooohed and ahhhed teasingly. Not embarrassed in the slightest, but rather smiling affectionately from ear to ear, she hugged me more for their benefit than mine.

"What?" I quickly asked. "Still not wearing that special perfume? Do you really think I'll get out of control in front of all these family members and embarrass you?"

She was starting to stand as I asked the question. Returning to the couch she leaned close to whisper her reply. "I'm saving it for our honeymoon. Or do you think I should leave it here in Ridgemont?"

"You're not going to keep on teasing me right through tomorrow's ceremony and into the honeymoon are you?"

"If that's what it takes", she replied, leaving me to ponder her remarks.

Before she got out of range I fired off a shot I know she had to explain to those who heard. "Sometime between now and tomorrow morning, you're going to have to get serious!"

The evening ended with the two of us in the parking lot embracing after a serious prayer of commitment to each other and unto God.

CHAPTER THIRTY

I looked at my watch more out of habit than a desire to know what time it was. After making what seemed like several attempts to determine what language my watch displayed, I realized it was 8:48 and thirty-three seconds. Jerry had earlier told me that Trish was in the building getting ready in his office. I waited silently in mine. Though finding it difficult, I attempted to pray in English. The resistance I encountered was more than I could surmount in my own strength. Relying on the Holy Spirit to overcome my fleshly inability to do what my spirit wanted, I started to pray in tongues. Even that seemed difficult at first and I recognized it was Satan's attempt to wedge his way into this special day. I was certain Trish was under an attack as well.

A few minutes later Pastor Glen knocked on my office door and while poking his head in he asked me if I was ready to gather in Studio A. Without a word I nodded and followed him and Jerry to the studio where nearly everyone else had already assembled. Everyone, that is except Trish, her Mom and Dad, and Susan. At nearly the same time I positioned myself at the appointed spot, in she came. She was preceded by Ruth, Susan and then arm in arm with her Father. Ed was grinning ear to ear as he slowly led my love toward me, passing Pastor Glen. As he did so he nearly knocked over the floor stand holding the microphone.

My eyes moved slowly and deliberately from Ed to Trish. It was like slow motion and yet I know it only took a split second. Our eyes met. She smiled a unique smile that seemed to say something that I was in no way capable of comprehending. To say she was radiant, exquisite or elegant would be totally inadequate. My mind instantly raced back to the portrait session at the now vacant photo shop, recalling how I beheld her beauty; capturing it on film. But now she reflected a beauty that made the previous encounter dim in comparison. *Isn't that exactly the way it should be for a bride*, I thought to myself. I was melting and I knew it. Just as quickly as my mind had traveled back in time I returned to the present, just in time to accept her arm as her father offered it to me. We turned to face Pastor Glen while those present seated themselves on the folding chairs positioned in a semi-circle around the microphone.

"Trish, David, relatives and friends, listening audience, let us approach the Throne of God in prayer." Pastor Glen started the ceremony. My feet felt as heavy as lead bricks. My knees seemed incapable of supporting me for another second, yet somehow they did. I felt each of a million drops of perspiration push their way through the pores of my forehead. My hands were as clammy as the cooler at nearby Sherman's Fish Market.

I took Trish's hand. She was as cool and composed as a seasoned veteran ball player at spring training.

Pastor Glen continued. "Our loving heavenly Father, we come together before You and each other with joy and expectation. Two of Your children, our brother and sister David and Trish, have sought your face, will and favor in Your holy sacrament of matrimony. You have said 'Yea and Amen' to them that they should become one in marriage. This we have assembled to do as You have ordained.

"Our words, though they may be important to us, are not the main ingredient to accomplishing Your will. It is Your blessing for which we ask, knowing, acclaiming and aspiring to the fact that You promised to give us the desires of our hearts.

"Father, Trish and David come to You to pledge to You and to each other their vows. We ask You to witness these promises. Bless these two citizens of Your kingdom, and enable them to do such as they promise for all the time that Your holy will has established. We ask boldly and confidently in the name of Jesus Your Son and our Lord."

Pausing only for a moment, turning to face her directly, he resumed the ceremony by saying, "Trish Ivey, with your hands holding David's hands, announce unto him your vows of marriage."

"David, my Love, these are the vows I make by which I take you as my husband. I have sought God, trusting in His gracious and constant voice of guidance in this regard. I pledge them to you in His presence, your hearing, and in the assembly of these witnesses.

"I, Trish, pledge to you, David, the very same unconditional love the Lord has given me. By that, I pray I have not over-simplified what it is that I promise. Just as we have a God shaped space within us that only God can fill, so it is that we have a love shaped space within us. It is that space within you, David that I vow to fill. I pledge a life of sincerely seeking God's wisdom in all that I think, all that I say, and all that I do in our union. I pledge to serve God First, placing Him preeminent in my life while allowing no one or nothing to come second in my life but you. I pledge my faithfulness, kindness, honesty, loyalty and understanding. I pledge to follow no ambition but the fulfillment of these vows and settle for nothing less than the accomplishment of the same.

"The ring I will soon place on your finger, as a symbol of these vows, indicates that I deliberately, voluntarily and joyfully join myself to you. I accept, now and forever, before God and man, the responsibility of accomplishing these vows. By God's grace and power, I marry you, David. You David are my mind's dream, my heart's love and my spirit's joy."

After receiving a nod from Trish that she had completed hers, Pastor Glen turned to me saying, "David Post, with your hands holding Trish's hands, announce unto her your vows of marriage."

Without hesitating, I began. "My Dear Trish, in a day and time when it seems man's words are nothing more than a means to accomplish personal gain; at a time when men speak words to cosmetically and systemically circumvent the situations of life in which they find themselves; and when a person's promise serves no lasting purpose but the immediate, I found it hard to find the words adequate to confirm my inner most feelings and to ratify so solemn a thing as marriage. In the search that has brought me to these words, I sought God's help, as rightly so great a promise demands. But rather, this is not so much a singular promise or even a series of promises, but a life of promises; each day, no—each moment, giving opportunity for the keeping or breaking. God will lead to be sure, provided we ask and then yield. God will empower to be sure, provided we seek and then employ. God will enrich to be sure, provided we acknowledge and then obey.

"With all that said, my Love, I enter marriage to you freely giving you all of me, with no hesitancy, no demands, no erroneous or preconceived ideas of how I think it should be for me. I enter committed, as I feel I should, to what I should be for you and what marriage should be for the both of us.

"I pledge to follow Christ and His example. I pledge to stay in fellowship with God and in tune with His Holy Spirit. I pledge my faithful love and all that you, Trish, call on that love to be.

"The Word of God says, 'He that finds a wife finds a good thing'. Trish, God has placed you in my life's path, not so much that I could find a wife, but that we, together, might find a life filled with His love and blessings. Before you, God and these assembled, I pledge to you my lifelong love, never diminishing, ever increasing, always faithful, never lacking, and always yours."

"David and Trish, mindful of God's presence here, you have promised these things to each other. Yours is not a marriage made to those conforms of this world nor its tradition. It started as the plan of God, confirmed by Him and now witnessed, ratified and blessed for success. This does not relieve the two of you of the responsibility, but rather increases your responsibility, individually and together. This is a Christian union, and as such, continues your Christian witness and testimony to believers and non-believers alike.

"This solemn yet simple ceremony may very well be a significant part of someone coming to a saving knowledge of Jesus Christ. What spiritual fruit could be greater? Only one thing, that being your married life, filled with faith and corresponding actions, should lead your children to Christ.

"David, do you have the ring?"

"I do."

"Then place it on Trish's finger and repeat after me. 'With this ring I thee wed. No limits of time, space or circumstance will alter this pledge, symbolized by a ring and lasting till death'.

"Trish, do you have the ring?"

"I do."

"Then place it on David's finger and repeat after me. 'With this ring I thee wed. No limits of time, space or circumstance will alter this pledge, symbolized by a ring and lasting till death'.

"By the power entrusted to me by our Creator and by the State of Michigan, I now pronounce you husband and wife. God bless you richly and give you exceeding abundantly above all that you ask or think, according to the power that works within us, in Jesus' name. Amen."

CHAPTER THIRTY-ONE

Jerry leaned over my right shoulder as I sat at the wedding party table. Whispering so no one but I could hear he said, "Someone's here who's not exactly dressed for the occasion but who wants to see you in the men's room. He would prefer that you see him alone but if you'd like, I'll come with you."

Immediately I surveyed the situation in the crowded break room. Everyone there, including Trish, who was on the other side of the room, was totally preoccupied with the food and festivities of the brunch reception. I turned back to face Jerry while quietly asking, "Do you have any idea who it is?"

"Yes, and you know him too. I suggest that you see what he wants in there rather than someplace else and run the risk of having a scene. I'll be in the hallway, right outside if you need me."

Slowly and casually I rose from the table. While smiling and trying not to display either a concerned look or be noticed by Trish, I left for the men's room. Moments later I found myself standing beside Jerry, right in front of the solid wood door, staring at the word MEN. I took a deep breath and entered. At first I didn't see anyone. Maybe whoever it was had left, I thought silently to myself. Then coming out from a privacy stall walked Frank. Not normally a victim of fear, I found myself frantically eyeballing him over for a gun. My imagination rapidly searched the archives of my mind, gearing up for a replay of some murder scene from a movie seen in years gone by. As for a gun, he had none that I could see.

"Hi David. Do you remember me?" he asked, nervously edging closer as he spoke.

"Yes Frank, I remember you." I reached out for a handshake, fairly certain at this point it was safe to do that much. As I gained a bit more control over my nerves, and while allowing time for my racing heart to return to a speed less conducive to a heart attack, I asked him what he wanted. Knowing that whatever it was specifically, it would surely pertain to Trish and I.

"First, I sure hope I haven't startled you or caused you any undue concern. If I have, I'm genuinely sorry for that. When I found out about your wedding plans for today I just had to get over here to let you and Trish know that I'm real happy for the two of you. I really mean that, and I wish you much happiness. My only concern was how to let you know that without upsetting Trish or causing an ugly scene. I didn't know if the two of you are going to be getting away for awhile or not, that's why I took a chance coming over here now. There's just two things I wanted to get off my chest before you and Trish started your life together."

At that point he paused much longer than I had anticipated so I prompted him on by asking, "Well, Frank I guess the first thing was that you wished us happiness. What's the other?"

For a moment it seemed as though he would never speak again. Then I feared the whole thing was a charade and that he was getting ready to say something derogatory, but that didn't fit the expression on his face. It became more and more obvious he was having a hard time holding back his emotions. Then, with a quivering chin and a tear tracing its way from his right eye down through his short stubby beard, he softly said, "When the time is right, and I trust you'll know when that is, would you please tell Trish that you and she can stop praying for me. I've accepted Jesus as my Savior, last weekend while I was at a church in Houghton Lake."

"Frank, I'm thrilled! How did it happen?"

"That's really not all that important, especially right now. You've got a bride to get back to. A beautiful bride at that I'll bet. Just know that I'm now on my way to heaven and also toward getting my life back in some kind of order. Now maybe I better leave before she wonders where you are or what's keeping you."

He started to leave but as he passed in front of me I gently grabbed his arm, stopping him. "Frank, I'll be sure to rely on the Holy Spirit for showing me the right time to tell Trish of your salvation, but one thing I'll not tell her is to stop praying for you. We'll both keep praying for you. After all, the Bible specifically states 'pray ye one for the other'. Could I ask you to pray for us?"

"Yeah David, you can ask me that. And I will!"

I released his arm and he continued his retreat. Within seconds he was out of the building and on his way.

As I came out of the men's room Jerry said, "I couldn't help but overhear the conversation. I only hope it's all true."

"Jerry," I said, "don't you believe in answered prayer?"

"Come on David, you know I do."

"Then look!" I emphatically remarked, pointing through the glass front door. "There goes an answered prayer driving through the parking lot. I'm convinced that he's now a brother in the Lord. Besides, I'd rather think of him as a fellow Christian than a potential threat or problem sometime out in the future."

We stood there looking through the front door of the station until he was well down the road and nearly out of sight. "Maybe this would be a good time to..." Jerry abruptly started, and then just as abruptly stopped.

"Good time to what, Jerry?"

"Oh never mind, let's get back to the reception." With his arm around my shoulders, we returned to the break room. I knew Trish would want to know about Frank's encounter with Calvary, but until the Holy Spirit revealed the proper time, she just wouldn't know.

Several hours later, with coats in hand, Trish and I made our way through the guests, more than sixty all total. Along the way we stopped to shake hands, get our hands shook, kiss cheeks and get cheeks kissed. Many of the older men had jubilantly slapped me on the back until it felt like I had a third-degree sunburn. I soon found it necessary to fight off a spirit of impatience, but by two o'clock we had successfully visited with everyone individually. Then we quickly escaped from the building, getting into my car, which was cleaned, tuned up and filled with gas for our honeymoon getaway.

On the dash Trish found an envelope; a pink envelope. To me it looked like the kind Madame DeVille used. It was. It bore her silver embossed initials. Trish opened the note and read it aloud while I maneuvered the car onto U. S. 41.

> Dear David and Trish,
>
> Jerome and I figured this would be a good way for the two of us to give the two of you a little special send off on your honeymoon. Enclosed is a small amount of money that we both want you to have. Enjoy yourselves and have a great time as you tour the shores of Lake Superior. We want you to know that you will be in our prayers for a safe trip and one that God blesses immensely. Be considerate and kind to each other, but at this critical time be especially patient. David, you be gentle! Trish, don't you be tense! After you get back to Ridgemont, Jerome and I have something real special to share with you.
>
> Love, Madame & Jerome

Trish folded the note and then started counting the money. "David, do you believe this? There's a thousand dollars here! And you know what it is she and Mr. Gramswald want to share, don't you?"

"Yeah. I'll just bet there's another wedding in the planning stages. No surprise there! With that much money, which is a surprise, we could go around Lake Superior fifty times," I joked. "Wasn't that extremely nice of them?"

She didn't answer the question, undoubtedly considering it rhetorical. I looked at her but she had since turned her attention to her purse. "Did you hear me Love?" I inquired.

"Yes David, you're right. That was very thoughtful of them," she replied matter-of-factly. As she spoke she continued fumbling with the contents of her purse. "Well finally; here it is!"

"Here what is?" I asked, keeping my eyes on the road.

"A note from Jerry to you. Would you like me to read it too?"

I thought for a moment. Certainly there shouldn't be anything too private in the note. He had plenty of time to talk to me. I wonder what he wrote that he couldn't tell me face to face. "When did he give you the note?"

"Just before we kicked him out of his office earlier this morning. That wouldn't make a difference, would it?"

"I really don't know. During the reception he was about to say something then stopped as quickly as he started. Go ahead, open it."

She had it opened before I finished, then started reading aloud.

> *Hi, David. I really don't know when you're going to find the time to read this, given the fact that you're now on your honeymoon. I didn't know how to say this to you even though I wanted to several times in the past fifteen hours since it happened. Because it didn't get said verbally though, I didn't want you to wonder what happened yesterday afternoon. Mr. G. and I had a very pointed conversation, if you know what I mean. We talked, we wept, we laughed, we forgave, and we promised to quit living the big lie. I know he wanted to personally thank you for the fine referee job you did, and for so tactfully reminding him that he'll 'never get too old for a good scolding', as he put it. He also told me the convicting power of the Holy Ghost took him on a trip to the woodshed. If he hasn't told you that yet, I'm sure he will as*

soon as you get back. As for my feelings, well, we'll have a combined AM/FM staff meeting to make the news release. Suffice it to say for right now though, "Dad" and I have got some big plans as we start working together with a different and improved relationship. It's also apparent he wants to spend more time up here in the coming months for two reasons. As you might guess, Madame is one of them. I'll let him tell you about that. And as you know, in about seven and a half months, either Karyn or Gabriel will be the other reason. Have an enjoyable and relaxing honeymoon.
God bless you and Trish abundantly.

Jerry

Trish reached over and placed the refolded note in my shirt pocket. Not wasting the opportunity, she placed a kiss on my cheek and then asked, "Am I supposed to be able to make sense out of that note?"

"Probably not, Love. Some of it relates to an on-going situation between Mr. G. and Jerry."

Looking more perplexed than ever, she fired off the next inevitable question. "Just what does the portion about Jerry and his "dad" mean?"

We turned west onto State Highway 38, forging our way toward Lake Superior. While doing so, I shared the entire story, as I knew it. She didn't say a word, listening intently to each fact as I unraveled for her the mystery. She wore an expression of amazement all the while I gave the account. I finished the saga at about the same time we reached our first stop in the small shoreline community of Ontonagon.

Feeling somewhat nervous, I walked to the office of the small motel to check in. It consisted of only twelve efficiency units on a densely wooded lot. Trish waited in the car while I registered. Unit number seven of the Pine Terrace Motel was ours. The motel was nestled between the village park and a small, nearly deserted looking shopping center. Trish asked that I forego the tradition of carrying the bride across the threshold, and I agreed. She said it had nothing to do with the amount of food she had consumed since meeting me. I brought our suitcases in while Trish searched the small yellow page section of the phone book for restaurants in the area.

She seemed calm and undaunted by our intimate surroundings and outwardly immune to the intensity of the approaching hours together. Setting my suitcase on the floor next to the side of the bed I had chosen, I stood, watching her scan all three half-sized pages that constituted the entirety of the restaurant ads. The room seemed to be getting warmer by the minute, and I was feeling more and more awkward. Finally out of near desperation to break the seemingly eternal silence I asked, "Did you find anything that appeals to you?"

She looked up at me, radiating all the love within her, saying, "Yes, of course, you!"

Her remark heightened my still uncomfortable condition. I walked around to her side of the bed, within arms length of her, setting her suitcase down. "I don't believe I've ever seen you look more beautiful and relaxed than you do today Trish. Look, you're not even perspiring in this warm room," I remarked while loosening my tie, hoping to gain some control over my out of control emotions. "And I find it even harder to believe that we're now married. Would you mind terribly if we wait for dinner until we've had a time of prayer, on our knees, before the God of the Universe who planned this whole thing from the beginning of the ages? I think I really need that right now."

Trish stood from the chair next to the table, delicately returning the phone book to its original position. "I can't think of a better thing to do first. Then David, I want us to be together. I think dinner can wait."

Taking each other's hand we knelt before the Lord and prayed silently. I firmly believe that our prayers were nearly identical for in a matter of about three, maybe four minutes, we both switched to our Holy Spirit inspired language, changing likewise, from silent prayer to praying out loud. As we stood at the end of our season of prayer, we held each other tightly and kissed.

"David, I sense your uneasiness. All the time I wrestled with that same spirit, sharing it with you in the woods of your back yard. I was nearly certain that it would interfere with us, and our special future moment. I always thought it would be me. Never did I think it would come upon you. We've just prayed. Let's trust in God to hear and answer that prayer, right now."

"Trish, just as you spoke, God gave me a revelation that I know came from deep within me. That revelation is that I really couldn't understand, on that day back in September, what I can now. I agree with you, let's claim the promise of God that '...all things work together for good for them that love God, to them who are called according to his purpose.' Maybe this will prove to be a way for me to better understand you and what you were experiencing at that time."

"I can agree to that David," she softly answered as our embrace continued.

Through each day, ours was a memorable honeymoon, as I'm sure nearly everyone's is. Each moment and special event we did became a mental snapshot for our memoirs. It's hard for an avid photographer to go anywhere without a camera. So it was with me. Though it was not intentional, Trish found herself contending for time with me, and against my many impulses to take pictures of every hill and valley we viewed. Lovingly she put my camera away after the tenth roll of film and nearly thirty shots of her standing next to this, that, and every other thing.

We drove around the big lake with little concern for the clock, stopping at virtually every scenic turnout or picturesque spot along the way. As we left Minnesota and entered Canada the air temperature became much colder. The wind from the north didn't receive the moderating effect of the slightly warmer waters of Lake Superior that the southern shoreline normally gets. Those falling temperatures prompted us to switch from fall to winter coats when we stopped at Thunder Bay, Ontario. We encountered a short period of snow squalls on the eastern shoreline as our direction turned to the south at Michipicoten Harbor.

When we reached Sault Ste. Marie, Ontario, six of the nine days we had were gone. We decided to limit our stops to just two more major tourist attractions, the Algoma Train ride into the Canadian Agawa Canyon, and a brief stop at Tahquamenon Falls, near Newberry, once back in the Upper Peninsula. Whatever time we had remaining after those two stops would be spent getting back to Ridgemont, and moving Trish's things from her apartment to the house.

Because no one knew exactly when we were going to return, we had all the time to ourselves. The first sign of us being back in Ridgemont came on Sunday morning at church. Pastor Glen made sure the entire congregation knew we were back from our honeymoon, they all applauded. I still wonder why. Certainly we weren't the first to complete and survive a trip around Lake Superior. After all, the people who built the road made it all the way around.

The alarm went off at 4:30 on Monday morning, jolting us both unkindly from the new habit we had developed of sleeping in. I reached first to the clock, shutting it off, then to my love, holding her close in the warmth of the waterbed. "I think it's time to get up Love," I softly spoke.

She moaned in unyielding protest to my gentle nudging until I turned on the light. "What time is it?" she quickly asked, springing to her feet.

"Four thirty five," I answered. "You can have the bathroom first. I'll get the coffee going."

Within 45 minutes I was out the door to warm up the car. Trish was standing in the living room putting on an earring as I returned. "We got a dusting of snow last night; probably just enough to make the roads slick. If you're ready, the car's warmed up."

I helped Trish with her coat, stopping long enough to bask for a moment in the fragrance of the fresh splash of 'Suddenly' she had applied. First she smiled and then shook her head. A moment later we were on our way to the station. Trish powered up the equipment and readied herself for her "Good Morning Lord Show", while I made the coffee. We went about our tasks as if we hadn't missed a day. It felt good to be back, rested, renewed, and ready for another week of broadcasting.

As I settled down with my second cup of coffee on the plush cushions of the break room couch, I heard the monitor speaker come alive, first with a pop, then a low hum. Next came the voice of my Love. It was the beautiful, soft, caring voice of my wife, with all the captivating qualities I'd first heard only months before.

"Good Morning Lord!" she enthusiastically started. "And good morning to you early morning listeners. This is WPFH, 101.9 FM, where people find Him—Him being Jesus Christ our Lord. This is Trish Ivey...oops, I mean Trish Post. Shall we start the day with prayer?"

Printed in the United States
1480700005B/1-54